Cloud VR

Cloud VR

Cloud VR
Technology and Application

Huaping Xiong

Dawei Li

Kun Huang

Mu Xu

Yin Huang

Lingling Xu

Jianfei Lai

Shengjun Qian

CRC Press
Taylor & Francis Group
Boca Raton London New York

CRC Press is an imprint of the
Taylor & Francis Group, an **informa** business

人民邮电出版社
POSTS & TELECOM PRESS

ISBN: 978-0-367-49167-3 (hbk)
ISBN: 978-1-003-09043-4 (ebk)

Typeset in Sabon
by codeMantra

Contents

2 Cloud VR Technologies 21

3 Cloud VR Service Platform Technologies 61

Prologue I

Virtual reality (VR) is a field of highly cross-integrated scientific and technical disciplines. It is the latest realm of human achievement toward simulating a real-world environment, with the development of technologies such as high-performance computing, computer graphics, and human–computer interaction. VR has been widely used across various scenarios and offers enormous social and economic benefits.

In the field of mass consumption, VR technologies have been applied in videos, games, tourism, e-commerce, and virtual social networking. They can create a new, immersive, interactive atmosphere and introduce a new sensory experience to users. On October 1, 2019, the military parade celebrating the 70th anniversary of the founding of the People's Republic of China (PRC) adopted a live VR broadcast. With this in mind, a new consumption field is growing based on VR.

After decades of development, remarkable VR achievements have been made in aerospace, equipment manufacturing, smart city, military, medical care, education, and many other physical industries. It has become a new IT support platform for industry development. VR+, like Internet+, has become a development trend and will have a large impact on related industries by promoting the transformation of industry product and service models and enabling the industry to be upgraded or enter a new generation. For example, in a realistic virtual battlefield environment, combat planning, confrontational drills, and effect evaluation can greatly improve the combat success rate, avoid the risk of real-world training drills, and reduce consumption. The field of medical care and medical education will greatly benefit through surgical planning, rehearsal, evaluation, and training on virtual human organs through surgical simulators. The application of VR technology in equipment manufacturing generates numerous new manufacturing technologies, such as immersive design, virtual prototype and evaluation, virtual assembly, augmented reality (AR) assembly and disassembly guidance, and equipment operation and maintenance training. In recent years, the digital twin, which has emerged in the manufacturing industry, applies VR technology to the entire life cycle of equipment from design to operation training and after-sales service. Digital twin and industrial Internet form the basis of smart manufacturing.

The popularization of 5G is expected to eliminate the data transmission bottleneck that currently restricts VR development, enabling breakthroughs in some key VR technologies and important platforms. This advancement will ensure that VR objects and environments are deeply realistic; VR interaction is highly natural; intelligence remains an important feature of VR systems; and VR cloud computing and services, VR/AR mobile phone applications, and VR edge computing develop rapidly.

Healthy development of the VR industry requires continuous breakthroughs in key technologies and requires long-term R&D investment in hardware platforms and devices, core chips and components, software platforms and tools, as well as standards and specifications. Through technological innovation, the VR experience is constantly moving closer to reality. To further our goals, we should explore market requirements, enrich VR+ industry applications, generate business returns, and drive enterprise investment through market requirements to ensure that enterprises are the main body of technological and business innovations. In addition, we should accelerate the development and training of professionals in various VR fields to address the shortage of R&D and product development talent. Currently, the global VR industry is moving from the initial to the rapid development period.

With the popularization of 5G technologies, the efficiency of fast data transmission and processing on the cloud has become increasingly high. Cloud VR has become an important infrastructure and mode for VR technology application and VR technical services, respectively. Cloud VR is a cross-industry convergence and innovation of cloud computing, network, and VR technologies, reflecting openness and innovation.

Cloud VR: Technology and Application introduces Huawei's technological innovation, system construction, and demonstration application in cloud VR. It represents the innovation achievements of technology enterprises and provides a useful reference for VR technology and industry development.

赵沁平, Qinping Zhao
Academician of Chinese Academy of Engineering,
Expert in Computer Software and Virtual Reality
November 2019

Prologue 2

Virtual reality (VR) is a new-generation computing platform currently driving a new round of technological innovation and industry transformation and one that has entered a steady new development phase, more so now than in previous years. Specifically, the overall performance of products is continuously improving, innovative business scenarios are continuously emerging, and technical conditions are ready for large-scale commercial use. As a result, VR has started to introduce huge social and economic benefits. Cloudification is an important VR industry trend; Huawei was the first in the industry to put forward the concept of cloud VR. By doing so, Huawei aims to associate VR with fast-growing networks and cloud computing technologies to implement wide and convenient VR access and accelerate its large-scale commercial use. As a world-leading information and communication technology (ICT) powerhouse and intelligent terminal provider, Huawei has delivered strong support for VR technology innovation and industry progress across networks, computing platforms, and terminals.

The time has come for large-scale commercial use of cloud VR. On June 6, 2019, the Ministry of Industry and Information Technology (MIIT) officially issued the 5G commercial license, indicating that 5G will become a part of our daily lives. In the era of 5G mobile networks, fixed networks have also implemented gigabit optical networks for home users. Gigabit mobile and fixed networks need to establish business models based on high-bandwidth and ultra-low-latency services to guide users to upgrade networks; cloud VR can successfully meet these requirements. The high bandwidth required for comfortable user experiences has exceeded that of 4K videos. In the future, higher user experience requirements will lead to higher cloud VR bandwidth compared with 4K videos. In terms of ultra-low latency, interactive cloud VR services have similar requirements on latency with cloud gaming. Therefore, cloud VR is a powerful tool for operators to develop dual-gigabit networks that can fully unleash the potential of VR.

Currently, services such as cloud VR+, movies and entertainment, cloud VR+ education, and cloud VR+ gaming have emerged in consumers' homes. Cloud VR+ industry scenarios are also being explored and are continuously improving our experience and cognitive efficiency. Cloud VR and gigabit mobile and fixed networks complement each other to achieve mutual success. Together, they enable VR+ for consumers, families, and industries, so that VR can quickly create tangible value for society.

The commercial use of cloud VR is continuously being promoted. In July 2018, China Mobile Fujian released a cloud VR service oriented to home scenarios, which is the first commercial example of cloud VR. Since 2019, China Telecom, China Mobile, and China Unicom have either started or gradually accelerated the commercial use of cloud VR. In June 2019, China Communications Standards Association (CCSA) approved the development of three cloud VR standards, including the General Technical Requirements for Cloud VR. This was the first time that the cloud VR series standards were approved in the standardization field, marking the official progress of the cloud VR industry from technical practice to large-scale commercial use.

Cloud VR has broad industry opportunities. Just as PCs ushered in the Internet era and smartphones ushered in the mobile Internet era, cloud VR will create opportunities to promote the emergence of many great business practices.

Cloud VR: Technology and Application can help more industry peers understand cloud VR and provide a useful reference for them to enter the cloud VR industry. In addition, it helps industry participants build an open and unified technical architecture. Let's create a prosperous era for the VR industry together!

汪涛, David Wang
Executive Director of Huawei,
President of ICT Strategy & Marketing

Preface

Next-generation virtual reality (VR) is driving a new round of technological and industrial transformation. VR is an engine for China's technological advancement and, since 2016, has actively been promoted by the government through various policies.

The emergence of cloud VR has freed VR from traditional computing restrictions, such as wiring and expensive hardware by using high-speed, stable dual-gigabit networks (5G+gigabit home broadband) to deliver cloud-based content, wirelessly, to VR terminals. It is not only cheaper for users, but also offers a better user experience, can be used in a wider range of scenarios, and features richer and more diverse content.

Huawei iLab, the pioneer of cloud VR, is dedicated to scenario and experience studies that investigate the industry and its ecosystem. As the developer of the first cloud VR system prototype, Huawei iLab has helped operators in China design, plan, and deploy cloud VR services. In Shenzhen, the VR OpenLab was built as a development and collaborative platform for global operators and industry partners to demonstrate cloud VR solutions and conduct greater in-depth research.

With greater understanding of the industry, Huawei iLab has developed a systematic methodology for cloud VR including E2E technologies and experience improvement. The 20th China Communications Standards Association (CCSA) meeting in June 2019 saw the cloud VR trend shift from technical practices to commercial use.

To accelerate the development of cloud VR and the industry, we will share valuable technical practices and research in cloud VR to stimulate the popularization of cloud VR technology.

Overview

This book comprises eight chapters, covering the technical principles, platform structure, network solutions, user experience, and business practices of cloud virtual reality (VR).

Beginning with VR development and evolution, we introduce the transformation to cloud VR and the technologies that encompass this revolutionary platform.

We then discuss the cloud VR platform, network solutions, and terminals.

The following chapters describe the methods of testing and evaluating cloud VR, as well as its commercialization.

Here is a brief introduction of each chapter.

Chapter 1 Cloud VR Overview
This chapter describes the unique features of VR, its history, and the challenges it faces. It also discusses the advantages of cloud VR and various application scenarios.

Chapter 2 Cloud VR Technologies
This chapter describes the technical architecture of cloud VR and its two key service types (strong-interaction and weak-interaction). This chapter also analyzes the key problems these two service types face and the various solutions to overcome them. Collaboration between cloud, pipe, and device is critical to the entire technological architecture of cloud VR.

Chapter 3 Cloud VR Platform Technologies
The platform determines the service types and features provided by cloud VR. In this chapter, platform technologies and their relationship with strong- and weak-interaction services are described in detail.

Chapter 4 Cloud VR Network Solution
This chapter focuses on how to improve the VR user experience by analyzing network requirements at the different phases of cloud VR. In addition, it describes the cloud VR network transport solution and the future of network evolution, providing a reference for cloud VR service deployment.

Chapter 5 Cloud VR Terminals
This chapter describes the implementation principles, classification, selection, key technological development, and platform interconnection functions of cloud VR terminals.

Chapter 6 Research on Cloud VR Service Experience
This chapter discusses a benchmark for analyzing and evaluating the user experience of cloud VR services.

Chapter 7 Cloud VR Business Practices
This chapter describes the current situation of the cloud VR industry, the advantages and roles of operators, and success cases, as well as provides suggestions for operators when deploying cloud VR services.

Chapter 8 Future of Cloud VR
The final chapter discusses and predicts the future that awaits cloud VR.

Acknowledgment

This document is written by Huawei iLab and the Transmission & Access Digital Information and Content Experience Team. We would like to express our sincere gratitude to the leaders of Huawei Network Products & Solutions and Transmission & Access Product Line for their guidance, support, and encouragement.

Chapter 1

Cloud VR Overview

Our sense of perception defines our virtual existence. As we advance through the digital world, our interactions with video games and what we experience in science fiction movies come together in virtual reality (VR). With higher network speeds and stability, we can bring users closer to powerful computing clouds which ignite the VR industry, facilitate cloud VR technologies, and provide new growth for the VR industry.

1.1 VR OVERVIEW

1.1.1 What is VR?

VR is a simulated experience of the real world. It uses digital modeling and simulation to generate a three-dimensional virtual environment, offering an immersive experience using display, sound fields, sensing, and motion capture technologies, as shown in Figure 1.1.

The ultimate goal of VR is true immersion and reproduction of all of our senses in a virtual environment by creating a digital twin of the human body and reading and writing brain waves and neural signals via brain–computer interfaces. For example, the transfer of consciousness explored in the film *Avatar* may someday become reality.

1.1.2 VR development

The concept of VR was born nearly a century ago and has now moved on to commercial production. A timeline is shown in Figure 1.2.

Earliest form: In 1935, Stanley G. Weinbaum released *Pygmalion's Spectacles*, a science fiction story. In his book, Weinbaum described a pair of goggles which allowed people to experience a fictional world through sight, sound, smell, and touch, which closely resembles what has emerged today.

Term coinage: The 1970s saw the first implementation of VR in the lab. In 1985, computer scientist Jaron Lanier co-founded VPL Research with Thomas Zimmerman and coined the term "virtual reality". In 1987, they launched the first VR headset and gloves priced as high as USD 9000.

Figure 1.1 VR user.

Early attempts: 1990 to 2013 saw technology companies dabble in the VR market without much success. Sega launched Sega VR for arcade games, and Nintendo launched the Virtual Boy game console. However, their attempts were not well received through sales, as these technologies lagged behind in terms of the VR vision. Only in 2012, when the Oculus Rift VR headset was crowdfunded with USD 2.4 million, did VR applications begin to grow in popularity.

Temporary prosperity: In 2014, Oculus VR's acquisition by Facebook for USD 2 billion was undoubtedly a boost for the VR market, motivating hundreds of companies to develop VR products. By 2016, PC VR headsets, standalone VR headsets, and smartphone VR headsets had become well-known. However, this popularity was short-lived, as the quality and user experience did not follow. The full potential of VR was nowhere to be seen.

Steady development: In 2017, while many VR companies exited the market and the VR craze faded away, some companies survived by improving the VR experience. These companies have benefited from major progress in terms of hardware, content, quality, and shipments. In 2018, the screen resolution of VR headsets had doubled, and global shipments reached 5.64 million units. According to a prediction from the International Data Corporation (IDC), the annual shipment of headsets was set to exceed 6.24 million units in 2019, an increase of 10.9%. As for content, 2018 saw the success of the VR rhythm game, Beat Saber, which became the highest-rated game on Steam three days after its launch, making 8.68 million USD in the following six months. In addition, high requirements on computer performance gave birth to cloud VR, which supports VR applications with cloud computing. After seeing the advantages of cloud, networks, and a large user base, telecom operators started to provide cloud VR services for individual users.

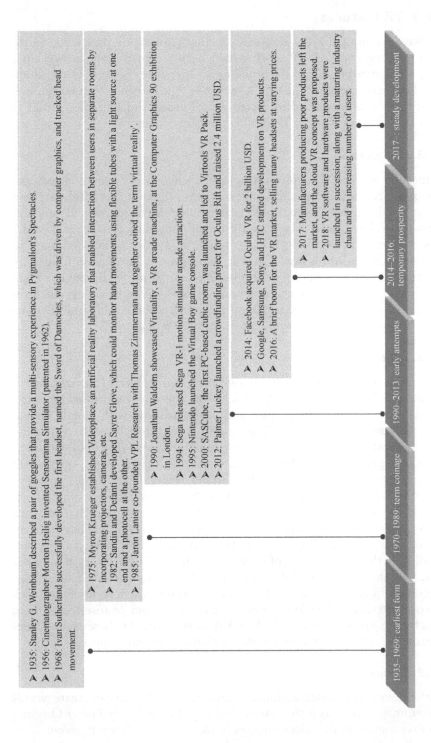

Figure 1.2 Development history of VR.

1.1.3 VR features

Unlike conventional HD video services that gained popularity due to the high-resolution visuals, VR services have been accepted in the market since their emergence because of the brand new experience they bring to consumers. This new experience features "three Is" (immersion, interaction, and imagination), as described by Grigore C. Burdea and Philippe Coiffet in their book *Virtual Reality Technology* published in 1994.

1.1.3.1 Immersion

Immersion is something that distinguishes VR services from conventional video services, which present images in 360°, making users feel part of a virtual environment. Virtual objects become clearer and more detailed as users move closer and can be viewed from all sides, just as in the real world; this is immersion of sight. Hearing, touch, and smell immersion are also included. Three-dimensional (3D) surround sound allows users to identify the direction and distance of a sound source, and force feedback gives them a feeling of touch when interacting with virtual objects. The more the users can perceive, the more they feel like they are in a real world, and the more likely they are to resonate with and be immersed in it.

1.1.3.2 Interaction

Interaction refers to the influence between users and objects in a virtual environment and how natural the feedback from this environment is. We interact with computers through mice and keyboards and with mobile phones through buttons and touch. These are all done through interfaces, rather than natural human movements, for example, the movements involved in drinking a glass of water. We don't do this through an interface – picking up and moving the glass is a natural human movement.

Natural interaction is the second feature that makes VR services stand out. Ideally, the VR experience should immerse all of the senses. That is, when users do something in a virtual environment, the surrounding environment should offer corresponding feedback. For example, if users pick up a cup, they should feel the slight change of weight in their hand. When they move their legs, they should feel the shift in position. When they turn their head, they should see in a new direction. Progress has been made in technologies such as voice interaction, motion capture, eye tracking, and gesture recognition, which have already been applied to VR interaction. As these technologies mature, the natural aspect of VR interaction will greatly improve.

1.1.3.3 Imagination

With immersion and interaction in a simulated world, we can create worlds of our imagination, as is the case with the OASIS in *Ready Player One* and the exotic space in the science fiction book *The Three-Body Problem*.

VR imagination allows users to create new concepts and environments with divergent thinking. VR gives users the power to set their own rules. Why prevent them from designing their own virtual worlds? As long as users can imagine it, VR technologies can make it in virtual reality, be it an adventure in the skies, underground, in the Jurassic period, or out in space.

1.2 VR INDUSTRY ENVIRONMENT

The immersive, interactive, and imaginative VR experience enables people to perceive the world in a brand new way. Benefiting from increasingly advanced technologies, favorable government policies, and a mature ecosystem, the VR industry has become a hotspot for investment and financing with great potential. VR is a historical opportunity and the most promising option for a new computing platform.

1.2.1 VR industry chain

The VR industry chain constitutes an ecosystem involving multiple domains, for example, near-eye display, content creation, network transmission, rendering, and perception and interaction, as described in the *Virtual Reality/Augmented Reality White Paper (2018)* released by China Academy of Information and Communications Technology (CAICT). Each of these domains is divided into smaller sections,[1] as shown in Figure 1.3.

The VR industry chain mainly consists of terminal hardware vendors, software tool providers, platform service providers, and content providers, as shown in Figure 1.4.

Terminal hardware vendors: Provide end user devices, including output and interaction devices. Output devices can be categorized into tethered, standalone, and smartphone VR headsets, while interaction devices mainly refer to peripherals used for interaction and perception, such as controller handles, base stations, motion capture apparatus, and haptic vests. Be it an output device or an interaction device, basic components are indispensable, including chips, sensors, screens, optical components (lenses and panoramic cameras), and casing.

Due to their more complex structure, it is harder to produce an output device for VR than for a smartphone. In contrast to the 40–50 components average in a smartphone, the Oculus Rift contains more than 200 components. Assembly and manufacturing of VR terminals are more difficult and thereby more costly. VR devices also have stringent requirements on screens due to displays being placed so close to the eyes, as well as on optical amplification systems. For consumer-grade devices, the pixels per inch (PPI) should be no lower than 800, while for professional devices, it should be higher than 1600 PPI.

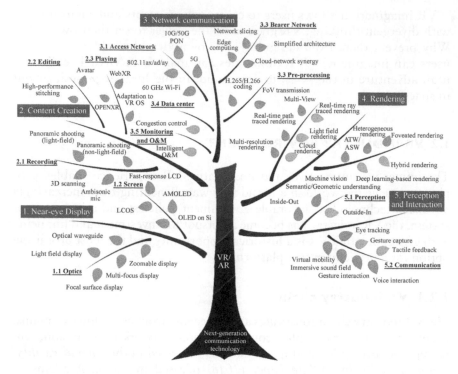

Figure 1.3 Hierarchy of VR technologies (CAICT). Note: The numbers in the figure correspond to chapters in the *Virtual Reality/Augmented Reality White Paper (2018)*.

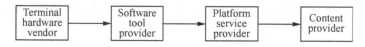

Figure 1.4 VR industry chain.

Software tool providers: Mainly provide operating systems and information processing systems to deliver sensing and collection, coding and decoding, rendering and display, and physical feedback. Software tools are indispensable for content development and application, while content development requirements also guide tool development. For example, VR photography and videography require image capture and stitching tools and content creation requires computer graphics (CG) and modeling tools, as well as rendering engines. In addition, VR content needs to adapt to different platforms and terminals due to the lack of unified industry standards.

Platform service providers: Perform distribution and operations that further relate to distribution platforms, content operation, and sales channels. Similar to the concept of mobile app stores, VR content is released, managed, and sold to users under a positive feedback loop.

Content providers: Generally speaking, no VR platform has enough content, let alone enough premium content. The scarcity of VR content can be seen by comparing the tens of thousands of PC games with only 1,600 VR games on Steam, the world's largest gaming platform.

Most content in the VR industry is bespoke, and most of it is applied to education. Although other industries such as public service, healthcare, real estate, and tourism marketing are catching up on VR content creation, most of this content is designed for instruction and training, and it seems to lack inspiration and so could be improved.

1.2.2 Investment in the VR industry

There has been a steady growth in the VR industry since 2017. According to the *Worldwide Quarterly Augmented and Virtual Reality Headset Tracker (2019 Q1)* released by IDC, the global headset shipments of 2019 Q1 reached 1.23 million, up 27.2% from the figure of the same quarter of the previous year. According to the report, shipments in China exceeded 270,000, up 15.1% from the figure of the same quarter of the previous year, mainly contributed by PC and standalone headsets, as shown in Figure 1.5.

IDC forecasts VR headset shipments of 34.6 million at a five-year compound annual growth rate (CAGR) of 43.7% by 2023. According to this forecast, standalone headset shipments will account for 64.6% of all shipments, followed by PC headsets (34.4%) and mobile headsets.

Encouraged by this strong momentum, VR will become a heated area for investment and financing. IDC predicted that much of the growth in the global VR market for the five years after 2019 was to be driven by accelerating investments from commercial and public sectors. The market expenditure of 16.8 billion USD for 2019 was estimated to reach 160 billion USD by 2023, at a five-year CAGR of 78.3%. The financial and infrastructure sectors

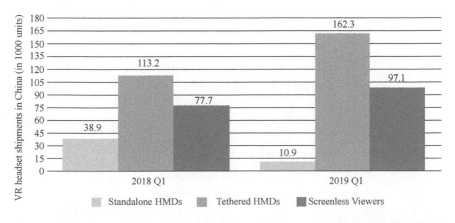

Figure 1.5 VR headset shipments in China from 2018 Q1 to 2019 Q1 (IDC China, 2019). Note: Q1 refers to the first quarter.

were estimated to lead the five-year CAGR rank with CAGRs of 133.9% and 122.8%, respectively, followed by manufacturing and public sectors. Consumer spending on VR was expected to deliver a CAGR of 52.2%.

Training (11.7 billion USD), film and television (4.5 billion USD), and industrial maintenance (4.1 billion USD) were estimated to receive the largest investments by 2023. In comparison, investment in the three consumer use cases (VR gaming, VR video, and Augmented Reality (AR) gaming) was estimated to reach 15.3 billion USD.

Investors are optimistic about emerging VR/AR technologies. According to the statistics organized by China Centre for Information Industry Development (CCID), from January to October 2019, global VR/AR investment and financing exceeded 6 billion USD (as shown in Figure 1.6). The annual growth rate was estimated to exceed 50%. Hardware and content are hotspots for investment and financing. In spite of less investment and financing events, China has witnessed larger amounts in single investments and more rounds of funding in 2019 than in the previous year. The amount of financing had exceeded 1 billion USD by October 2019, close to the total for 2018.

1.2.3 VR industry policies

In recent years, governments in multiple countries have promoted the VR industry at state level.

In as early as the 1990s, the U.S. government had made VR one of the key areas of support in the National Information Infrastructure (NII) plan. In 2000, the U.S. Department of Energy (DOE) formulated the Long-Term Nuclear Technology Research and Development Plan, which underlined the development, application, and verification of VR technologies. In 2017,

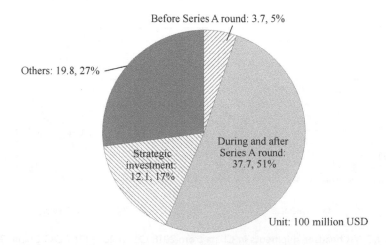

Figure 1.6 Global VR/AR investment from January to October 2019.

multiple U.S. senators announced the establishment of a VR steering group to support the VR industry at Congress. The U.S. Health and Human Services (HHS) and Department of Education (ED) have also made efforts to launch pilot programs for VR application in the treatment of mental illness, and primary and secondary education.

Meanwhile, Europe began to fund the VR industry in the 1980s. Tens of millions of euros were subsidized for the VR industry in the Horizon 2020 program that started in 2014. Japan launched the long-term strategic guidelines of *Innovation 25* (2007) that extends to 2025 and the *Comprehensive Strategy on Science, Technology and Innovation 2014-Bridge of Innovation toward Creating the Future,* which aims to make Japan a global innovation center. Both regard VR as a key direction for technological innovation. In 2016, South Korea set up a special fund of approximately 40.2 billion KRW to list VR, autonomous driving, and artificial intelligence (AI) technologies into their nine emerging fields. In addition, the Ministry of Science, ICT and Future Planning of South Korea has planned to invest approximately 405 billion KRW from 2016 to 2020 to develop VR industries. The emphasis is on ensuring the original technology R&D and industrial ecosystem improve and shortening the time required to catch up with the U.S. from two years to half a year.

Overall, enterprises are the main force developing VR in the U.S., while the government acts as a coordinator, focusing on setting a pattern of VR application development. The EU, South Korea, and Japan are mostly concerned about top-level design and R&D of new technologies and offer guidance in key areas by means of special funds.

In China, the government has included VR in its *Outline of the 13th Five-Year Plan for the National Informatization* and *Guiding Opinions of the State Council on Vigorously Advancing the "Internet Plus" Action,* and other national departments have followed suit. Since 2016, VR policies have been implemented in cities to facilitate VR industry development.

1.3 DILEMMAS OF VR

The popularization of VR as an emerging industry is built on a mature and open ecosystem, with affordable pricing, and an acceptable service experience. However, there is still a long way to go for the VR industry.

1.3.1 Fractured ecosystem

In the initial phase of VR development, hardware and software are heavily coupled. They are not only linked together, but also highly dependent on each other. Figure 1.7 gives a glimpse into the ecosystem of VR terminals.

Sony has a closed ecosystem for PlayStation software and hardware, ranging from headsets and PCs to accessories and content. Users who purchase

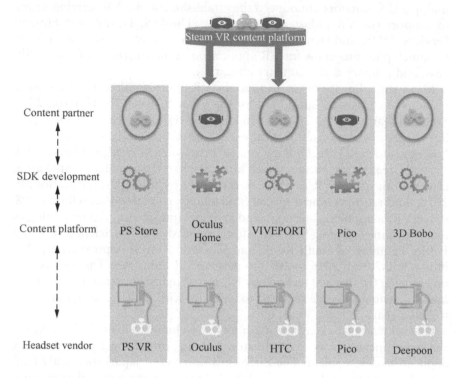

Figure 1.7 Industry ecosystem centering on terminal hardware. Note: SDK refers to software development kit.

PlayStation hardware can experience VR content on Sony's platform only. Although this may seem unreasonable, the PlayStation appeals to a large number of consumers for its premium content that can be lacking elsewhere.

Oculus and HTC are looking beyond their independent content platforms for interconnection with Steam, offering users more VR content. HTC goes further to open the VIVE development software for their VIVE headset, to allow developers to build up their content, streamlining the ecosystem that is centered on VR headsets. Latecomers like Pico and Deepoon are also working to accumulate more VR content by constructing their platforms and establishing connections with other content platforms. Not only VR companies, but also vendors like Huawei and Skyworth are striving for richer content.

This is a fractured ecosystem, where terminal vendors are in need of content cooperation, while content providers crave the adaptation of VR terminals, as shown in Figure 1.8. This kind of fracture undoubtedly restricts the development of the industry.

Open platforms and rich content are what is needed for a thriving industry ecosystem. However, Yivian reported that by the end of 2018, there were only 6,000 items of VR content, which was far less than the number of

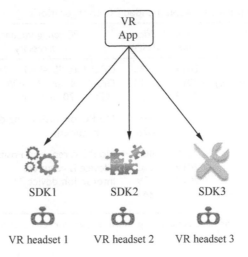

Figure 1.8 VR applications adapting to terminals and software.

common PC and smartphone applications. A lack of unified standards is the root cause; this deeply concerns standards organizations worldwide, such as China Communications Standards Association (CCSA) and OpenXR. Their VR/AR working groups are aiming to establish interface specifications and standards.

1.3.2 Unaffordable

VR terminal hardware can be very expensive. To enjoy the PC VR experience, a consumer also needs a computer with high-end performance that usually costs nearly 1,500 USD. A complete set of VR terminals costs even more. For details, see Table 1.1.

Due to the computing and graphics processing capabilities of computers, PC VR headsets are able to provide consumers with a smooth experience in large-scale interactive games, overshadowing standalone VR headsets. Although they are at a disadvantage, standalone VR headsets are winning some consumers over with their lower prices. As for smartphone VR headsets, they come at a variety of prices and provide patchy user experiences that depend on the processing performance of mobile phones.

In addition to hardware constraints, a lack of content also contributes to the expense of VR content for individual users. The price issue becomes more noticeable for industry users who require customized content. This is because VR content requires more complex technologies, more costly rendering, and a longer development period than common apps and videos. This was the case with the VR documentary "VR China", jointly produced by the Chinese National Geography (CNG) film center and Whaley VR. The production used 360° 8K on-site filming, was very expensive, and took two years to make.

Table 1.1 Headset price and recommended PC configurations

Brand	GTM time	Price (USD)	PC configuration or accessory	Accessory price (USD)
Oculus Rift S	2019	595	CPU: Intel i5-4590 or later	> 715
HTC VIVE Pro 1.0 (suite)	2019	1414	Graphics card: NVIDIA	
Deepoon E3 4K	2019	555	GTX 970 or later	
HTC VIVE Focus Plus	2019	810	No PC or positioning device	N/A
Oculus Quest	2019	676	is required.	
Oculus Go	2018	405	No PC is required. Positioning	NOLO
Pico G2	2019	(64G)	device is required.	suite: 185
Skyworth V901	2019	329	Interaction device	
		343		

Note: These are prices on the e-commerce platform and are for reference only.

1.3.3 Limited experience

Although VR promises a brand new panoramic, 3D, and fully interactive experience, technological limitations indicate that there is still room for improvement in the VR industry.

1.3.3.1 Image quality

Many people have gone through deteriorated user experiences caused by visual fatigue from low image quality. This low quality can be attributed to many factors, such as definition, smoothness, color, and production means. Flat videos have nearly hit the threshold of what human eyes are capable of by offering 4K ultra-HD videos. However, VR panoramic videos in 4K only provide an experience equivalent to a 240P flat video at best. This lags far behind the experience of ultra HD videos. VR terminal hardware also affects image quality depending on its display performance, decoding capability, and anti-distortion processing. Furthermore, some headsets have implemented 4K resolution for both eyes and 8K hardware decoding, improving display quality and reducing the screen-door effect – a mesh-like appearance that occurs when visible gaps between pixels are seen on an electronic screen.

1.3.3.2 Dizziness

A key problem facing VR experience, dizziness, or motion sickness, is caused by an inconsistency between the user's vision and the motion state sensed by the brain. Symptoms commonly include a loss of balance, nausea, vomiting, sweating, and so on. There are many causes of motion sickness, among which motion-sensing conflict and vergence-accommodation conflict are two key factors.

Motion-sensing conflict refers to dizziness resulting from a mismatch between physical motions and vision due to missing motion feedback output. In order to avoid this conflict, when users walk forward in a virtual environment, the images in their view should move backward at an equal speed; when users turn their heads, the view should follow the rotation. Motion-to-photon (MTP) latency is the time needed for a user movement to be fully reflected on a display screen. The industry consensus is that MTP latency should be less than 20 ms, otherwise motion sickness will become an issue. It should be noted that not everyone gets motion sickness, just as some people do not suffer from carsickness.

Vergence-accommodation conflict is also known as focusing conflict. In principle, the crystalline lens needs to get thicker or thinner to project images precisely on the retina for objects at different distances. Yet this change cannot be achieved in VR headsets, as they cannot provide the desired depth perception for human eyes to view the world in 3D. Specifically, the light rays emitted by the headset screen do not contain the depth cues of an object, and so the eye stays focused on the screen. The crystalline lens remains unchanged even if objects are at different distances. This results in a conflict, and often dizziness, which may be reduced by improving image quality, providing 3D surround sound, reducing MTP latency, and giving force feedback.

1.3.3.3 Poor usability

Another prominent issue with the VR experience is poor usability. After VR devices are purchased, users need to go through a complex process of setting them up, including installing the base station, calibrating the center, pairing the controllers, and downloading the games. For stand-alone VR headsets, users may need to install a positioning kit that is not very user-friendly. Only products that are ready to use are popular among users.

1.3.3.4 Cumbersomeness

PC VR headsets are connected to computers via cables. Due to limited cable length and tangled cables, users are confined to a limited range of motion. Therefore, cable-free designs can help free users with wireless access through Wi-Fi or 5G. In addition, a security barrier needs to be set up to prevent users from bumping into objects in the real world. In Oculus Quest, the super FoV (field of view) sensor and computer vision algorithm are used to distinguish the virtual world from the real world by providing what Oculus calls a playspace for obstacle avoidance.

1.4 EMERGENCE OF CLOUD VR

1.4.1 Cloud is the future

Cloud computing is a revolutionary technology that accelerates the pace of cloudification, offering three platforms: infrastructure as a service (IaaS), platform as a service (PaaS), and software as a service (SaaS). They not only reduce costs, improve efficiency, unify management, and bring security and control to enterprises and individuals, but they also energize parties in the cloud service industry chain.

In recent years, infrastructure based on cloud computing has been powering global services, and governments have been encouraging this market. According to data released by Gartner in early 2019, the worldwide public cloud service market reached USD 136.3 billion in 2018, up 23.01% from that in 2017. Gartner also forecasts that in the next five years, the CAGR will approach 20%, and the market will double to more than USD 270 billion by 2022.[2]

1.4.2 Cloud-based applications are supported by network infrastructure

Network infrastructure is indispensable for cloud-based applications. With the rollout of 5G networks and fast development of broadband networks, particularly optical broadband networks, the network infrastructure is being prepared for cloud applications, such as cloud VR.

1.4.3 Cloud VR will drive the industry

Cloud VR revolutionizes VR by transferring host rendering, computing, and storage to the clouds, which then transmit these video streams to VR headsets.

Cloud VR offers the following advantages:

1. Affordable prices: Cloud VR maintains all the advantages of VR but reduces the burden of computing on terminals. High-performance and expensive terminals are no longer needed, saving consumers 70% on hardware costs.
2. Content aggregation and click-and-play: A unified cloud VR platform can accommodate different VR content for different VR terminals, transforming the way content is stored and transmitted. VR content developers only need to adapt their content to the platform rather than to different terminals, and therefore this can improve the quantity and quality of VR content. Furthermore, once content is integrated to a unified platform, users can obtain premium content in one click.
3. Stronger copyright protection: It is difficult to enforce copyright protection for VR content that is purchased and played in its physical form.

However, by making VR content available through the cloud, the content can be centrally managed to ensure that VR is not tampered with, modified, or pirated.

4. Better synergy between big data analysis and AI: By storing data on the cloud, the computing and analysis capabilities of the cloud can be fully leveraged to bring larger value and boost innovation.

5. Improved user experience: Cord-free headsets grant users barrier-free control in virtual environments.

6. Accelerated popularization of VR: A larger user base lowers costs for users and creates an ideal environment for VR content and business to flourish.

Cloud VR is the ultimate form of large-scale VR development. The goal is to build a cloud VR platform through device-cloud synergy to efficiently and securely distribute VR content.

Telecom operators are the best candidates to run cloud VR services. Smartphones have completely changed people's work and living habits, as such VR will stand at the forefront of gigabit home broadband and 5G technologies, becoming the first major commercial application.

1.5 APPLICATION SCENARIOS OF CLOUD VR

VR technologies have been widely used in various industries. This section lists several typical cloud VR use cases in home and industry scenarios.

1.5.1 Application scenarios at homes

1.5.1.1 Giant-screen cinema

VR technology and traditional cinema technology can create a more immersive viewing experience for the audience. A panoramic viewing experience can be achieved by combining VR headsets with large cinema screens, as shown in Figure 1.9. Moreover, with the maturity of video conversion technologies, traditional two-dimensional (2D) films will be easily converted into VR video.

1.5.1.2 VR live broadcast

VR live broadcast distinguishes itself from common TV live broadcast as it goes beyond traditional videos and allows users to view live broadcasts from any angle, as if they were physically present, as shown in Figure 1.10.

In addition to using VR cameras to take photos and stitch images, the production process of VR live broadcast is similar to a traditional one, which includes VR shooting, real-time stitching, transcoding and distributing,

Figure 1.9 VR IMAX cinema.

Figure 1.10 GVR live broadcast (GVR).

as well as video on demand (VoD) playback. VR live broadcast has greater potential due to its ability to penetrate a number of fields, including sports events, concerts, product launch events, and variety shows. These kinds of live broadcasts are both frequent and attract a large audience, thereby justifying the commercial feasibility of VR live broadcast.

1.5.1.3 Panoramic VR video

Panoramic videos combine the technologies of VoD and VR. When users watch videos through their VR headsets, they are able to adjust their AoV as if they were physically on-site, as shown in Figure 1.11. However, shooting panoramic videos requires a range of professional devices. After multi-angle images are captured, stitching is required to ensure that each frame

Figure 1.11 Panoramic VR video.

forms a 360° panoramic image. Depth information may be added to a video to make it more immersive, so users can actually feel that they are approaching or moving away from an object in the virtual world.

1.5.1.4 VR gaming

VR games hold the most potential for cloud-based strong-interaction services. They not only attract users, but also embody the concept of full immersion.

First-person shooters and racing games are fun and highly immersive as they allow players to do things they are unable to do in reality. Therefore, these kinds of games are highly marketable (Figure 1.12).

1.5.2 Application scenarios of industries

1.5.2.1 Education

VR education focuses primarily on campus education. It enhances the teaching and learning experience by allowing ideas that cannot be observed in reality, such as astronomy, as well as geological and geomorphological changes to be reproduced. Additionally, VR technologies and AI can facilitate other educational activities, such as generating realistic and immersive situational dialogues to provide students with authentic language practice.

VR technologies can break time and space restrictions and present knowledge in a more vivid and intuitive manner, thereby stimulating student's interest and enhancing learning, as shown in Figure 1.13.

1.5.2.2 Enterprise and vocational training

VR technologies can provide virtual training to employees, reducing significant energy, heavy equipment, and rail costs for enterprises. Employees can receive on-the-job skills training in virtual environments, eliminating hardware costs, and improving safety and security, as shown in Figure 1.14.

Figure 1.12 Interactive VR games (7663 VR).

Figure 1.13 VR education (Growlib).

Figure 1.14 VR welding training (Shenzhen GTA Education Tech Ltd.).

Figure 1.15 VR fire evacuation training (Elernity).

VR training can be beneficial in chemical and medical environments where traditional training methods may cause risk to an employee's welfare. By using VR technologies, enterprises of these industries can ensure employee safety while also making sure they are well-trained.[3]

1.5.2.3 Public services

Government agencies have long been striving to provide better welfare and services to the public. Through technology, these services have become more accessible to the public and are available across networks and mobile platforms.

In scenarios such as earthquake response training, fire safety training, traffic accident simulation, environmental protection publicity, and urban planning, VR can be of great use due to its ability to recreate reality, offer an immersive experience, and lower construction costs, as shown in Figure 1.15.

1.5.2.4 VR experience center

VR experience centers are physical stores that combine traditional entertainment with VR technologies, such as motion capture, haptic, and force feedback devices. They can be highly immersive, fun, and cost effective, as shown in Figure 1.16.

Theme parks are extremely popular with thrill-seekers and children, but the main issue is that they are often located in rural areas. Yet, with VR, consumers can enjoy the thrill of theme park rides from more convenient locations, such as in a shopping mall or even at home.

VR centers can also be built near historical and cultural attractions to reproduce important past events. And so, through VR, tourists can develop a better understanding of the history and culture of a place.

Figure 1.16 Throwing snowballs at VR theme halls (Realis).

In conclusion, there are many more scenarios where VR can be applied, be it at home or in industrial environments. Opportunities to open up new ideas and solutions are endless.

Chapter 2

Cloud VR Technologies

Cloud virtual reality (VR) moves content and rendering to the cloud, lowering costs and improving user experience. Cloud VR also supports a wide range of application scenarios and copyright protection, which are key to promoting large-scale development of the VR industry.

Cloud VR requires comprehensive development and advancement of services, experience, and technology. A high-quality VR experience and support for a wide range of service scenarios are important for promoting cloud VR. The content layer, platform layer, network layer, and terminal layer need to form a four-in-one technical architecture and system to support cloud VR services and guarantee a good experience.

2.1 CLOUD VR SERVICE AND EXPERIENCE

2.1.1 Cloud VR service types

Section 1.5 describes the diversified services of cloud VR and their application in business scenarios. However, the implementations are quite similar. VR services fundamentally change the way humans interact with machines, transforming the traditional two-dimensional (2D) interface to a three-dimensional (3D) one so that a user can interact with a virtual environment in real time and with three dimensions of information. Cloud VR services are classified into weak-interaction services and strong-interaction services depending on the interaction between users and the virtual environment, as shown in Figure 2.1.

1. Weak-interaction VR services
   Weak-interaction services include VR panoramic videos, VR live broadcast, and VR video on demand (VoD). Weak-interaction services are further classified into VR VoD or VR live broadcasting services depending on how time sensitive they are. Weak-interaction cloud VR services have the following characteristics:
   • They mainly focus on providing immersive audio and video experiences, with little interaction between users and the content.

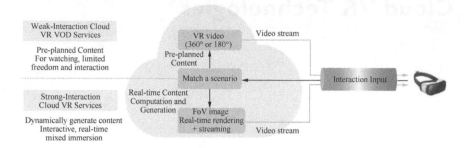

Figure 2.1 Cloud VR service types.

- They have limited degrees of freedom. The user may, to some extent, select a fixed viewpoint in the virtual environment from which to watch surrounding or panoramic content.
- The interaction between users and virtual environments is limited. In general, users can only move their head and look around. Some videos with light interaction allow users to choose the plot direction, but they have no interaction with objects in the virtual environment.

Weak-interaction cloud VR service content is deployed on the cloud and pushed as video content to user terminals in real time as requested.

2. Strong-interaction cloud VR services

In strong-interaction services, a user may use an additional device to interact with the virtual environment, such as a handheld controller. Objects in the virtual environment respond to interaction by the user, and this is rendered in real time, providing direct feedback. Strong-interaction services include VR games and interactive education. Strong-interaction cloud VR services have the following characteristics:

- A user may use devices to actively interact with the virtual environment, another user, and so on. Therefore, in addition to an audio and video experience, the user may be further immersed by interacting with the virtual environment.
- The virtual environment and objects in the environment respond to user interaction in real time. Content in strong-interaction services needs to be computed and rendered in real time according to interaction by the user but only in the immediate field of view (FoV). In contrast, weak-interaction services do not require as much processing and cover 180° or 360° of view. Strong-interaction cloud VR services are deployed in the cloud where they undergo computing and real-time rendering. These rendered images are continuously streamed as video to terminals.

2.1.2 Cloud VR key elements for experience

The sustainable development of the cloud VR service depends on good user experience. In the Internet era, various industries have been evolving from providing products and services to providing user experience. This has created an experience-driven economy and encouraged improvement to user experience. Traditional videos provide users with a limited experience in terms of quality content and high definition. From its conception, VR has created an experience that integrates more of our senses and more technology, creating a much more immersive experience than is possible with traditional video. According to the theory[4] proposed by J. J. Gibson, human perception may be divided into orienting, auditory, haptic, taste–smell, and visual systems. Virtual reality should continuously develop its use of multiple senses to provide an all-round experience for users.

Chapter 1 describes the three "i"s of the VR experience: immersive, interactive, and imaginative. These three features accurately summarize VR and are known in the industry as important requirements for the VR experience. Cloud VR introduces elements such as cloud processes and networks. Cloud VR needs to pay attention to the factors that may be introduced with cloud transformation in addition to the local VR experience.

Figure 2.2 shows a breakdown of requirements for an immersive and interactive VR experience. The requirements systematically summarize the main factors that concern users. For details, see Chapter 6. The requirements model for user experience will be continuously updated and improved alongside the development of cloud VR technology.

According to the cloud VR user experience requirement model, many factors affect the cloud VR experience. In the current phase of development, the main factors are as follows:

- Definition: Determined by the number and quality of pixels visible to the user and affected by such factors as content resolution, coding, terminal resolution, decoding capability, and FoV. Insufficient content

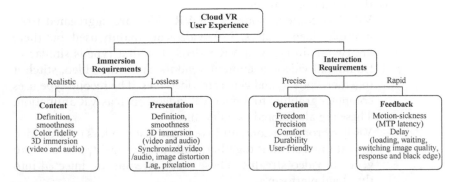

Figure 2.2 Cloud VR user experience requirement model.

and terminal resolution can easily result in a loss of immersion, as the eye will be able to see individual pixels. This is currently the main problem affecting VR definition.

- Smoothness: The main factors that affect fluidity are the frame rate of the content and the refresh rate of the terminal. If the frame rate or refresh rate is insufficient, the picture may be unreliable, and lag may occur.
- Field of view: If FoV is insufficient, such as when it is smaller than is perceived by human eyes, users will feel that they are observing the scene through a window instead of in a virtual environment. Immersion will be reduced.
- Motion sickness: It is widely accepted that motion sickness can be caused when the delay from VR terminal movement to display (motion-to-photon) is greater than 20 ms.[5] This can be avoided if this latency is reduced to less than 20 ms.
- Lag: Lag occurs when a user moves or interacts in a virtual environment and does not receive prompt feedback, for example, a delay between when the user clicks a button and when the image responds, such as the delay when changing the video or channel. Lag greatly affects the reality of VR interaction.

2.2 OVERALL TECHNICAL ARCHITECTURE

The overall technical architecture of cloud VR must support different types of services and guarantee a good service experience. The overall technical architecture of cloud VR consists of the content layer, platform layer, network layer, and terminal layer, as shown in Figure 2.3.

1. Content layer
   The content layer provides source content for weak- and strong-interaction cloud VR services.
   1. Weak-interaction content
      - VR VoD content: Sources for VR video are aggregated from multiple video vendors. 360° videos are mainly used, but there are two main types of VR videos. The first type is similar to traditional video, as content vendors shoot the video, stitch it together, code it, and generate video files. The second type uses computer graphics to render VR videos, such as VR animation. These are also stored as video files.
      - VR live broadcast content: Live broadcast vendors record video in real time, stitch it together, code it, package it, and use it to generate video streams. These video streams are injected into the cloud platform.

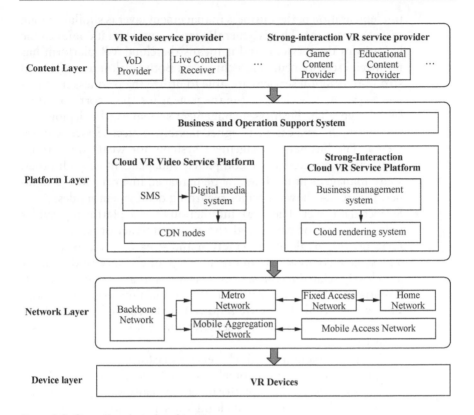

Figure 2.3 Overall technical architecture.

2. Strong-interaction content

VR games and interactive education. The VR software development kit (SDK) is provided by content developers. Developers create VR content using mainstream game engines such as Unity and Unreal Engine and build executables for an operating system. PC VR content can generally be migrated to a cloud platform with the same running environment after some adjustment.

2. Platform layer

Cloud VR features and processes are different for weak-interaction and strong-interaction services, especially for real-time interaction and compute processing. Therefore, a differentiated service platform is required. A mature service platform generally covers both business management and service data.

- Business management layer: Before data services can be provided for users, services such as content management, user rights management, and user login and authentication are provided. The implementation of the business management layer is similar among service platforms. This is generally irrelevant when it comes to the features of the services, and it means the cloud VR platform has no special requirements for technology. Both weak-interaction and strong-interaction services are able to utilize the business management system, as well as self-management for their corresponding service type. The business management system can be deployed in various modes and can be designed flexibly to meet service requirements. The business management systems for weak and strong-interaction services can be completely independent of each other, share management modules, or be managed in a centralized manner. Figure 2.4 shows specifics regarding deployment modes.

- Service data layer: The weak-interaction service platform provides video services for users, and the strong-interaction service platform provides real-time interaction and streaming video services. The system composition and technology of the service data layer are closely related to the service features and are the core for differentiating the service platforms. It is important to carefully consider which technologies are required at the core of the cloud VR service platform, to support services and guarantee a good user experience.

  1. Weak-interaction cloud VR service platform
     Current Internet Protocol television (IPTV) platforms and over the top (OTT) video platforms are already very popular and mature. Weak-interaction cloud VR services are essentially an evolution of traditional video services. If a traditional video platform such as IPTV or OTT video has been deployed on the live network, the weak-interaction cloud VR services can extend from this to create a platform. The weak-interaction cloud VR service platform consists of the business management system, digital media system, and content delivery network (CDN) nodes.

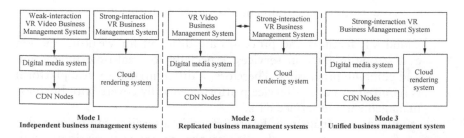

Figure 2.4 Deployment mode of the weak- and strong-interaction business management systems.

- Business management system: This system supports weak-interaction services and is oriented to VoD and live broadcast of VR video. It manages users, products, content, subscriptions, and charging, and helps with service logic such as user authentication, service authentication, and list management. The system can be connected to a business and operation support system to implement functions such as creating new users and synchronizing business management information.
- Digital media system: The digital media system provides video content as a service. It is the core of the weak-interaction service platform and is responsible for ingesting, transcoding, storing, and distributing on-demand and live video content.
- CDN node: The CDN node is a downstream distribution node for the digital media system. It is deployed close to users and is responsible for caching and accelerating content, connecting video users, responding to scheduling requests of the digital media system, and quickly providing media streams to users. A digital media system may be connected to multiple CDN nodes, and nodes may be divided into more layers to meet service coverage for an area or another service requirement. This facilitates hierarchical management and distribution of content. The relationship between a digital media system and CDN nodes is shown in Figure 2.5.

2. Strong-interaction cloud VR service platform

   The strong-interaction cloud VR service platform cannot reuse the traditional video platform for service data and needs to be reconstructed.

   - Business management system: This system manages users, products, content, subscriptions, and charging and helps with service logic such as user authentication, service

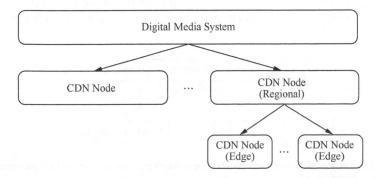

Figure 2.5 Relationship between the digital media system and CDN nodes.

authentication, and list management. The system can be connected to a business and operation support system to implement functions such as creating new users and synchronizing business management information. The strong-interaction business management system can reuse some functions from the weak-interaction business management system or combine them to construct a centralized business management platform.

 – Cloud rendering node: The cloud rendering node provides content as a service. It is the core of the strong-interaction cloud VR service platform. The cloud rendering node is mainly responsible for responding to interaction by a terminal and functions such as logic computation, real-time rendering, stream coding, and data transmission. Because strong-interaction services are time sensitive, cloud rendering nodes need to be deployed close to users to reduce end-to-end network latency. In most situations, a unified business management system will manage multiple cloud rendering nodes on the strong-interaction cloud VR service platform. Figure 2.6 shows the relationship between the business management system and the cloud rendering nodes.

3. Business and operation support system
   The business and operation support system provides centralized service operation, including user management, product management, resource management, customer service, channel management, charging, accounting, and settlement. As the unified management platform for multiple services, the service operation support system synchronizes business management information with the business management systems of weak- and strong-interaction services.

3. Network layer
   The cloud VR service is transmitted from the cloud platform to terminals through the network in the form of video streams. VR terminals

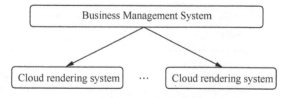

Figure 2.6 Relationship between the business management system and cloud rendering nodes.

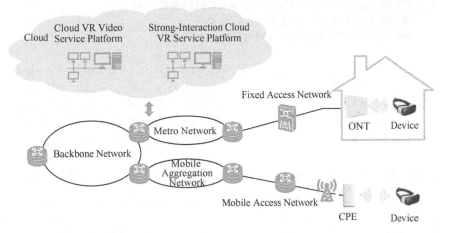

Figure 2.7 Cloud VR network.

access the cloud platform through a wireless network to communicate interaction and obtain video streams.

The business management system for the cloud platform can be deployed in regional centers, a provincial center, or a municipal center as required. CDN nodes and cloud rendering nodes need to be deployed close to users. Figure 2.7 shows the network structure of cloud VR, including the backbone network, metro network, fixed access network, home network, and mobile access network.

4. Terminal layer

The terminal layer consists of VR terminals and additional external positioning devices. Cloud VR terminals mainly come as either one or a pair of VR devices (such as a VR headset+a mobile phone). Built-in positioning or external positioning devices are used for multi-degree positioning.

VR terminals have the following native functions: capturing actions and operations, decoding video streams, and refreshing and displaying images. To provide cloud VR services for users, VR terminals must have modules that interconnect their underlying hardware with the cloud platform. These modules mainly perform the following functions:

- Provide an entry point for users to access the cloud platform.
- Interconnect with the action and operation capture module of the VR terminal, encapsulate action and operation information, connect to the cloud platform, and upload this information.
- Connect to the cloud platform to obtain video streams and connect to the decoding module of the VR terminal to decode, refresh, and display video images.

2.3 CLOUD VR TECHNICAL ARCHITECTURE AND KEY TECHNOLOGIES OF WEAK-INTERACTION SERVICES

The technical architecture for weak-interaction cloud VR services is mostly focused on the digital media system and CDN nodes, which are closely related to the service data layer. Compared with traditional videos, weak-interaction services have a large amount of data. Therefore, efficient transcoding and transmission is a key technical issue to be resolved.

2.3.1 Core technical architecture

Cloud VR VoD and live broadcasting services require service processes such as transcoding, storage and caching, and distribution and streaming, much like traditional VoD and live broadcasting services. In addition, VoD and live broadcasting services have different requirements for real-time performance. VoD services require previously prepared video content, and live broadcasting services require collection of video content in real time. Figure 2.8 shows the core technical architecture of the weak-interaction cloud VR service.

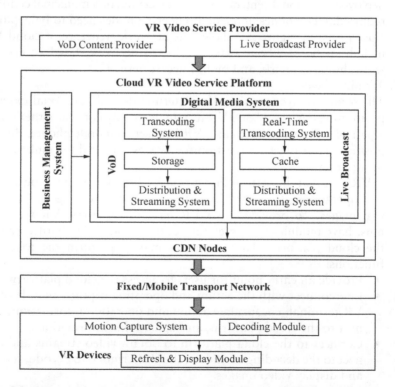

Figure 2.8 Core technical architecture of weak-interaction cloud VR services.

The processing modules of the digital media system vary according to the features of the two types of services.

The core components of the VoD system are as follows:

- Transcoding: Transcodes ingested video content, including slicing, coding, and encapsulating video content, to ensure it complies with the storage and transmission specifications of the platform.
- Storage: Stores a large number of video files for distribution after transcoding.
- Distribution: Responds to instructions for content management and distributes video files from the storage component to the CDN Nodes.

The core components of the live broadcast system are as follows:

- Real-time transcoding: Connects to the broadcasting side to transcode video content in real time as it is collected. This mainly involves video slicing, coding, and encapsulation, to meet platform specifications.
- Caching: Caches and stores live video files.
- Distribution: Distributes video files from the caching component to CDN nodes.

The components of a VR terminal are as follows:

- Motion capture system: Responsible for capturing the movement of the user and the terminal.
- Decoding module: Decodes video streams transmitted from the cloud in real time.
- Refresh and display module: Refreshes and displays images on the terminal screen.

2.3.2 Key issues: coding, decoding, and transmission of large-volume VR video data

Content quality is imperative to the immersive experience of cloud VR. Content quality is mainly affected by factors such as definition, smoothness, color fidelity, and stereo effect. Compared with traditional videos, VR video services bring large data volumes and have higher requirements with regard to aspects such as resolution, frame rate, and color depth.

Taking definition as an example, when the resolution of a VR terminal matches that of content, pixel density is measured by the pixels per degree (PPD) that are visible from each angle of the typical industry VR terminal. Figure 2.9 is a schematic diagram of this concept. The larger the PPD value, the higher the pixel density within the FoV and the better the definition experienced by the user, making it difficult for the human eye to distinguish the difference. In terms of the visual capabilities of the human eye, 1.0 visual

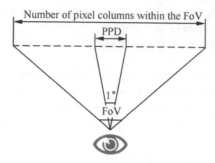

Figure 2.9 PPD schematic diagram.

acuity corresponds to a PPD requirement of 60. In general, the human horizontal and vertical monocular FoVs are 160° and 150°, respectively. (There is a slight variation in the data provided by different institutions.) A PPD value of 60 requires a VR screen display that attains a single-eye resolution of 9,600×9,000, and the corresponding full-view content resolution needs to attain 21,600×10,800 (almost 24K). Even if coding technology continuously develops, there is a steep increase in VR video data volumes compared with the traditional TV, which is already capable of providing high-quality experience with content at a 4K resolution (4,096×2,160). If improvements in other dimensions such as frame rate, color depth, and stereo effect are also taken into account, then there will be larger data volumes, ultimately improving the required bitrate for video streaming. Taking the current and relatively good level of VR terminals as an example: FoV is 100°, single-eye resolution is 1,920×2,160, and PPD is approximately 19.2. As a result, the required full-view resolution for content is 8K, and the required bitrate exceeds 100 Mbit/s, which is a multi-fold increase of the 25 Mbit/s bitrate requirement for traditional 4K videos with good user experience.

As the resolution of weak-interaction cloud VR services increases, the corresponding huge data volumes pose significant challenges to aspects such as coding, decoding, and transmission. Especially with regard to cloud VR live broadcast, the enormous computing power required in real-time transcoding must be taken into account. Therefore, the key technologies of current weak-interaction cloud VR services lie in finding the right balance of capabilities such as coding, decoding, network transmission, and rendering output, as well as exploring efficient transmission technologies.

2.3.3 Key technologies: cloud VR video transmission technology

The focal point of cloud VR video transmission lies in optimizing the data volume of VR video transmission. This means decreasing the bitrate of videos while ensuring the same level of video quality to reduce network bandwidth and terminal processing performance requirements.

2.3.3.1 Full-view transmission

Full-view transmission is the transmission of entire VR full-view images from a cloud to a terminal. When a user moves their head to view an image at a specific angle, the terminal instantly completes processes such as bitstream parsing, video decoding, and image displaying.

Depending on whether the terminal performs full-view image decoding, full-view transmission can be classified into two solutions: cloud full-transmission + terminal full-decoding and cloud full-transmission + terminal partial-decoding.

1. Two types of full-view transmission
   In the cloud full-transmission + terminal full-decoding solution, a full-view VR video source is deployed on the cloud, full-view content is coded and then transmitted to the terminal with the same quality, and the terminal decodes all of the full-view content, as shown in Figure 2.10.

   The advantage of this solution is that the same content quality is displayed to users no matter which direction their heads rotate. The main limitations are as follows:
   - Full-view content is transmitted and decoded, but only portions of VR videos are displayed to users. In general, the human horizontal and vertical monocular FoVs are 160° and 150°, respectively. The spherical signals effectively seen by the human eye are approximately 37% of the spherical full-view signals. However, the FoV that is supported by current VR terminals is between 90° and 110°, and the spherical full-view signals that can be effectively seen by the human eye are less than 19% of spherical full-view signals.
   - Terminals are required to have decoding capabilities with the same resolution as the content. Currently, VR terminals have decoding capabilities that support 4K content, and a few VR terminals can support 8K content. Terminal decoding capability is one of the current shortcomings of developing ultra-high-resolution VR video services.

   In the cloud full-transmission + terminal partial-decoding solution, when high-quality full-view video sources are prepared on the cloud, full-view videos are divided into multiple video tiles;

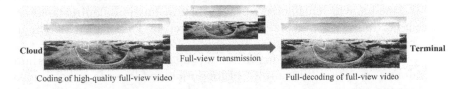

Cloud   Terminal

Full-view transmission

Coding of high-quality full-view video   Full-decoding of full-view video

Figure 2.10 Full-view transmission solution: cloud full-transmission + terminal full-decoding.

Figure 2.11 Full-view transmission solution: cloud full-transmission+terminal partial-decoding.

then each tile is coded and transmitted to the terminal by the cloud with the same quality. The terminal can locate corresponding tiles based on the current view, and it can decode and stitch the tiles and display the images, as shown in Figure 2.11.

Compared with the full-decoding solution, the advantage of the terminal partial-decoding solution lies in the fact that the terminal only needs to decode VR content in the angle of view (AoV) area. This reduces decoding capability requirements while still transmitting full-view content.

In general, the advantage of the full-view transmission solution lies in the fact that compatibility is relatively good and images transition smoothly when users move their heads. During the initial stage of cloud VR development, with an emphasis on 4K VR videos, network bandwidth and terminal processing are still capable of supporting full-view transmission. However, the improvement of VR video quality to a resolution of 8K or higher introduces higher requirements in terms of network bandwidth and terminal decoding capabilities. Currently, extensive research is being conducted by the industry on challenges brought by full-view transmission.

2. Full-view transmission solution based on projection optimization
In reality, the reason full-view transmission results in higher data volumes is not only because VR videos have higher resolutions and frame rates than traditional videos, but also because projection technology leads to more redundant pixels.

Projection technology converts the spatial spheres seen by users into 2D media, which facilitates storage and transmission. Equirectangular projection (ERP) and platonic solid projection (PSP) are the two main projection methods.

Currently, ERP is the mainstream projection method. This method draws on the traditional idea of longitude and latitude projection to expand spheres into 2D rectangles, as shown in Figure 2.12. The ERP longitude and latitude lines intersect at 90°, and this angle is mainly

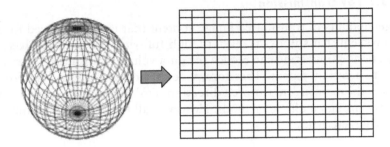

Figure 2.12 Equirectangular projection.

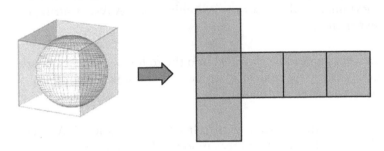

Figure 2.13 Platonic solid projection (taking a hexahedron as an example).

maintained through increasing area deformation. Low distortion is attained after the spatial sphere image is projected and expanded at the equator; however, the closer the projection is to the two poles, the larger the image distortion. This method increases the area of images and leads to more pixels that are redundant, which in turn reduces the compression efficiency of files.

PSP is a new trend within the industry. As shown in Figure 2.13, some longitude and latitude lines are set as boundaries, the surface of the spatial sphere is divided into multiple sections, and then the sphere of each section is projected onto to the different surfaces of a polyhedron, which can be a tetrahedron, pyramid, or cube. PSP is based on projecting the different sections of a sphere onto the surfaces of polyhedrons with different areas. Distortion is extremely low due to each section being projected separately.

According to industry test results,[6] the number of pixels per frame can be reduced by 25% compared to ERP by selecting a cubic plane for PSP and converting the top 25% and bottom 25%, along with the middle 50%, of a longitude and latitude diagram into two cubic planes and four other planes, respectively. As a result, coding efficiency can be increased and decoding capability requirements effectively decreased.

2.3.3.2 FoV transmission

Large amounts of transmitted image content that is not displayed to users is a problem that still exists, even though full-view transmission based on projection optimization can reduce the data volume transmitted over a network to a certain extent. Therefore, video transmission based on FoV has become the mainstream research direction. FoV transmission can be implemented through multiple methods. However, all these methods exhibit two main characteristics:

- High-quality images are used in users' AoV areas to ensure image quality within users' FoVs.
- Low-quality images are used for non-FoV areas to enable users to view images when they are switching their AoVs, ensuring good user experience.

FoV transmission can be classified into the following three categories based on whether full-view content is segmented and how high-quality and low-quality images are coordinated:

1. Full-view transmission with self-adaptive quality: FoV area in high definition (HD)+other areas in low definition (LD)

   In the traditional full-view transmission solution, full-view VR videos in HD with the same quality (that is, identical quality across the entire image area) are transmitted to the terminal. In the full-view transmission with self-adaptive quality solution, full-view VR videos with different quality (that is, varying quality across each image area) are transmitted to the terminal. In the latter solution, varying degrees of compression are performed on different areas of full-view images. This means that high-quality images are maintained in the FoV areas whereas low-quality images are created for non-FoV areas through quality degradation, as shown in Figure 2.14. The cloud needs to separately prepare one full-view video stream with non-uniform image quality for and centered on each AoV. The terminal requests a full-view video stream from the cloud that corresponds to the user's current AoV, and when that AoV changes due to the user rotating their head, the terminal requests a video stream that corresponds to the new AoV. If the new AoV video stream does not reach the terminal in time when the user switches their AoV, the terminal will continue to display the original AoV video stream to the user, and low-quality images of the original AoV video stream's non-FoV area will appear within the user's new AoV, affecting switching experience. The pyramid-projection transmission solution[7] falls within the scope of this type of FoV transmission.

   In the pyramid-projection transmission solution, different areas of the VR sphere are projected to different surfaces of the pyramid model,

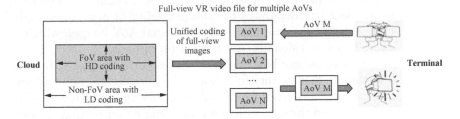

Figure 2.14 Full-view transmission solution with self-adaptive quality.

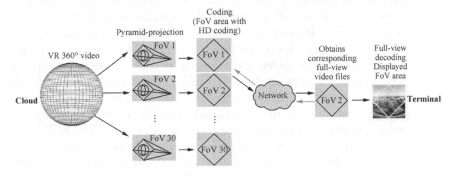

Figure 2.15 Pyramid-projection transmission solution.

and images for different surfaces are processed differently, as shown in Figure 2.15. The bottom of the pyramid model maps the user's AoV area using high-quality images. The other surfaces of the pyramid map the user's non-AoV areas using images that have reduced resolution through subsampling. The full-view videos that are mapped onto the pyramid model will be transmitted to the terminal in full. When the user switches to a new AoV, a new full-view video file is requested from the cloud.

According to data released by vendors, the pyramid-projection transmission solution divides full-view images into 30 AoVs. Each AoV file is only 20% the size of the original file, and the corresponding transmission bitrate is also only 20%[6] of the original. While ensuring the quality of images within AoVs, this solution can reduce the bitrate of full-view videos and lower requirements for bandwidth and terminal decoding capabilities. However, some aspects of this solution can still be improved.

- Increased pressure on cloud storage: The total size of video files from all AoVs is six times that of the original files due to the fact that a full-view video is prepared for each AoV.
- Burst traffic: An entirely new full-view video file is requested from the cloud every time a user switches their AoV, which easily leads

to bursts in network traffic. Buffering might occur when there is insufficient bandwidth, or the image quality of new AoVs might reduce due to the continued use of original AoV images, which is caused by new video files not reaching terminals.

2. Tile-wise transmission: FoV area in HD tiles+other areas in LD tiles
   In this solution, high-quality full-view images are divided into multiple tiles that are coded separately. In addition, corresponding low-quality tiles are obtained through fallback processing based on high-quality images or tiles, as shown in Figure 2.16.

   Based on the posture and position of the user's original AoV, the terminal requests the cloud for multiple high-quality tiles of the corresponding FoV as well as multiple low-quality tiles of the non-FoV areas, and then it completes images by decoding and stitching the tiles. High-quality tiles of the FoV area are used to guarantee image quality within users' AoVs, and low-quality tiles of non-FoV areas are used to ensure images are displayed when users switch their AoVs. To reduce the volume of data transmitted, low-quality tiles of non-FoV areas are not all transmitted. Instead, only low-quality tiles of some angles (greater than the FoV) are transmitted. In addition, instead of transmitting all the low-quality tiles of non-FoV areas, only the tiles that have higher quality than that of the FoV are transmitted in some solutions. As a result, no images are displayed in newly added AoVs when users turn their heads sharply.

   When a user changes their AoV, the terminal requests the new corresponding video tiles from the cloud, and there are two implementation

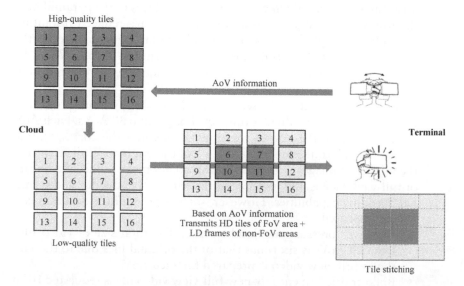

Figure 2.16 Tile-wise transmission solution.

solutions depending on whether the terminal reuses the original AoV tiles.

1. Solution 1: The terminal clears all the cached tiles of the original AoV tiles and requests the cloud for all the high-quality and low-quality tiles again. In reality, the new and original AoVs overlap, and some tiles can be reused.

2. Solution 2: The terminal determines which video tiles can be reused, preserves them, and preferentially requests the cloud for new high-quality tiles of the new AoV. This enables the cloud to respond faster and deliver the key new tiles, which in turn reduces the delay in displaying high-quality images when the user switches their AoV, improving the switching experience of users.

   In general, the tile-wise transmission solution is more advanced than the full-view transmission with self-adaptive quality transmission solution in the following aspects:

   – Reduced cloud storage requirements: There is no need to create a separate video file for each AoV, and suitable tiles are selected from a combination of similar tiles from different AoVs.

   – Reduced transmission requirements: When a terminal reuses video tiles, the cloud does not need to transmit all of the tiles to the terminal.

   – Improved AoV switching experience: The cloud is enabled to respond faster and deliver key new tiles by the terminal preferentially requesting it for new high-quality tiles of new AoVs. This reduces the delay in displaying high-quality images when users switch their AoVs.

In the tile transmission solution, real-time stitching needs to be performed at the terminal. This leads to the following key issues:

- Higher cloud computing requirements: In addition to decoding video tiles, terminals also need to stitch high-quality and low-quality tiles, which requires more computing.

- Higher real-time stitching requirements: In the full-view image transmission solution, relatively good stitching quality can be ensured by the stitching or converging of the high-quality and low-quality areas of full-view images on the cloud. However, issues such as image stitching misplacement as well as unnatural stitching of high-quality and low-quality tiles might occur in the tile transmission solution, if the stitching algorithm is inefficient or of insufficient quality.

3. Full-view+combined tile-wise transmission: HD FoV tiles+LD full-view In this solution, the cloud prepares one low-quality full-video video stream as well as multiple video stream tiles. The specific process is shown in Figure 2.17. First, the cloud performs fallback processing on the original high-quality full-view VR video to create a low-quality

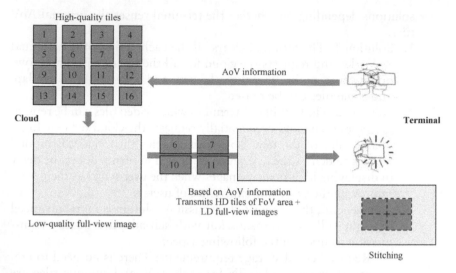

Figure 2.17 Full-view+combined tile-wise transmission solution.

full-view VR video. At the same time, spatial cutting is performed on the original high-quality full-view images, creating multiple high-quality tiles. Each tile is then coded separately to create a segmented video stream. According to the AoV information, the terminal obtains a low-quality full-view video stream as well as a high-quality segmented video stream of the AoV area from the cloud. The terminal then decodes the video stream, stitches high-quality tiles, and converges them with low-quality full-view images.

This solution transmits high-quality images in AoV areas according to requirements, ensuring image quality within users' AoVs. At the same time, this solution can ensure that images are displayed to users when they quickly switch their AoVs with no interruptions, which in turn diminishes their discomfort. An efficient stitching algorithm is required for this solution to stitch high-quality images and converge the transition area of high-quality and low-quality images.

The tile-wise streaming (TWS) solution, which is based on video tiles, represents the full-view+combined tile transmission solution (Figure 2.18).

The TWS solution was adopted by the Omnidirectional Media Format (OMAF) working group of the Moving Picture Experts Group (MPEG), and it was included in the most recent ISO/IEC 23090-2 standard.[8] In this solution, a full-view video stream and a high-quality tile video stream that meet basic quality requirements are prepared on the cloud. According to terminal AoV information, the cloud transmits full-view video streams and multiple tile video streams from within AoVs, and then the terminal decodes, stitches, and displays the video streams.

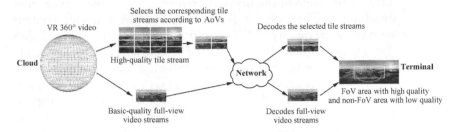

Figure 2.18 TWS transmission solution.

When there is insufficient network bandwidth, only high-quality tile videos and low-quality full-view videos are transmitted in this solution, effectively ensuring that bandwidth resources are preferentially allocated to the tile videos within the AoVs. When there is sufficient network bandwidth, the cloud can transmit tile videos with higher quality than that of AoV areas, enabling users to rapidly view high-quality images when they switch their AoVs.

In general, and similar to the other FoV transmission technologies, the full-view+tile transmission solution ensures user experience while reducing network transmission and terminal decoding pressure. Further advantages of this solution include:

- Reduced terminal computing pressure in stitching: Low-quality images are also stitched in the tile transmission solution. In reality, low-quality full-view images are not restricted by network transmission and terminal decoding bottlenecks. The differences with high-quality images within AoVs are that low-quality full-view images are definitely transmitted and terminals do not need to stitch them in real time. Instead, they only need to stitch high-quality images, which reduces terminals' computing pressure in stitching as well as processing delay.
- VR video smoothness ensured more easily: When network bandwidth is suddenly insufficient, the inability to ensure rapid downloads of entire video tiles in the full-view transmission with self-adaptive quality solution might cause buffering. In the tile transmission solution, the inability to ensure rapid downloads of high-quality video tiles might lead to buffering. Low-quality full-view video streams in the full-view+tile transmission solution have relatively low bandwidth requirements. As such, when bandwidth is insufficient, video streams can be rapidly downloaded to terminals, enabling smooth playback of videos with basic-quality images.
- Easier to cast to other terminals: In casting scenarios, the content of the VR terminal is synchronized to the screens of other types of terminals (for example, televisions). This makes it easier to share VR content. In comparison with VR terminals, other terminals

have lower content-quality requirements and lower computing capabilities. Therefore, it is not advisable to transmit content with the same quality to VR terminals and other terminals. Video streams can be directly transmitted to other terminals to decode and display due to the low-quality full-view video streams of the full-view+tile transmission solution. Therefore, video streams can be directly transmitted to other terminals to decode and display. From one aspect, the cloud does not need to prepare other low-quality video streams for other terminals, and from a different aspect, the terminals do not need to meet the extra computing requirements necessary for processes such as real-time stitching.

2.3.3.3 Evolution of FoV transmission

FoV transmission technology requires that terminals are capable of rapidly displaying high-quality images when users change their AoVs. This means that the delay when switching low-quality images of newly added AoVs to high-quality images needs to be as short as possible. There are two main optimization methods with regard to further improving the switching experience of users.

- Viewpoint prediction: This involves predicting the next viewpoint based on the pattern of users' previous AoVs, transmitting the predicted AoV information to the cloud, and the cloud delivering the images of the predicted AoVs.

  Currently, some VR terminal chips integrate functions such as six degrees of freedom (DoF) visual–inertial ranging and eye tracking. These types of tracking can effectively guide VR transmission systems to pre-download and pre-cache new AoVs.
- Terminal rendering prediction: To create new AoV images when users switch their AoVs, terminals rotate and wrap existing downloaded or cached high-quality images of previous AoVs in accordance with users' new AoVs and based on the difference between them. Original low-quality images are displayed for newly added AoVs, and technologies such as super-resolution (SR) imaging can be used to improve their quality. In essence, this type of technology is based on the process of predicting high-quality rendered images through low-quality rendered images.

2.4 TECHNICAL ARCHITECTURE AND KEY TECHNOLOGIES OF STRONG-INTERACTION CLOUD VR SERVICES

The focus of the technical architecture of cloud VR interaction services is on cloud rendering nodes with a strong correlation to the service data layer. The cloud VR technical architecture has extremely high requirements for delay because strong-interaction cloud VR services are highly delay sensitive.

2.4.1 Core technical architecture

In the conventional local VR architecture, the VR terminal collects motion and instruction information, then sends it to the terminal driver installed on the PC via a universal serial bus (USB) cable. The driver delivers the information to the upper-layer application running system, which then performs logic computing and real-time image rendering based on the instructions, and losslessly sends the rendered images to the VR terminal via a high-definition multimedia interface (HDMI) cable. Local VR comprises three parts: server (PC), VR terminal, and instruction and image transmission processing.

By contrast, cloud VR advances the connection between the server and the terminal while adhering to the basic server–terminal processing of local VR. Thus, the way information about the user's movement is processed and rendered images are transmitted is different to local VR in two key areas.

- Terminal–cloud connection: In local VR, information from a VR terminal is transmitted to an application running on a server through a direct cable. In cloud VR, as the VR terminal is wireless and the server has moved to the cloud, the terminal must encapsulate information which is then transmitted to the cloud. The cloud must then decapsulate the packet before computing this information.
- Image rendering and streaming: In local VR, a rendered image is transmitted from the server to the VR terminal through an HDMI cable; therefore, coding and decoding of the rendering image are not involved. In cloud VR, an image rendered in the cloud needs to be coded into a video stream and then transmitted to a terminal through a network for decoding and displaying.

Figure 2.19 shows the core architecture of the strong-interaction cloud VR service.

1. Cloud rendering node
   - Application running system: This performs logic computing based on motion capturing and renders real-time FoV images.
   - Cloud rendering engine: This includes the cloud driver and real-time streaming functions. The cloud driver is responsible for decapsulating the latest posture and location information uploaded by the terminal, converting it into the necessary format, and then transmitting the information to the upper application. The real-time streaming function is responsible for coding, compressing, encapsulating, and transmitting the real-time rendered image data back to the terminal.

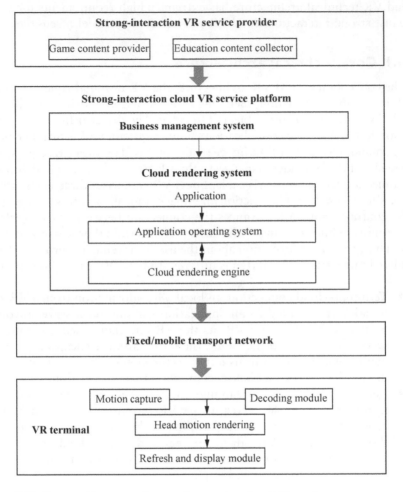

Figure 2.19 Core architecture of strong-interaction cloud VR services.

2. VR terminal
- Motion capture system: It is responsible for capturing the movement of the user and the terminal.
- Decoding module: Decodes video streams of rendered images transmitted from the cloud to terminals in real time.
- Head motion rendering module: When the rendered images on the cloud are not retransmitted to the terminal in time, the terminal warps the existing images on the terminal to create new images.
- Display refresh module: Refreshes the screen and displays images.

2.4.2 Key issues: meeting MTP delay requirement

Strong-interaction cloud VR services have stronger interactive character-istics than weak-interaction cloud VR services; therefore, they place high bandwidth and latency requirements on networks to reduce the motion sickness and lag experienced by users as much as possible.

- Motion sickness is related to the MTP delay. Currently, it is widely accepted in the industry that when the MTP delay is within 20 ms, lag-inflicted motion sickness can be reduced.
- Lag is related to the operation response delay (the time from when a user starts an operation to when the screen responds). The industry has proposed the RAIL (Response, Animation, Idle, Load) model[9] for user-centric application performance evaluation. The model's study shows that for normal operations, when the delay is within 100 ms, the user does not feel the delay.

Compared with lag, avoiding motion sickness has higher real-time perfor-mance requirements for cloud VR. For local VR, it is challenging to achieve an MTP delay of less than 20 ms. The main processes of local VR include motion capturing, logic computing, image rendering, and screen refresh-ing and display. Figure 2.20 shows the relationship between the processing times of these steps. MTP delay is calculated as follows:

- The smallest MTP delay is at the moment before a new screen refresh cycle begins, image rendering has just been completed, and the image can be refreshed and presented as soon as possible.

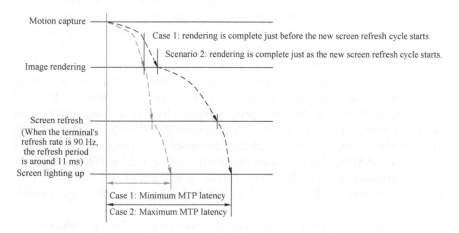

Figure 2.20 Minimum and maximum MTP delays.

- The biggest MTP delay occurs when image rendering gets completed at the same time as the new screen refresh cycle begins. In this case, the image can only be refreshed and presented just before the next screen refresh cycle begins.

For example, the refresh rate of the VR terminal is 90 Hz, and in this case, the refresh period of the terminal screen is about 11 ms. According to tests and research, under good conditions, the motion capture delay is about 1 ms, the computing and rendering delay is about 5–10 ms (which is closely related to the quality of the application development and the complexity of the content image), and the display time delay is about 3 ms. Therefore, the overall MTP delay range is 9–25 ms. It is therefore challenging for local VR to ensure MTP delay is less than 20 ms. However, cloud VR will bring about extra delays due to the transmission, coding, and decoding of rendered images. As such, this poses a major challenge for cloud VR: How can an MTP delay of less than 20 ms be ensured to reduce motion sickness?

2.4.3 Key technologies: cloud VR real-time rendering technology

Cloud VR real-time cloud rendering technology is at the core of strong-interaction service architecture, which includes terminal–cloud asynchronous rendering and end-to-end low latency.

2.4.3.1 Terminal–cloud asynchronous rendering technology

Cloud VR processing includes motion capturing and reporting, cloud rendering and streaming, and terminal screen refresh and display, as shown in Figure 2.21. The action information is transmitted from a terminal to a cloud via a network, and then the cloud completes logic computing, real-time rendering, coding, and compression, and transmits video streams to the terminal through a network for decoding.

The local VR terminal needs to perform a series of operations, such as motion capturing, logic computing, image rendering, and screen refreshing and display, which are challenging for MTP latency requirements. If cloud VR continues to follow the serial processing of cloud rendering and streaming and terminal refresh and display processes (as shown in Figure 2.22), whereby the terminal refresh and display process is completely dependent on cloud rendering, this increases the likelihood of a delay. This is because network transmission, coding, and decoding will occur in both cloud rendering and streaming processes; thus, the MTP delay requirements cannot be achieved.

In the terminal–cloud asynchronous rendering technical solution (as shown in Figure 2.23), rendering and processing is performed separately on the cloud and a terminal.

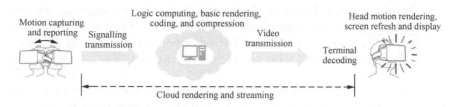

Figure 2.21 Main cloud VR processes.

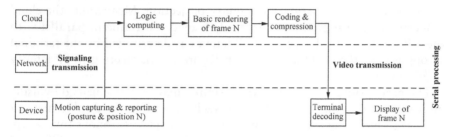

Figure 2.22 Serial processing solution that cannot guarantee MTP delay.

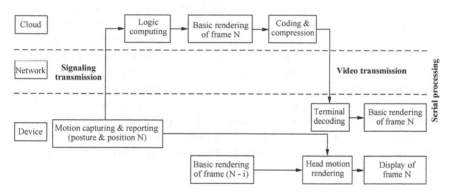

Figure 2.23 MTP delay guarantee solution: Terminal–cloud asynchronous rendering.

- Basic rendering on the cloud: The complete basic image is rendered based on the logic computing result. Specifically, the cloud executes the logic computation for the application periodically according to the dynamic capture and operation information reported by the terminal. The cloud then renders an image, generates a frame, performs real-time coding, and transmits the information to the terminal for decoding.
- Head motion rendering on the terminal: Based on real-time head position and rotation, the basic image that is displayed on the screen is initially rendered to generate a real-time display image. Specifically, the terminal periodically caches a frame of the rendered image when rotation and positioning change. When the cloud renders the next

frame, which is based on the terminal's current positioning, the terminal rotates, translates, and warps the cached frame to produce a smoothed intermediate frame between the past and present positioning. This then forms a new image on the display.

The terminal–cloud asynchronous rendering technology converts two serial processes, namely, cloud rendering, streaming, and terminal refreshing, to parallel processing. Specifically, when refreshing the picture, the VR terminal uses the nth rendered frame sent by the cloud rendering platform as the basic frame to perform secondary projection. Meanwhile, the cloud rendering platform processes the (n+1)th rendered frame in parallel with the VR terminal. In this case, MTP latency is determined by the terminal as opposed to the cloud (as shown in Figure 2.24), meeting MTP latency requirements.

The head motion rendering of the terminal may be implemented by using an asynchronous warping technology such as rotation or displacement of the image, including asynchronous time warping (asynchronous time warp, ATW), asynchronous space warping (asynchronous space warp, ASW), and so on. The asynchronous warping technology is designed to reduce the rendering latency. In VR rendering, the complexity of content varies. Therefore, the rendering of complex content cannot possibly be completed within the refreshing period of one frame. As a result, no new content is generated after screen refreshing, and the user is left feeling disorientated and uncomfortable. Asynchronous warping technology works by intervening every frame to warp the last generated image based on the difference in head posture and movement between the current and previous posture. Specifically, ATW only tracks the user's head rotation, while ASW captures animation and movement within the scene. These two technologies combine to achieve a full VR experience of the VR 6DoF. The main features of ATW and the ASW include the following:

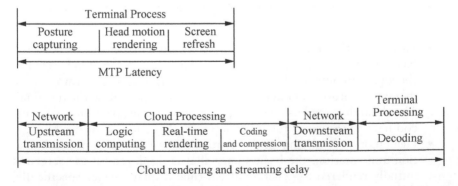

Figure 2.24 MTP latency and cloud rendering and streaming latency of the terminal–cloud asynchronous rendering.

- ATW technology: Rotating and adjusting a rendered image based on head positioning between the present and past posture.
- ASW technology: More complex than ATW and requires the use of depth information and motion vectors of the image, where the depth of field describes the distance of the object in the image to the user's eyes, and the motion vector describes the displacement of an object. Based on the difference between a header position at the current moment and a header position at a past moment, the depth information at a past moment is adjusted as a prediction of the current depth information. In addition, a position of the pixel block is adjusted according to the motion vector. The three-dimensional image is adjusted by combining the depth information and the motion vector.

The terminal–cloud asynchronous rendering technology ensures that cloud rendering and streaming delays do not affect the MTP latency; however, these delays will affect the image quality and user experience.

1. Black edge problem

When the VR terminal warps basic rendered images to a new angle of view based on head posture changes, no image will be displayed in the new FoV which can cause black edges to appear around the image, as shown in Figure 2.25. The form of black edges varies depending on the header rendering algorithm used by the VR terminal. In addition to typical black areas, some algorithms fill the black edge part with pixels. Filling it will form a phenomenon similar to a smear. Black edges have impact on the quality of cloud VR images when a user moves their head, thereby affecting user experience.

The size of the black edge changes depending on the delay or the speed in which the user turns their head. According to the principle of the terminal–cloud asynchronous rendering technology, the display screen of the terminal is always based on the posture and movement before a delay period (motion capture and uplink delay+cloud rendering and streaming delay+head motion rendering delay). The basic rendered image is generated after head motion rendering, as shown in Figure 2.26. Therefore, the difference between the current pose and the previous pose determines the angle of deviation of the basic rendered image and the size of the black edge. The black-edge angle is essentially the user turning their head too quickly during a delay period. Cloud rendering and streaming delay are the biggest causes of the delay period.

To minimize the impact of black edges on user experience, super FoV image can be performed on the cloud, where the angle of basic images can be increased to ensure that the image is displayed in the angle of view, even when the user moves their head, as shown in Figure 2.27. However, this consumes cloud rendering resources and increases

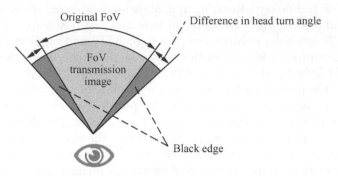

Figure 2.25 Schematic diagram of forming black edges.

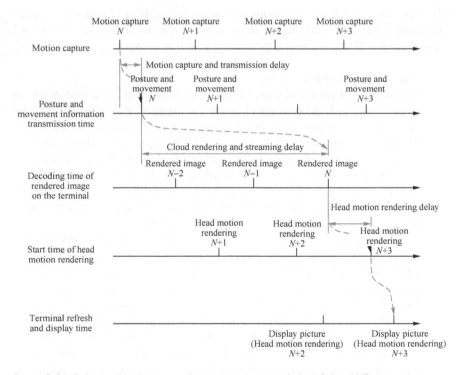

Figure 2.26 Relationship between the main processing links of cloud VR.

cloud rendering and streaming latency. For example, if 5° is added to each direction of basic rendering for each image, cloud resource consumption will increase by about 20%. Therefore, the cost of cloud rendering and improved user experience must be considered for super FoV image rendering. If the cloud uses super FoV image rendering, the black edges can be removed from the angle of the rendered image in each direction.

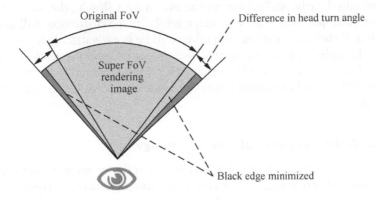

Original FoV

Difference in head turn angle

Super FoV
rendering
image

Black edge minimized

Figure 2.27 Rendering effect of a super FoV image.

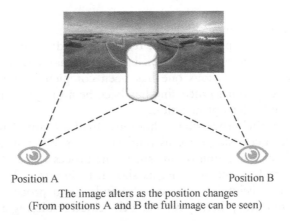

Position A

Position B

The image alters as the position changes
(From positions A and B the full image can be seen)

Figure 2.28 View of screen object from different user Point of View (PoV).

2. Picture quality

When a user moves, they will view the object from a new angle, and the relative position of the object changes which causes the user's FoV to be obstructed, as shown in Figure 2.28.

For an image that includes depth of field and motion vectors, the VR terminal performs head motion rendering by using ASW to adjust the position of an object in relation to the position of a user, so as to quickly respond to the user's movement. Although head motion rendering can adjust the relative positional relationship between objects, it cannot create the blocked part of the object out of thin air. At this time, only the background can be used. In this situation, it can only be replaced by the surrounding picture, which causes picture quality issues such as distortion and an unnatural look. If cloud rendering and streaming latency is low, a basic rendered image can reach the terminal early, and providing the user moves slowly, the blocked part of an object will not be so clear while image distortion will also be less. Otherwise, the image quality will be greatly affected.

In addition to using terminal–cloud asynchronous rendering technology to solve the problem that MTP latency is unable to meet, cloud rendering and streaming latency needs to be controlled to reduce black edges.

2.4.3.2 End-to-end low-latency technology

End-to-end low-latency technology is used to optimize latency during cloud rendering and streaming. It improves the comprehensive performance of rendering, coding, decoding, and transmission, including parallel processing, fast coding and decoding, VR transmission protocol, and low-latency transmission network.

1. Parallel processing technology
   For a complete picture frame, rendering, coding, transmission, and decoding are generally performed in a serial manner. Each frame must wait until the previous one has been completed before beginning. Therefore, parallel processing has become an important direction of end-to-end delay optimization.

   The parallel processing technology divides a complete picture into multiple slices and performs rendering, transmission, and decoding on each slice in a unit of one slice. The processing of different slices is independent and parallel, as shown in Figure 2.29. The parallel processing technology reduces the end-to-end processing time of a complete frame, thereby reducing the cloud rendering and streaming delay.

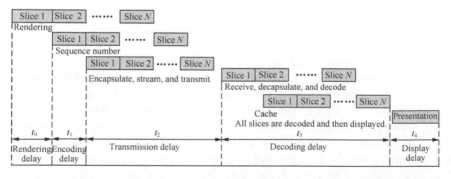

Figure 2.29 Parallel processing technology.

2. Fast coding and decoding

Currently, the efficiency of general video coding and decoding technologies is too low for cloud VR.

Optimized coding practices for real-time rendering of cloud VR include the following: simplifying motion estimation algorithms, reducing methods for intra-frame prediction, simplifying motion vector algorithms, reducing coding unit division, adopting improved processing methods such as parallel inter-frame and intra-frame slicing, and the development of a dedicated chip for video coding. In order to guarantee consistent quality across images, low-compression coding can be used.

3. VR transmission protocol

Currently, the bandwidth and retransmission mechanism of Transmission Control Protocol (TCP) is suitable for normal internet services. For strong-interaction cloud VR, VR terminals access the network via Wi-Fi, and thus random packet loss can occur on air interfaces due to ambient interference. On the one hand, when TCP transmission is used, upstream packets such as acknowledgments compete with downstream packets over a half-duplex channel, which increases the load and packet loss rate. On the other hand, when packet loss occurs, the sender retransmits packets and the receiver reorders them, thus increasing the end-to-end delay by hundreds of milliseconds. The problem is more serious in the event of Wi-Fi interference.

With the development of cloud VR, a new VR-oriented transmission protocol which can quickly send a frame of data to a terminal on a protected network is needed. Such a protocol is critical for both weak- and strong-interaction cloud VR services and must have the following characteristics.

- The transmission rate reaches the bitrate required for transmitting upper-layer frames.
- Redundancy error correction and packet retransmission ensure the delivery rate of data within a specified period is extremely high. For cloud VR video services, full-view/FoV transmission technology is required to transmit core video data and global/edge basic quality video data in a differentiated manner. Furthermore, different redundancy error correction mechanisms/packet retransmission mechanisms are used to ensure an ultra-high delivery rate (such as 99.9999%) of core data within a specified time, as well as the general delivery rate of global/edge basic quality video data (for example, 99%). When bandwidth is limited, core video data, including its redundancy error correction packets, has a higher transmission priority.
- The packet loss model of the network can be detected and automatically adjusted in real time.

- The network status is reported in milliseconds, including but not limited to the network throughput and packet loss rate, so that the upper-layer application can better adjust the codec policy.

2.5 CLOUD, PIPE, AND DEVICE TECHNICAL REQUIREMENTS

The two key technologies of cloud VR, video transmission and real-time rendering, are end-to-end technologies covering the cloud, pipe, and device. These technologies require efficient collaboration among the cloud platform, network, and terminal.

2.5.1 Cloud VR development phases

The development of cloud VR is a collaborative process of improving services, technologies, and experience. Along with the continuous innovation of cloud, pipe, and device technologies, the development of cloud VR can be divided into the following four phases:

1. Initial phase
   At the initial phase, the content is 4K VR, and the typical screen resolution is 2K–4K. The quality of the image is almost equivalent to 240P PPD on a traditional TV screen. The full-view transmission scheme, which supports 3DoF, is used at this stage as weak-interaction VR services are usually passive. In contrast, users are more involved in strong-interaction VR services through the use of handheld controllers.
2. Comfortable-experience phase
   At the comfortable-experience phase, content is typically 8K VR, while the resolution of terminals is 4K. Chip performance and ergonomical design are better, and the quality is similar to a 480P TV. For weak-interaction VR services, full-view transmission scheme and FoV scheme coexist. Strong-interaction VR services usually use inside-out position tracking, and the user's hand interacts with the environment and objects via a handheld controller.
3. Ideal-experience phase
   At the ideal-experience stage, user experience will further improve. Terminal displays will feature 8K resolution, the FoV will expand to 120°, 12K VR will become more widespread, and the experience will be close to HD (720P). The user experience is good and can meet the requirements of most users. At this stage, reducing traffic volume and terminal decoding requirements are critical. Weak-interaction VR services will mainly adopt the FoV scheme, while cloud rendering and streaming delays will be further reduced in strong-interaction VR services with improved interaction and tactile feedback.

4. Ultimate-experience phase

At this stage, content resolution will reach 24K, terminal screens will be equipped with 16K resolution, the FoV of some terminals will expand to 140°, and the overall visual experience will be similar to an ultra HD 4K TV. Likewise, the cloud rendering and streaming latency of strong-interaction VR services will be further reduced to enable users to interact with the virtual world more closely than ever.

Currently, solutions are only available for the key problems that hinder the development of cloud VR. Moreover, platform, network, and terminal technologies are continuously innovated and include panoramic 8K content, high bandwidth and low latency through Gigabit broadband, as well as 4K terminal screens and 8K decoding. Cloud VR service is already at the comfortable-experience phase. The following sections focus on the technical and solution requirements in the comfortable-experience phase and discusses the direction needed to enter the ideal-experience and ultimate-experience phase.

2.5.2 Key service metrics

The development of cloud VR technology will be well perceived by the end users. The requirements of the service are built around the experience of VR and are an important basis for constraining the technical requirements of the platform, network, and terminal.

Multiple factors, such as cloud, pipe, and terminal, can affect the user's experience of cloud VR. Table 2.1 lists the key service metrics for cloud VR based on experience, industry tests, and analysis. With further research, the expectations of cloud VR services will be updated.

Table 2.2 describes the general requirements for key business indicators.

1. Resolution

The evolution of terminal screen resolution and content resolution reflects the advancement of TVs from SD (480P), HD (720P), and UHD (4K), as shown in Table 2.2.

2. FoV

Generally, the horizontal FoV of one eye is 160°, the vertical FoV of one eye is 150°, and the horizontal FoV of two eyes is about 200°. Therefore, to improve the immersive experience, a VR terminal's FoV angle needs to align with that of the human eye.

3. Color depth

The greater the color depth, the more detailed and delicate images can be produced. Color depth, resolution, and frame rate affect the quality of images; therefore, all of these factors need to be improved to achieve an immersive experience.

4. Frame rate

The frame rate affects the image smoothness of weak- and strong-interaction services, and it is determined by the content's source.

Table 2.1 Key service metrics of each development phase

Phase		Comfortable experience	Ideal experience	Ultimate experience
Full-view resolution of typical content		8K	12K	24K or higher
Screen resolution of mainstream terminals		4K	8K	16K or higher
FoV of mainstream terminals		100°–110°	110°–120°	120°–140°
Color depth		8 bits	10 bits	≥ 12 bits
Coding mode		H.264/H.265	H.265/H.266	H.266
Frame rate		30 FPS (weak-interaction service) 60 FPS (strong-interaction service)	60 FPS (weak-interaction service) 90 FPS (strong-interaction service)	≥ 60 FPS (weak-interaction service) ≥90 FPS (strong-interaction service)
Weak-interaction cloud VR services	Recommended bitrate	FoV:≥80 Mbit/s	FoV:≥280 Mbit/s	FoV:≥760 Mbit/s
Strong-interaction cloud VR services	Recommended bitrate	≥ 65 Mbit/s	≥ 270 Mbit/s	≥ 770 Mbit/s
	Cloud rendering and streaming delay	70 ms	50 ms	30 ms

Table 2.2 VR terminal and content resolution and equivalent TV experience

Dual-eye resolution of VR terminal screen	Resolution of equivalent TV experience	Full-view resolution of VR services
4K (3,840×1,920)	480P	8K
8K (7,680×3,840)	720P	12K
16K (15,360×7,680)	4K	24K

Generally, the video image is shot in an actual scenario, and the exposed image includes motion smearing of an object. The image generation principle of the strong-interaction service is different from that of the video. The image is generated by the graphics card rendering, and there is no movement track information of an object in the image. Therefore, to achieve the same smoothness, the frame rate requirement of a strong-interaction service is higher than that of a video.

5. Coding standard

The high bitrate of VR services has high requirements on network bandwidth. Compared with H.264, H.265 or updated coding standards can improve the coding and compression efficiency and reduce the bitrate while ensuring the image quality or provide better image quality at the same bitrate.

6. Bitrate

The weak-interaction cloud VR service bitrate is calculated as follows:

Bitrate=Image pixels×bits per pixel×frame rate×compression ratio

The code rate of the strong-interaction cloud VR service is calculated as follows:

$$\text{Bitrate}=\text{Pixels of terminal screen}\times(1+\text{super FoV rendering ratio})^2\times$$
$$\text{bits per pixel}\times\text{frame rate}\times\text{compression ratio}$$

7. Cloud rendering and streaming delay

Cloud rendering and streaming delay are related to black edges in terminal–cloud asynchronous rendering and image quality. Based on the service test results and theoretical analysis, suggestions on cloud rendering and streaming delay are as follows: Within 70 ms, black edges and quality deterioration are acceptable. Within 50 ms, black edges are eliminated. Within 30 ms, the distortion of the image will be imperceptible when the position moves.

2.5.3 Platform, network, and terminal technology requirements

1. Key technical requirements for the platform

Different cloud service platforms need to be constructed to account for the difference in features between weak-interaction and strong-interaction VR services. The network's role in end-to-end technical architecture is to transparently transmit data between both sides, the cloud and the terminal. The terminal is mainly responsible for capturing actions and operations, decapsulation and decoding, and refresh and display. Although requirements are higher for head motion rendering in strong-interaction services, the requirements on terminal function are basically the same for both types of services. Therefore, the cloud service platform is the biggest differentiating factor in the end-to-end technical architecture and is the determining factor for both service types.

1. Weak-interaction cloud VR service platform

Key technologies of the weak-interaction cloud VR service platform include transcoding (including coding) and content distribution technologies. The transcoding technology transcodes FoV-based tiles. Different development phases have different requirements on technologies for the weak-interaction service platform. These are based on key service indicators for cloud VR and are shown in Table 2.3.

Table 2.3 Key cloud VR requirements for the weak-interaction service platform

Phase		Comfortable experience	Ideal experience	Ultimate experience
Weak-interaction cloud VR service platform	VR video transmission technology	Full-view transmission/ FoV transmission	FoV transmission	FoV transmission
	Transcoding in FoV transmission	Supported	Supported	Supported
	Coding standard (coding/ transcoding)	H.264/H.265	H.265/H.266	H.266
	Supported video bitrate (transcoding/ distribution/ streaming)	FoV:≥80 Mbit/s	FoV:≥280 Mbit/s	FoV:≥760 Mbit/s

2. Strong-interaction cloud VR service platform

The key technologies of the cloud VR interaction service platform include rendering, coding, and streaming technologies. In addition, end-to-end low-latency technologies such as parallel processing are gradually introduced to reduce the system latency and improve interaction experience. Table 2.4 lists the technical requirements in each development phase for the strong-interaction service platform.

3. Key technical requirements for the network

Transmission networks relevant to cloud VR include the data center network, backbone network, metro network, fixed access and home network, and wireless cellular access. The cloud VR service requires ultra-high bandwidth, ultra-low latency, and ultra-low packet loss. Table 2.5 lists the requirements of the cloud VR service.

The development of cloud VR drives the evolution toward ultra-broadband access networks, high-quality home networks, and simplified networks. In the comfortable-experience phase, the cloud VR transmission network is mainly composed of gigabit home broadband access, 5G cellular mobile access, high-quality home network, and simplified metro networks. As cloud VR enters the ideal and ultimate experience stages, it will need to evolve into an intelligent and simplified network with ultra-gigabit broadband access, 5G and next-generation cellular mobile access, intelligent home network, and simplified network architecture to ensure a high-quality cloud VR experience.

Table 2.4 Key cloud VR requirements for the strong-interaction service platform

Phase			Comfortable experience	Ideal experience	Ultimate experience
Strong-interaction cloud VR platform	Terminal–cloud asynchronous rendering	Super FoV image rendering (ATW)	Supported	Supported	Supported
		Streaming video, including depth information and motion vectors (ASW)	Optional	Supported	Supported
	Coding standard		H.264/H.265	H.265/H.266	H.266
	Supported video bitrate (coding/ streaming)		≥ 65 Mbit/s	≥ 270 Mbit/s	≥ 770 Mbit/s

Table 2.5 Network KPIs

Phase		Comfortable experience	Ideal experience	Ultimate experience
Weak-interaction cloud VR service	Recommended bandwidth	FoV:≥ 120 Mbit/s	FoV:≥ 420 Mbit/s	FoV:≥ 1140 Mbit/s
	Network round-trip time (RTT)	≤ 20 ms	≤ 20 ms	≤ 10 ms
	Packet loss	≤ 1×10^{-5}	≤ 1×10^{-6}	≤ 1×10^{-6}
Strong-interaction cloud VR service	Recommended bandwidth	≥ 130 Mbit/s	≥ 540 Mbit/s	≥ 1.5 Gbit/s
	Network RTT	≤ 20 ms	≤ 10 ms	≤ 8 ms
	Jitter (maximum RTT)	≤ 40 ms	≤ 20 ms	≤ 15 ms
	Packet loss	≤ 1×10^{-6}	≤ 1×10^{-7}	≤ 1×10^{-7}

4. Key technical requirements for the terminal

The key differences between cloud VR terminals and local VR headsets are that cloud VR terminals are wireless and lightweight. Similar to these headsets, cloud VR terminals require technologies such as display, motion capture and positioning, and distortion correction. In addition, cloud VR terminals also need to have high-performance wireless transmission technology, fast decoding technology, and head motion rendering technology such as ATW. The continuous improvement of the cloud VR experience requires continuous improvement and optimization of VR terminal functions and performance, as shown in Table 2.6.

Table 2.6 Key terminal requirements

Phase		Comfortable experience	Ideal experience	Ultimate experience
Screen resolution		4K	8K	16K or higher
FoV		100°–110°	110°–120°	120°–140°
Wireless connections	Wi-Fi	802.11ac/ 802.11ax	802.11ax/ 802.11ay	802.11ay Further generations of Wi-Fi technology
	Cellular access	5G cell	5G cell	Further generations of cellular technology
Head motion rendering		ATW	ATW, ASW	ATW, ASW
Decoding	Decoding slices for FoV transmission	Supported	Supported	Supported
	Coding standard	H.264/H.265	H.265/H.266	H.266

Chapter 3

Cloud VR Service Platform Technologies

To optimize efficiency, cloud virtual reality (VR) requires seamless collaboration between the platform, network, and terminal. This chapter focuses on the key technologies used in service platforms, which are categorized as either strong-interaction or weak-interaction, depending on their characteristics. However, it will not discuss the service operation and support system.

3.1 WEAK-INTERACTION CLOUD VR SERVICE PLATFORM

Key services require seamless processes and collaboration between key end-to-end (E2E) technologies, including the platform, network, and terminal. These key technologies were expanded upon in Chapter 2.

3.1.1 Service platform overview

The service platform is key in operation management as well as content production, ingestion, and distribution. It consists of the service management system, digital media system, and content delivery network (CDN) nodes, as shown in Figure 3.1.

In the service platform, the business management system is used to perform routine operations, such as product management, content management, service authentication, electronic program guide (EPG) development, quality management, subscription management, user management, access authentication, casting management, and charging management. By contract, the digital media system is used for weak-interaction cloud VR services, and it provides service processing capabilities such as content ingestion, storage, production (transcoding and encapsulation), distribution, and CDN scheduling. Although the VoD service's content distribution and transmission share similarities with live broadcast services, the content ingestion mode is where they differ. This means that weak-interaction cloud VR services, as an extension of traditional Internet Protocol television

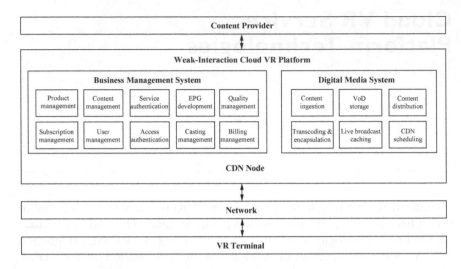

Figure 3.1 Weak-interaction cloud VR service platform.

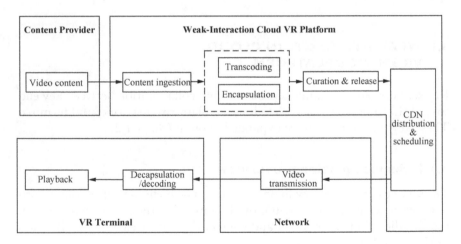

Figure 3.2 Weak-interaction cloud VR service process.

(IPTV)/over the top (OTT) video services, are processed in a way similar to that of traditional video services, as shown in Figure 3.2.

- Content ingestion: Video on demand (VoD) or live broadcast content is ingested into the digital media system after video content shooting, stitching, projection, coding, and encapsulation. Although the VR VoD content is ingested into the cloud platform as MP4 or Flash Video (FLV) video files, VR live content is encapsulated using a streaming media protocol such as the Real-Time Messaging Protocol (RTMP), before being ingested into the cloud platform in real time.

- Transcoding/encapsulation: Ingested content is segmented, trans-coded, and encapsulated. Then, coded and encapsulated video streams are converted into another type of video stream. That is, the ingested video content is decapsulated and decoded and then coded and encapsulated. Transcoding/encapsulation involves coding and streaming technologies.
- Curation and publishing: Processed content is curated and published to CDN nodes for users to request.
- CDN distribution and scheduling: When a user initiates a video service request, the CDN schedules a proper node using an algorithm.
- Video transmission: Video content is streamed from a CDN node to a terminal.
- Decapsulation/decoding and playback: The terminal decapsulates, decodes, and plays the received video.

Even though traditional video service platforms feature mature coding and decoding, streaming, and CDN technologies, weak-interaction cloud VR services, by contrast, need to meet new requirements to inherit these technologies. These requirements include the following:

- Higher transmission and processing rates, due to increased definition
- Support for field of view (FoV) transmission.

3.1.2 Coding/decoding technologies

Both video and audio data are used during coding and decoding, whereas transcoding only involves video data. During coding and decoding, the original spatial spherical VR video images are mapped to flat images for storage. As such, the technologies used for coding and decoding VR video are similar to those used for traditional flat video. In this case, weak-interaction cloud VR services continue to pose the following requirements on coding and decoding (codec) technologies:

- More efficient coding and decoding are required to optimize the content bitrate.
- The ability to divide full-view images into tiles based on the FoV in FoV transmission is needed to enable the independent coding and decoding of tiles and to ultimately improve efficiency.

3.1.2.1 Basic principles

Raw video data consumes large amounts of bandwidth and storage space. Therefore, it must be compressed using standards such as the advanced video coding (AVC or H.264), high efficiency video coding (HEVC or H.265), or versatile video coding (VVC or H.266) standard (currently being developed).

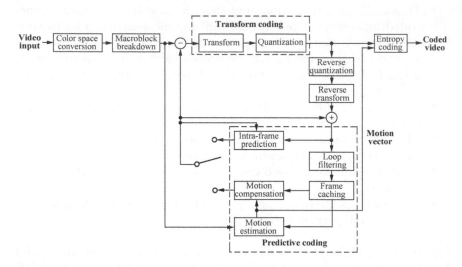

Figure 3.3 H.26x coding standard architecture.

Even though H.264's architecture is the same as that of H.265 and H.266, as shown in Figure 3.3,[10,11] each generation has improved coding efficiency and stability, when compared to the generation before.

To compress data, redundant information must be removed. To do this, the video coding process' core algorithms include the intra-frame coding and inter-frame coding algorithms.

Intra-frame coding involves compressing each frame in order to generate intra-coded frames (I-frames). An I-frame is a frame that carries all required information and can be decoded by itself without referencing any other frames.

Inter-frame coding leverages the correlation between frames to generate predictive-coded frames (P-frames) and bidirectionally predictive-coded frames (B-frames). P-frames store the differences from the preceding I-frame and must be coded by referencing the preceding I-frame. By contrast, B-frames not only store the differences from the preceding frame, but also the following frame, thereby generating a final image that references both frames.

As shown in Figure 3.3, color space conversion (converting RGB to YUV) is performed on raw video. It performs chroma subsampling to achieve less resolution for chroma information than luma information, taking advantage of the human visual system's lower acuity for color differences than for luminance. Then, each frame is broken down into multiple macroblocks (e.g. 4 pixels×4 pixels), which are delivered to the coder for coding.

Key processes of coding include transform coding, predictive coding, and entropy coding. Transform coding includes transform and quantization, while predictive coding includes intra-frame prediction and inter-frame prediction (motion compensation and motion estimation). By contrast, intra-frame coding involves intra-frame prediction, transform coding, and entropy coding, while inter-frame coding involves inter-frame prediction, transform coding, and entropy coding. Video decoding is an inverse process of entropy, transform, and predictive coding.

1. Transform coding

   Transform: The macroblock information is transformed from a spatial domain representation to a frequency domain representation using discrete cosine transform (DCT) or discrete sine transform (DST). It generates a series of transform coefficients, and its key image information includes direct current components and low-frequency components (energy in a frequency domain) in the frequency domain. It also stores information that is not easily perceived by the human visual system in the high-frequency component.

   Quantization: The transform coefficients produced in transform processing are divided by a quantization step to convert them to an integer multiple of the step or a value of zero. At the same time, high-frequency components that include small coefficients are removed or minimized.

   In general, the transform coding process eliminates spatial redundancy (correlation among pixels within one frame) and redundant visual information.

2. Predictive coding

   Intra-frame prediction: Multiple similar coded image blocks within a frame are weighted to estimate uncoded macroblocks, thereby removing spatial redundancy between adjacent image blocks.

   Inter-frame prediction: Coded images are used as reference frames to predict the current image. Its core algorithm is the motion estimation and motion compensation algorithm, which is used to remove time redundancy (different frames that share similar content).

   Motion estimation is a process that involves generating motion vectors. In this process, a reference frame is selected to code the current frame, and the same displacement value is used for all pixels of each image block in a frame. Then, in the reference frame, the best matching block is located for each image block of the current frame according to the matching criteria, and the relative displacement between the matching block and the current block becomes the motion vector, as shown in Figure 3.4. What's more, in the video decoding process, the image block can be restored by using the reference frame and motion vector.

   Efficient matching algorithms are crucial to the motion estimation process. Block matching algorithms are most commonly used, including the diamond, regular hexagon, uneven multi-hexagon, and exhaustive search algorithms. However, matching algorithms have different computing efficiency. To ensure that motion estimation is completed accurately, the appropriate algorithm needs to be selected based

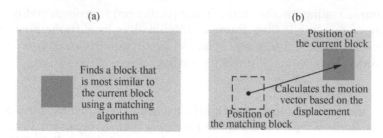

Figure 3.4 Motion estimation process. (a) **Reference frame** (coded image frame) and (b) **Current frame** (displaced pixel block).

on computing resources and capabilities, as well as coding time requirements. For example, the video coding process in predictive coding is the most complex process, and the most critical and computing-intensive part is the motion estimation search process. Therefore, in situations where computing resources and capabilities are not abundant, these algorithms are not recommended.

In addition, motion compensation, performed during video decoding, is used to predict and compensate the macroblocks of the current frame by using those of the reference frame and data such as motion vector and residual.

Loop filtering: The distortion caused by the coding processes, such as prediction, transform, and quantization, is eliminated through filtering.

3. Entropy coding

Entropy indicates the average rate at which information is produced by a source of data and depends on the information and its probability of occurrence. The entropy coding process ensures that information is not lost and involves coding according to an entropy principle, as well as converting video data into bit streams for storage and transmission purposes.

3.1.2.2 H.264, H.265, and H.266

This section compares H.264 and H.265 and briefly expands upon the development of H.266.

1. Comparing H.264 and H.265

H.265, when compared with H.264, has a greater selection of algorithms used to improve coding efficiency. These algorithms are expanded upon below:

- Image segmentation

When using H.264, images are divided into blocks of a unified size (for example, 4 pixels×4 pixels or 8 pixels×8 pixels) as well as slices. However, the image segmentation method used in H.265 is more adaptive and flexible, as it supports tile-wise image segmentation and uses a quadtree (a data structure where each node has four sub-blocks) division method.

In image segmentation, slices and tiles are distinguished based on their shape. That is, a strip is observed as a slice, and a rectangle as a tile, as shown in Figure 3.5. What's more, a frame of an image may be divided into multiple slices or tiles, while a slice may be further divided into multiple tiles, and a tile divided into multiple slices. By doing this, slices and tiles can be coded separately in parallel, improving coding efficiency.

Slice and tile are spatial division of frames and are useful in, for example, the tile division mode of H.265 that supports more flexible rectangular segmentation as well as motion-constrained tile set (MCTS) coding. This makes it suitable for weak-interaction cloud VR services and the FoV transmission solution. In addition, by limiting the motion vector search range, the motion vector does not cross a tile boundary, thereby implementing independent coding and decoding of each tile.

What's more, slices and tiles can be further divided into image blocks for coding. For example, H.264 uses macroblocks of a unified size, in contrast to H.265, which supports macroblocks of different sizes. And by using a quadtree structure, H.265 supports the division of an image frame into coding tree units, coding units, prediction/transform units, and coding blocks level by level, as shown in Figure 3.6.

By using adaptive, flexible multi-layer division, H.265 optimizes the different coding phases, such as prediction, transform, and entropy coding.

- Transform coding
  In transform processing, H.264 and H.265 perform DCT or similar transform on the predicted residual. H.265, however, supports

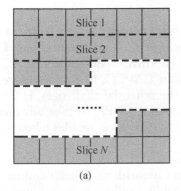
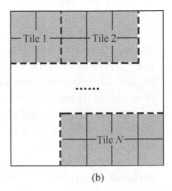

(a) (b)

Figure 3.5 (a) Slice division and (b) tile division.

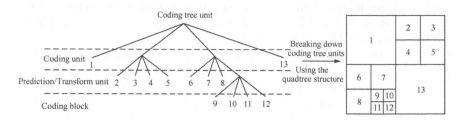

Figure 3.6 Quadtree structure and coding tree unit division.

DST on a 4×4 small block of the coding tree to implement intra-frame prediction and residual coding of small blocks, thereby improving prediction accuracy.

In terms of quantization processing, H.265 uses a rate-distortion quantization (RDOQ) technology. For the same bitrate, H.265 reduces the distortion of a restored image by selecting another quantization coefficient.

- Predictive coding

  For intra-frame prediction, H.265 uses multi-direction intra-frame prediction based on image blocks. Compared with H.264, H.265 has a more adaptive and refined image block division and more flexible intra-frame prediction, improving prediction precision and efficiency.

  Additionally, in terms of inter-frame prediction, H.265 supports image blocks with more flexible sizes and shapes. This ensures that the shapes of reference blocks can be more accurately matched during motion estimation and compensation.

  Meanwhile, to achieve loop filtering, H.264 uses deblocking filter (DBF) to reduce the blocking effects at boundaries of various units. By contrast, H.265 performs sample adaptive offset (SAO) filtering before DBF to reduce distortion by adding an offset to pixels of different categories.

- Entropy coding

  H.264 has two entropy coding modes, namely context-based adaptive variable length coding (CAVLC) and context-based adaptive binary arithmetic coding (CABAC). Although CABAC has a higher coding performance than CAVLC, it involves more complex calculations. To mitigate the potential challenges, H.265 also adopts wavefront parallel processing (WPP) to take advantage of the correlation between boundaries of slices or tiles when they are independently coded.

  In general, H.265 has a finer and more flexible image block division and uses more efficient algorithms in each coding phase when compared with H.264. Additionally, research shows that,[12] for conventional video of the same resolution, H.265-coded video

Table 3.1 Lower average bitrate of H.265

Definition	Lower bitrate of H.265 compared to H.264(%)
480P	52
720P	56
1080P	62
4K	64

Note: 1080P=1,920 pixels×1,080 pixels.

has a significantly lower average bitrate than H.264-coded video, as shown in Table 3.1.

2. H.266 development

The H.266 standard is designed for 4K HD video or video with 10-bit depth definition. The standard, which is currently under development, is more suitable for weak-interaction cloud VR services. The following section expands upon the direction that H.266 is taking.

In terms of image block division, H.266 is more flexible than H.265, as it uses a mixed tree structure that includes quadtree, binary tree, and ternary tree structures.

In addition, H.266 features more improved transform coding by using adaptive multiple core transform (AMT) technology to further improve its inter-frame residual coding accuracy.

H.266 also improves its intra-frame prediction accuracy by using technologies such as position-dependent intra-prediction combination (PDPC), linear mode (LM) prediction, wide angle intra prediction (WAIP), and multiple reference line (MRL) intra-prediction.

H.266 achieves improved inter-frame prediction accuracy by using technologies such as affine motion compensation prediction (affine mode), adaptive motion vector resolution (AMVR), alternative temporal motion vector prediction (ATMVP), and spatial temporal motion vector prediction (STMVP).

It also uses new technologies such as decoder-side motion vector refinement (DMVR) and bidirectional optical flow (BIO).

In general, each standard, from H.264 to H.265 and then to H.266, delivers higher accuracy than its previous generation to optimize bitrate for VR videos.

3.1.2.3 VR video coding and decoding

During the early development of weak-interaction cloud VR services, it was 4K content, full-view transmission, and H.264 standard that were used as vendors' mainstream solution to ensure there was no impact on network bandwidth and storage space. However, as resolution continues to increase, VR video data poses new data storage and transmission challenges. As such, new coding technologies are needed to the requirements set by FoV transmission. To this end, H.265 and next-generation video standards will be more suited to support VR video coding by providing the following benefits:

- Higher coding efficiency: A lower bitrate (generated using compression) ensures the same or even higher image quality. This is especially useful when using high-resolution images.
- Flexible tile division and independent coding: Although H.264 is suitable for full-view transmission, FoV transmission requires tile-wise division and MCTS coding to achieve independent coding and decoding, both of which are available only using H.265 and next-generation video standards.

Following the selection of a coding standard for the coding module (coder) of the transcoding system, coding parameters must be selected to determine the technologies and algorithms used. For example, H.265 requires that the profile, level, and tier need to be specified. In this example, profile determines the coding technology and algorithm, while level defines parameters such as the coder processing load and storage capacity, and tier defines the bitrate at each level. In this case, H.265 will contain Main, Main 10, and Main Still Picture profiles, as shown in Table 3.2.

The coding performance, which is measured by image quality and computing complexity, varies according to the specified coding standard and parameter settings. Additionally, image quality is evaluated by definition, luminance, and chrominance, while computing complexity is measured by computing cost and time. That is, a higher image quality usually correlates with higher computing complexity. Therefore, when selecting technologies and algorithms, actual conditions and requirements need to be considered.

Table 3.2 H.265 coding profile examples

Supported technology/algorithm	Profile		
	Main	Main 10	Main still picture
8-bit depth	V	V	V
Sampling rate of 4:2:0.	V	V	V
Coding Tree Block (CTB) size from 16×16 to 64×64	V	V	V
Six-frame decoding buffer limit	V	V	V
Wavefront or slice division (not both)	V	V	V
Inter-frame coding	V	V	X
10-bit depth	X	V	X

3.1.3 Streaming technology

To view VR videos while streaming, weak-interaction cloud VR services need to be transmitted to terminals over the network in streaming media.

For VR videos transmitted in full-view mode, the requirements on streaming technologies are similar to traditional videos. However, when transmitting VR video in FoV mode, the angle of view (AoV) information of slices is involved.

3.1.3.1 Basic principles

By being encapsulated into packets, data may arrive on the receiver out-of-order due to latency. Therefore, streaming protocols are used to address two key challenges: latency and time sequence. In general, streaming media protocols involve pre-processing transmission data at the transmitting end to reduce delay, carrying time sequence information in data, and buffering the received data on the receiving end to restore the time sequence.

Streaming technologies are separated into two categories: progressive and real-time. In progressive streaming, media is downloaded progressively, and users can watch downloaded content but not content that has not been downloaded. However, real-time streaming transmits content in real time based on user requests, allowing users to fast forward or rewind through videos. As such, real-time streaming transmission is more suited to weak-interaction cloud VR services. Real-time streaming protocols include the RTSP/RTP/RTCP protocol suite, RTMP, and HTTP-based streaming protocols (such as HLS and DASH):

1. RTSP/RTP/RTCP protocol suite

   The Real-Time Streaming Protocol (RTSP), Real-Time Transport Protocol (RTP), and Real-Time Transport Control Protocol (RTCP) work together to form one of the first developed video transmission protocol suites.

   RTSP is an application-layer protocol based on Transmission Control Protocol (TCP) that establishes and controls (plays) sessions, and publishes streaming media file information, but cannot transmit multimedia data (which is transmitted using RTP), as shown in Figure 3.7.

   By contrast, RTP and RTCP are both protocols based on User Datagram Protocol (UDP). RTP transmits multimedia data and encapsulates data into multiple UDP packets that carry timestamp information. However, it cannot ensure that data is delivered in order or control data traffic or congestion. In cases where these requirements need to be satisfied, RTCP is used instead.

   And as RSTP, RTP, and RTCP cannot guarantee network transmission's quality of service (QoS), the Resource Reservation Protocol (RSVP) is used to reserve network resources (bandwidth) and guarantee QoS.

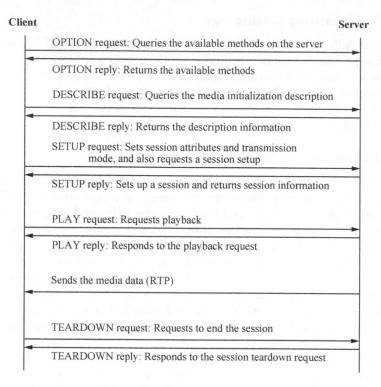

Figure 3.7 RTSP interaction process.

The benefits of the RSTP protocol suite include its use of UDP to ensure high transmission efficiency on a stable network (an IPTV network, for example). Additionally, it does not perform video pregrouping or slicing, and can control video frames, delivering real-time performance. Its drawbacks, however, include its complex implementation on the server side and route traversal of UDP on complex networks.

2. RTMP

RTMP is a TCP-based application layer protocol developed by Adobe. It is used to transmit multimedia data between a Flash server and clients in real time. It has multiple variations, including RTMP Tunneled (RTMPT), RTMP Secure (RTMPS), Encrypted Real Time Messaging Protocol (RTMPE or RTMPTE) , all of which are guided by basic principles such as fragmentation and multiplexing. RTMP's main processes are shown in Figure 3.8.

• Fragmentation on the server side: The server encapsulates the original data into messages, which are further divided into multiple chunks for transmission over TCP.

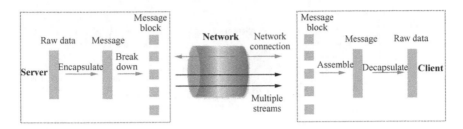

Figure 3.8 RTMP interaction process.

- Multiplexing: The server sets up a network connection with a client. Then, fragments from different streams are multiplexed over a single connection.
- Reassembly on the client: After receiving the data, the client reassembles the chunks into messages and decapsulates the messages to restore the multimedia data.

RTMP uses TCP to ensure transmission quality in poor network environments. By contrast, RTMP (with its short delay) is often used in live broadcast scenarios. However, it requires large amounts of server resources to maintain persistent TCP connections.

3. HTTP-based streaming protocols (such as HLS and DASH)

Hypertext Transfer Protocol (HTTP) is a TCP-based application layer protocol. There are multiple HTTP-based streaming protocols, including HTTP Live Streaming (HLS), HTTP Dynamic Streaming (HDS), and HTTP Smooth Streaming (HSS), and Dynamic Adaptive Streaming over HTTP (DASH) protocols.

Multiple different vendors and standards organizations have proposed the above-mentioned protocols (HLS, HDS, HSS, and DASH), but their basic principles remain similar: A server breaks down the content into a sequence of small HTTP-based file segments, while the client downloads a segment, decodes it, and plays it.

As the HLS protocol is developed by Apple, support for it is widespread in media players, web browsers, mobile devices, and streaming media servers. In fact, an annual video industry survey consistently found HLS to be the most popular streaming format. Additionally, in an attempt to unify the various different streaming protocols, the DASH protocol (currently recognized yet not mature) was developed by MPEG. These two protocols (HLS and DASH) share similar processes, as shown in Figure 3.9.

- Coding and encapsulating: The video source is directly coded or transcoded and encapsulated into video files in storage format (Transport Stream (TS) in HLS and MP4/TS in DASH).

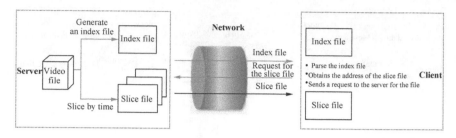

Figure 3.9 Interaction process of HLS/DASH.

- Segmentation: The video file is broken into a sequence of segments of equal length. The server prepares versions of different bitrates or resolutions of the same segment to adapt to different network environments.
- Index generation: During video playback, the corresponding segment files need to be obtained and reassembled to form a sequence that can be continuously played. That is, an index file (text file that records each segment's index information, including its video length, type, resolution, and address) needs to be generated during file segmentation. The index files of HLS are M3U8/M3U files, while DASH uses Media Presentation Description (MPD) files to record index information.
- Distribution: The server sends the index file and segmented files to the client using HTTP.
- Download and playback: Firstly, the client software downloads the index file, and downloads available media files of the right bitrate based on the address in the index file. Next, the playback software assembles the sequence to enable uninterrupted viewing to the user. In live broadcast scenarios, the client needs to continuously obtain index files from the server. However, a VoD program only requires the client to obtain the index file once.

Compared with RTSP and RTMP, HTTP-based streaming protocols can fall victim to delay due to the video being broken into a sequence of segments. Even with that being the case, however, HTTP-based streamlining protocols offer the following advantages:

- Better network compatibility: The standard protocol HTTP is used to transmit data and prevent data from being blocked in special network environments. In addition, as HTTP is based on TCP, it does not involve route traversal (unlike UDP).
- Load balancing on the server side: HTTP is a stateless protocol that does not record processed transactions. Instead, each request is independent. Therefore, the client can request segments from

different times and different servers to implement distributed download, enabling load balancing on the server side. By contrast, RTSP and RTMP are stateful protocols that need to maintain the status of each client, thereby making it difficult to switch between servers when using these two protocols.

- Adaptive bitrate: Multiple versions of different bitrates can be prepared for the same segment. That is, the client can request segments with the right bitrate based on the actual bandwidth.

3.1.3.2 VR video streaming technology

Full-view transmission features the same requirements as traditional video streaming. This means that different streaming protocols can be selected based on actual requirements as well as the advantages and disadvantages of different protocols. In this case, most vendors use RTMP for live content ingestion, while HLS or DASH are normally chosen for VoD and live content distribution.

In FoV transmission, the AoV information of each segment file needs to be identified. Therefore, this function is key when selecting the right streaming protocol. MPEG is currently developing the Omnidirectional Media Format (OMAF) standard, which defines Spatial Relationship Description (SRD) in the MPD file of the DASH protocol. SRD describes the position and size of a sub-image sequence and presents the relationship between a sub-image sequence and the FoV. Due to its proposed benefits, OMAF is often used by vendors in FoV transmission.

3.1.4 CDN technology

Although traditional video services' CDN technology is used for weak-interaction cloud VR services, higher requirements need to be satisfied:

- Higher throughput is required to handle the higher bitrate of VR videos.
- Tile-wise FoV transmission requires fast download of multiple segments between CDN nodes and user devices.

3.1.4.1 Basic principles

A typical CDN network consists of the central, regional, and edge nodes, as shown in Figure 3.10. The central node (which includes the digital media system of the service platform) is responsible for content management, ingestion, processing (involving transcoding), storage, and distribution. Meanwhile, the regional and edge nodes are used as content distribution nodes that cache and accelerate content and provide media services. In addition, to satisfy the needs of different users, the hierarchy of CDN nodes can be easily modified. For example, a CDN can be modified to not include any

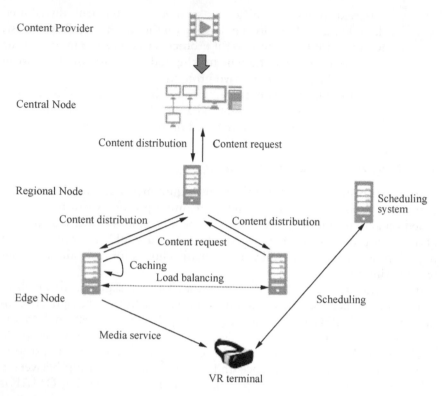

Figure 3.10 Typical CDN networking.

level-3 nodes (edge nodes) or to include level-4 nodes. A CDN's interaction process is as follows:

- Firstly, the content provider ingests content to the central node, which then distributes the content to regional and edge nodes.
- Secondly, a terminal sends a video service request to the CDN. The CDN finds the node where the requested video resides and returns the address of the edge node.
- Finally, the terminal requests the video service from the corresponding edge node. Then, if the edge node has the requested video, it streams the video to the terminal. However, if the content is unavailable, the edge node retrieves the content from an upper-layer node.

Key CDN technologies include content distribution, scheduling, load balancing, caching, and media services.

1. Content distribution
   Content distribution technology transfers content from an upper-level node to a lower-level node until it is delivered to the requesting

terminal. The content distribution mechanism, which can be either pull mode, push mode, or both, will be expanded upon below.

Pull mode: The request of a terminal is scheduled to a proper edge node; however, if the edge node does not have the requested content, it requests it from the upper-level node. This process continues until the requested content is found from either the proper edge node or upper-level node. It is simple to implement the pull mode because there is no need to consider where the content is stored. Rather, the CDN only needs to schedule a nearby edge node. However, if content storage is not yet optimized and lower-level nodes need to continually request content from upper-level nodes, latency will increase, and edge nodes' rapid response advantages will be forfeited. What's more, user experience may be impacted when using tile-wise FoV transmission, as it introduces high levels of latency when users change the AoV.

Push mode: To help users quickly obtain content from nearby nodes, upper-level nodes push content to lower-level nodes in advance. However, both terminal location and content storage location must be considered in CDN scheduling. Otherwise, latency might be experienced if the node where the requested content resides is not nearby the requesting terminal. In cases like this, implementation becomes far more complex.

Push and pull mode: In this mode, frequently requested content items are pushed to corresponding edge nodes in advance, while other items are pulled level by level when requested. To ensure this mode is optimized, content popularity management is required. That is, the requested items and request frequency data need to be collected to determine which items are popular on an edge node, allowing these items to be pushed to the node in advance. The push and pull mode combines multiple advantages from the two individual modes to implement more efficient distribution, making this the most commonly used mode.

When an upper-level node transmits media data to a lower-level node, the throughput (the rate at which data is transmitted) is used to indicate and measure data transmission performance. As weak-interaction cloud VR services have higher bitrates than traditional video services, they require a higher CDN throughput.

2. Scheduling

After a user sends a video request to the CDN, the CDN schedules a proper edge node for the user. Then, to establish optimal scheduling policies, factors such as proximity, service availability, load, and QoS must be considered. The Domain Name System (DNS) servers' redirection technology uses scheduling to parse the request of a user and allocates the IP address of the optimal node based on the loads of nodes and the distance between the nodes and the user.

Scheduling also determines the latency experienced by users. In traditional video services, latency is experienced as video buffering time. If latency is too long for weak-interaction cloud VR services, especially the FoV transmission scheme, new tiles may not be delivered to the terminal when a user switches the AoV.

3. Load balancing

   Load balancing technology dynamically adjusts the load of different nodes or different servers within a node based on load information, such as utilization of hardware resources (e.g. CPU and memory), network traffic load, and number of connected users. This technology can be implemented either globally or locally and based on either hardware or software.

   It is used to optimize efficiency, performance, and response speed and enables better service quality and user experience.

4. Caching

   To enable quick download, items that are frequently requested can be cached on CDN nodes. These cached items can be dynamically adjusted depending on their popularity as well as available storage capacity. The most commonly used cache algorithms include Least Recently Used (LRU) and Least Frequently Used (LFU).[13] Meanwhile, its basic function is to determine whether to cache or delete an item by collecting and analyzing information such as access time, count, and frequency.

   As caching shortens latency, it is highly suited to FoV transmission. The caching technology can also be combined with the posture prediction function of terminals to predict the posture of the user and cache the corresponding data in advance.

5. Media service

   Media service involves delivering media content from an edge node to a user. In this process, the edge node must support requested service types, such as VoD and live broadcast, as well as corresponding acceleration and streaming protocols, such as RTMP, RTSP, HLS, and DASH. Additionally, to adapt to different network conditions, the edge node must prepare versions of different resolutions or bitrates for the same content.

   For the tile-wise FoV transmission scheme, multiple tiles must be downloaded in parallel from the edge node to the user terminal.

3.1.4.2 New requirements of weak-interaction cloud VR services on CDN

The CDN of traditional video services is suitable for weak-interaction cloud VR services. However, with the increase in video resolution and bitrate as well as FoV transmission technology application, new requirements are required to implement CDN.

- Support for DASH protocol

  As the tile-wise FoV transmission scheme uses DASH to encapsulate content, the transcoding and media service modules of the CDN must also support DASH.

- Parallel download of multiple tiles
  The tile-wise FoV transmission scheme requires parallel download of multiple tile streams to ensure user experience when the AoV changes.
- Adequate network resources for HD and high-bitrate content
  The higher resolution and bitrate of weak-interaction cloud VR services compared with traditional video services requires adequate network resources to meet bandwidth and concurrency requirements.
- Optimal node deployment to minimize transmission latency
  In full-view transmission mode, weak-interaction cloud VR services are similar to traditional video services because AoVs are not involved. As such, content can be downloaded to user terminals in advance without raising latency requirements. By contrast, in FoV transmission, CDN nodes need to deliver content in real time based on the AoV of users. However, this ensures that its latency requirements are higher. Meanwhile, as the distance between CDN nodes and terminals remains essential, the location of CDN nodes must be properly planned based on the survey and analysis of target users and their geographic distribution.

3.1.5 FoV transmission technology

In the full-view transmission scheme, panoramic video is produced using equirectangular projection (ERP) or platonic solid projection technologies. Although its coding and streaming protocols are similar to those used in traditional video services, FoV transmission technology instead involves slicing on the cloud, stitching on the terminal, and selection of the proper coding and streaming technologies. The three FoV transmission technologies, which vary in implementation, are described in more detail in Chapter 2.

1. Adaptive transmission: high-quality images in FoV areas + low-quality full-view images in non-FoV areas
   This solution, which combines FoV and full-view transmission technologies, codes and encapsulates full-view video data on the cloud. Using this solution, vendors employ either the H.264 or H.265 coding standard for low-definition VR videos, while they use H.265 as well as new streaming protocols such as HLS and DASH as definition increases. The different ways that full-view videos can be generated are expanded upon below.
   - Using projection: The cloud selects a proper projection mode, degrades the quality of the images in non-FoV areas, and codes and encapsulates the complete projection plane that contains both high-quality and low-quality images. Then, the terminal requests a corresponding full-view video file from the cloud based on the current FoV information, as shown in Figure 3.11. (The hexahedron projection is used as an example.)

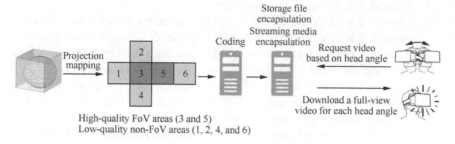

High-quality FoV areas (3 and 5)
Low-quality non-FoV areas (1, 2, 4, and 6)

Figure 3.11 Adaptive full-view transmission process based on projection technologies.

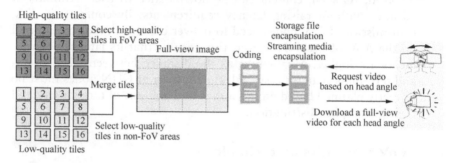

Figure 3.12 Adaptive full-view transmission process based on stitching.

- Using stitching: The cloud compresses high-quality full-view images into low-quality images of equal definition and breaks the original high-quality images and compressed low-quality images into multiple tiles. Then, it selects the high-quality tiles in FoV areas and low-quality tiles in non-FoV areas and stitches them into complete, full-view images for coding and encapsulation. The terminal requests a corresponding full-view video file from the cloud each time based on the current FoV information, as shown in Figure 3.12.

2. Tile-wise transmission: High-quality tiles in FoV areas+low-quality tiles in non-FoV areas

   To prepare both high-quality and low-quality full-view images, the cloud breaks them into multiple tiles and codes them separately.

   H.265 supports tile-wise coding and decoding, as well as parallel tile processing. The cloud, after breaking a full-view image into tiles, delivers the tiles to the same H.265 coder for parallel coding and encapsulates them separately. If there is only one coder, the coder processes high-quality tiles first before processing low-quality tiles or vice versa. However, if there are two coders, one coder can process high-quality tiles while the other coder processes low-quality tiles. As the tiles need to be independently encapsulated during coding and decoding, they do not need to reference each other for intra-frame prediction. Therefore, the MCTS coding of H.265 is used to independently

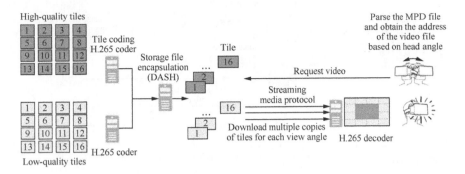

Figure 3.13 Tile-wise transmission process.

code the tiles. Then, after being independently coded, each tile needs to be encapsulated into an independent file and streamed to the user terminal using DASH where the SRD in the MPD file records the AoV of the tile. Upon receiving the file, the terminal parses the MPD file, finds the address of the tile in the MPD file according to the current AoV information, and requests the corresponding video tile from the cloud. To optimize transmission efficiency and reduce transmission latency, user terminals need to support parallel download of multiple streams. User terminals, upon receiving the code streams, reassemble them and send multiple tiles to the decoder for decoding and final stitching. The entire process is shown in Figure 3.13.

3. Full-view+tile-wise transmission: high-quality tiles for FoV areas+ low-quality full-view images

The cloud prepares both low-quality full-view images and high-quality tiles. Full-view images are coded using H.264 or H.265, whereas the tiles are coded using H.265 and encapsulated using DASH. As user terminals need to independently decode the full-view images and the tiles, two decoders are needed. The process is show in Figure 3.14.

In general, H.265 can independently code and decode tiles in parallel, and the implementation is simple. In terms of streaming, the SDR defined in the MPD file of DASH can describe the position information of a tile relative to the entire picture to identify the tiles of different AoVs. As such, most vendors use H.265 for coding and DASH for encapsulation in tile-wise FoV transmission.

3.2 STRONG-INTERACTION CLOUD VR SERVICE PLATFORM

Unlike weak-interaction cloud VR service platforms that provide pre-set video files for users, strong-interaction cloud VR service platforms need to use different technologies to generate content in real time based on user movements.

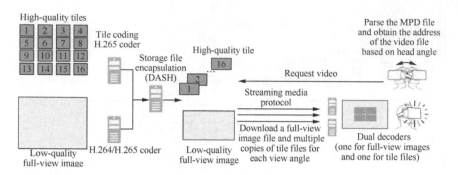

Figure 3.14 Full-view+tile-wise transmission process.

3.2.1 Service platform overview

A strong-interaction cloud VR service platform consists of a service management system and cloud rendering nodes, as shown in Figure 3.15.

The service management system is responsible for the routine operation of strong-interaction cloud VR services, including user management, subscription and billing, application management, EPG curation, authentication management, node management, service invoking, and task management. The cloud rendering nodes are mainly responsible for application rendering, coding, and streaming.

A strong-interaction cloud VR service platform needs to allocate an independent cloud rendering node for each user to provide an independent application running environment, as shown in Figure 3.16.

Virtualization can divide a server hardware cluster into multiple independent software running environments, which is critical for promoting the wide use of strong-interaction cloud VR services.

Figure 3.17 shows the key process of strong-interaction cloud VR services.

- Content ingestion, curation, and release: The VR content provided by content providers is loaded to the service platform as applications. The service platform curates these applications and releases them to the cloud rendering node for installation and adaptation.
- Computing and rendering: The cloud rendering node performs computing and rendering on the applications based on the instructions sent from the cloud VR terminals in order to immediately generate images that are displayed to users.
- Fast coding: The rendered images are quickly coded, compressed, and then transmitted over the network.
- Encapsulation and streaming: The coded video streams are encapsulated and streamed to users using streaming protocols.

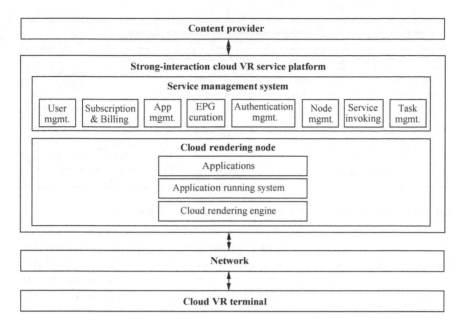

Figure 3.15 Architecture of a strong-interaction cloud VR service platform.

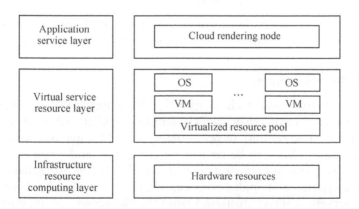

Figure 3.16 Deployment of a strong-interaction cloud VR service platform.

- Data transmission: The encapsulated video streams are transmitted from the cloud rendering node to VR terminals.
- Motion capture and instruction sending: The terminals report user movements to the cloud rendering node during play (for example, when users are playing games).
- Decoding and playback: The VR terminals decapsulate, decode, and then play the received video streams.

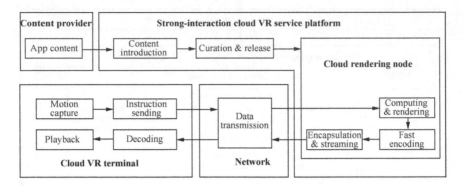

Figure 3.17 Key process of strong-interaction cloud VR services.

The key technologies used include virtualization, rendering, fast coding/ decoding, and streaming. Low latency is critical to ensuring optimal user experience in strong-interaction cloud VR services. And so optimizing the processing latency of technologies in each phase is key to the service platform.

3.2.2 Virtualization technology

The virtualization technology creates multiple virtual and isolated operating environments on shared physical resources for cloud services.

3.2.2.1 Basic principles

The core of virtualization technology is the virtual machine monitor (VMM, also referred to as hypervisor), which is an intermediate software layer running between a server and an operating system. Multiple independent virtual machines (VMs) can be created on the server, and resources such as CPU, memory, and storage are allocated to each VM, ensuring that multiple operating systems and applications can share a set of hardware resources (such as servers or server clusters). Currently, x86 servers are used for cloud construction. There are four types[14] of x86-based hypervisor architecture, of which the bare metal virtualization architecture and hybrid virtualization architecture are commonly used.

1. Host virtualization architecture
   A host operating system is installed on the server, and then applications are directly installed onto the operating system, or a hypervisor layer is constructed on the operating system. Multiple VMs can be created on the hypervisor layer, and a guest operating system or applications are deployed on each VM, as shown in Figure 3.18.

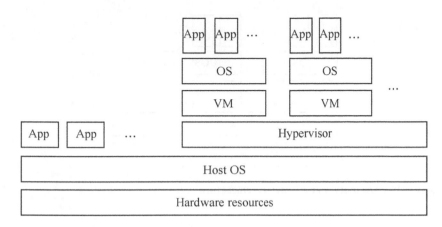

Figure 3.18 Host virtualization architecture.

2. Bare metal virtualization architecture

Multiple VMs are created on a server using the hypervisor, and an operating system is installed and run on each VM, as shown in Figure 3.19. This architecture is used by mainstream virtualization products, such as VMware ESX Server, Microsoft Hyper-V, and Citrix Xen Server.

3. Operating system virtualization architecture

A host operating system is installed on the server and divided into multiple containers, as shown in Figure 3.20.

4. Hybrid virtualization architecture

A host operating system is installed on the server, and a driver is inserted into the host operating system kernel to coordinate hardware access between the VMs and the host operating system (Figure 3.21).

3.2.2.2 Mainstream virtualization solutions for strong-interaction cloud VR services

Currently, most strong-interaction cloud VR service platforms use the bare metal or hybrid virtualization architecture. Each server is virtualized into multiple VMs; each VM has an installed operating system that is capable of deploying cloud rendering applications. The cloud rendering nodes move from the host to the cloud. Like PC VR, only one cloud rendering instance can run on one operating system at a time, meaning that a single VM supports only one user. Virtualization is implemented at the operating system level, as shown in Figure 3.22.

Applications of this architecture directly run on the operating system, and the solution can be easily implemented. In addition, each VM provides resources (such as the CPU, GPU, memory, and storage) for only one user

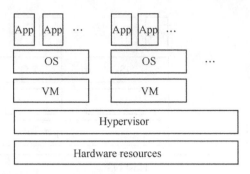

Figure 3.19 Bare metal virtualization architecture.

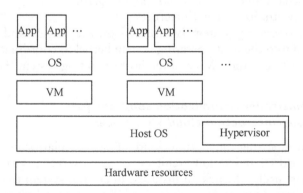

Figure 3.20 Operating system virtualization architecture.

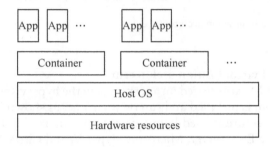

Figure 3.21 Hybrid virtualization architecture.

as needed, ensuring both smooth experience and high hardware resource utilization.

Currently, some vendors use technologies such as sandbox to implement single-VM multi-user access. This solution is virtualized at the application layer, as shown in Figure 3.23.

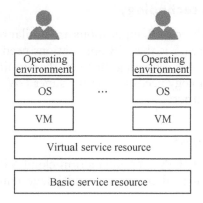

Figure 3.22 Single-VM single-user solution.

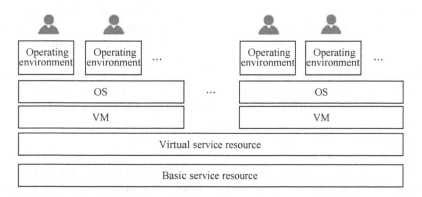

Figure 3.23 Single-VM multi-user solution.

In this solution, multiple independent environments need to be created on the operating system to allow applications to run in each environment. Sandbox technology is able to isolate applications in a restricted environment and can be implemented in two modes. One mode involves converting and storing an operating system's resources into a sandbox as virtual resources, where applications can directly write to them. In contrast, the other mode involves redirecting the write operations to the related applications or interfaces of the operating system.

The single-VM multi-user solution allows multiple users to share the same VM. Therefore, each VM needs to provide more resources than in the single-user solution. However, the multi-user solution requires only one operating system and one IP address and so has higher overall resource utilization. Resource utilization can be further improved by pooling resources so that they can be dynamically adjusted.

3.2.3 Rendering technology

The principles of rendering VR applications are similar to those of PC games; however, a key difference is that VR applications need to render binocular images. Additionally, the rendering phase in the terminal–cloud asynchronous rendering technology needs to support super FoV image rendering and depth information output.

3.2.3.1 Basic principles

The core functions of the strong-interaction cloud VR service application running system are logical computing and image rendering, as shown in Figure 3.24.

Logical computing is the process of determining the content to be rendered or removed based on information, such as the state machine, background animations, and interactive animations. State changing includes a character standing, sitting, or running in a game. When the user changes the state of an in-game character, the state machine responds to this change and subsequently renders a new image. The state machine is determined by the user's input, whereas background animations are related to time. For example, when a game reaches a specific period or moment, it will begin to rain in-game. Meanwhile, interactive animations are related to both user input and object collisions within the game itself and can include special effects or the movement and transformation of in-game objects. Logical computing is implemented by CPUs and simplifies image drawing.

Image rendering is drawing specific content in an image. Specifically, the rendering module extracts the objects from the material library to the corresponding positions in the screen according to logical computing instructions. The material library contains objects like various backgrounds and object models present in the application. Unity 3D is a prime example of

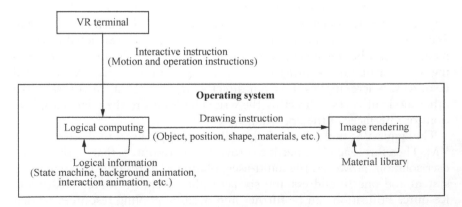

Figure 3.24 Logical computing and rendering.

this as it provides core functions, such as the terrain system, physical engine, model import and animation production system, as well as the special effects of games. The processing of these functions brings and generates a large number of objects; for example, the terrain system provides various background objects, such as terrains, environments, and buildings. The shape, materials, and texture of these objects will be packaged into the application. Image rendering requires the cooperation of the CPU and GPU, which is the most complex process in application running.

The foundation of rendering technology is the graphics pipeline or rendering pipeline, which is a process of converting data from a three-dimensional (3D) scenario into a two-dimensional (2D) image and then finally displaying a 2D image on a screen. This process can be divided into the application, geometry, and rasterization stages.[15]

1. Application stage

   The application stage is controlled by the CPU. At this stage, the data (including vertices and textures) of an original 3D scenario is loaded from a hard disk to a memory disk and then to a display memory, so that the GPU can quickly access the data. In computer graphics, triangles are used to form the shape of a 3D model, and any triangle or combination of triangles are called primitives. A primitive is composed of vertices, as shown in Figure 3.25. Texture is a structured image pasted to a 3D model primitive, as shown in Figure 3.26, to describe the object (such as a brick wall or wood) represented by the model.

2. Geometry stage

   The geometry stage is controlled by the GPU. At this stage, the 3D spatial coordinates of the vertices are converted into the spatial coordinates

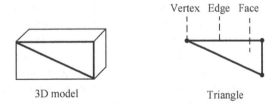

Figure 3.25 Relationship between the 3D model, triangle, and vertex.

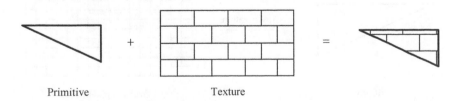

Figure 3.26 Texture and its relationship with primitives.

displayed on screens. The conversion process mainly includes the following aspects:

First, the original vertex space is converted into the view space. The original vertices are represented by an object coordinate system (the coordinates chosen for object drawing). There is a plurality of objects in a scenario which have their respective object coordinate systems. Therefore, different object coordinate systems need to be moved to a world coordinate system (which represents the location and object coordinate system of objects). The pictures users can see depends on their position and the direction they are looking in the world coordinate system, which needs to be converted to the view space of a virtual camera (this describes the position at which the user watches the pictures). This process also involves illumination calculation of vertices. The object color is transmitted to the user's eyes through light reflection, and so it can be seen. The illumination attribute of the vertices can be determined by means of illumination calculation.

Second is primitive assembly and clipping. The processed vertices are assembled into complete primitives. However, not all primitives are within the user's (camera's) field of vision, and therefore the primitives outside this view need to be clipped and culled.

Third, screen space conversion. The clipped 3D primitives need to be cast onto the 2D coordinates of the screen display space, and the texture coordinates also need to be converted.

3. Rasterization stage

Rasterization is mainly completed by the GPU. At this stage, primitives are converted into pixels that are then displayed on the screen (which may be considered as a grid lattice), so as to complete image drawing, as shown in Figure 3.27. The primitives are first converted into fragments, which contain attributes such as positions, colors, depths, and texture coordinates. However, not all of these fragments are converted into pixels for display. Visible surface determination is performed so that invisible surfaces are not rendered. For example, for two objects placed back to back, the part that is blocked by the front object is an invisible surface that does not need to be displayed. The primitives of such a surface are finally generated into pixels and stored

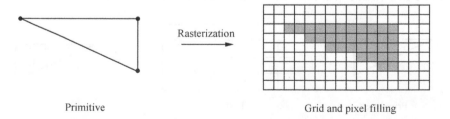

Primitive   Grid and pixel filling

Figure 3.27 Rasterization processing.

in a pixel buffer, and pixels here are drawn in the back buffer. Once drawing is complete, the pixels in the back buffer are exchanged with those in the front buffer and are then displayed on the screen.

In certain situations, logical computing and image rendering are completed by an application development engine. The development engine utilizes the graphics card driver through a bottom-layer graphics application interface such as DirectX or OpenGL and completes rendering in the graphics card, as shown in Figure 3.28.

3.2.3.2 Rendering optimization

Strong-interaction cloud VR services have high requirements on real-time interaction. As part of the cloud processing latency, the rendering latency should be controlled within a certain range. In addition, VR services need to render binocular images, which consumes greater resources and is more costly compared to traditional PC image rendering. Therefore, how to optimize resource consumption for rendering is also a key issue for VR rendering.

Currently, the following technologies draw most attention:

1. Binocular image merging and rendering
   Current cloud rendering nodes perform rendering sequentially by using binocular images. To be specific, the rendering node renders the images for each eye one by one, as shown in Figure 3.29. As the content of both eyes is very similar, the images from each eye can be merged, rendered, and drawn together. Through this method, both eyes will then select content from the rendered images at different angles to produce monocular images, as shown in Figure 3.30. By utilizing combined rendering to generate binocular images, content from both the left

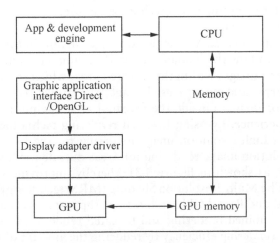

Figure 3.28 Software and hardware mapping involved in rendering.

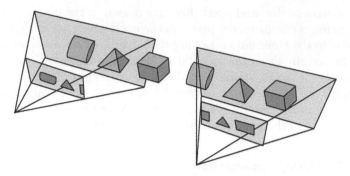

Figure 3.29 Binocular image sequential rendering.

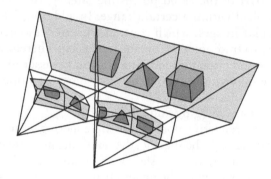

Figure 3.30 Binocular image combined rendering.

and right eyes can be recycled to avoid repeated rendering of similar content, while also reducing rendering latency. The Single Pass Stereo (SPS) rendering of NVIDIA's Pascal GPU architecture is an example of this rendering optimization technology in use.

2. Foveated rendering

At present, all cloud VR rendered images maintain the same quality, contrary to how the human eyes work. Human eyes are in fact more sensitive to images within the foveated area, which in turn would create a sharper and more focused image, impacting user experience. The quality of images outside the foveated area has minimal impact on user experience. By using foveated rendering technology, the system performs high-resolution image rendering for the foveated area and low-resolution image rendering for areas outside the foveated area of the user, as shown in Figure 3.31, thereby improving rendering efficiency. The Multi-Resolution Shading (MRS) technology of NVIDIA's Maxwell and Pascal GPU architecture supports foveated rendering.

The combined rendering and foveated rendering technologies can improve rendering efficiency by reducing the amount of rendered data required. However, implementing these technologies is dependent on

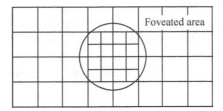

Figure 3.31 Foveated rendering.

GPUs, as these technologies are not supported on mainstream server graphics cards (such as NVIDIA M60).

In addition to the optimization of rendering technologies, platform resource configurations and content also affect rendering latency and resource consumption. On one hand, cloud rendering nodes need to provide sufficient resources, especially for high-performance graphics cards, based on factors such as resource requirements, user scale, and concurrency rate, to ensure the smooth running of applications and avoid higher rendering latency caused by sluggish applications and response delays. On the other hand, rendering complexity and latency are determined by applications when resources are sufficient and the running environment is determined. During application development, unnecessary rendering objects can be removed and rendering times reduced to improve resource utilization. When recruiting applications to the service platform, applications with in-depth rendering optimization can be prioritized if possible.

3.2.4 Fast coding/decoding technologies

After images are rendered, the strong-interaction cloud VR service platform codes the image sequences into video streams and transmits these streams to terminals. Strong- and weak-interaction cloud VR services use the same coding/decoding standards (such as H.264 and H.265). A key difference between these interactions is that strong-interaction VR services code images in real time, placing high requirements on latency (particularly on cloud rendering and streaming latency, as explained in chapter 2). Coding/decoding latency accounts for a significant part of cloud rendering and streaming latency, and therefore the question of how to reduce coding/decoding latency is critical to achieving optimal strong-interaction cloud VR services.

Coding/decoding latency can be minimized using the following methods:

3.2.4.1 Select proper coding parameters

Section 3.1.2 explained how the different coding/decoding standards, in addition to the different parameters and implementations under the same standard, will lead to different coding efficiency. After coding standards are selected, vendors may flexibly select and combine coding parameters (such as technologies and algorithms) based on actual conditions (including hardware resources, network bandwidth, and capabilities of other links) when designing and implementing service platforms. The following are examples.

Example 1: Avoid B-frames

An I-frame is coded independently of all other frames, and a P-frame is coded by referencing the previous frame, whereas a B-frame is coded by referencing both its previous and following frames, as shown in Figure 3.32. Consequently, a B-frame can be coded only after the subsequent frame is generated, which increases the latency.

Example 2: Select a proper motion estimation algorithm

As mentioned in Section 3.1.2, motion estimation is the most complex phase in video coding and is the most demanding for computers, causing heavy latency. Block matching[16] is a widely used motion estimation algorithm, and its performance is driven by search algorithms and matching criteria. Search algorithms mainly relate to the search policy and scope and include the full search (FS) and diamond search (DS) algorithms. The FS algorithm is global, but the DS algorithm focuses on optimal local resolution. The matching criteria includes the mean square error (MSE) and sum of absolute difference (SAD).

Coding quality and latency vary according to the selected search algorithm and matching criteria. Let's assume that the FS and DS algorithms work with the MSE or SAD criteria. Research[17] shows that for the same video test sequence, under the same conditions (such as image block division, transformation, and quantization), and using the same search algorithm (FS or DS), MSE coding delivers higher image quality but requires longer calculation time; when the same matching criterion (MSE or SAD) is used, DS coding has a lower latency than FS coding. This shows that coding quality and latency are a common trade-off when selecting algorithms.

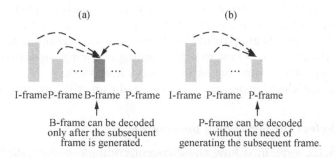

Figure 3.32 (a) Coding involving B-frames vs (b) coding involving no B-frames.

3.2.4.2 Optimize coding/decoding technologies

Academic circles have carried out extensive research on technology and algorithm optimization, for example, improving intra- and inter-frame prediction. Vendors are also improving coding technologies and algorithms based on their own software and hardware implementation.

Another form of optimization focuses on the synergy in the overall implementation of service platforms, such as the synergy between rendering and streaming. In strong-interaction cloud VR services, a complete image frame is rendered, coded, transmitted, and decoded in serial mode. That is, the processing of a phase starts only after the previous phase has finished processing. By using slice coding, which is supported in H.264 and H.265, a rendered image can be divided into multiple slices. Here, each slice is independently coded, encapsulated, transmitted, received, and decoded in parallel mode, thereby reducing E2E processing time, as shown in Figure 3.33. Currently, sliced images cannot be rendered and output; however, if this is possible in the future, the E2E processing efficiency will improve further.

3.2.4.3 Select soft coding and hard coding properly

Soft coding is implemented by using software encoders such as H.264 and H.265 in CPUs. Soft coding can be independently developed or controlled by service platform vendors. Its implementation is flexible, and parameter adjustment is simple. It can easily meet customization requirements and be embedded with self-developed optimization algorithms of vendors. Despite this, soft coding can lead to a high CPU load and slow coding speed.

Hard coding is performed by non-CPU hardware, such as GPUs, digital signal processors (DSPs), field-programmable gate arrays (FPGAs), and application-specific integrated circuits (ASICs). Mainstream GPU computing frameworks that support hard coding include the Compute Unified Device Architecture (CUDA) of NVIDIA and the Accelerated Parallel Processing (APP) architecture of AMD. Hard coding uses the encoders embedded into the bottom-layer hardware, and is faster than soft coding. Service platform vendors need to invoke the application program interfaces (APIs) provided by hardware chip vendors. Hard coding is not as flexible as soft coding in

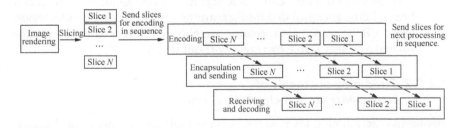

Figure 3.33 Pipeline-based coding optimization.

parameter adjustment, and algorithms need to be optimized based on available APIs. However, since cloud VR rendering requires high bitrate and low latency, hard coding is the popular choice.

3.2.5 Streaming technology

To ensure the real-time interaction of strong-interaction cloud VR services, the output of video streams requires the real-time input of instruction streams. Therefore, it is crucial to select the right protocols for the transmission of instruction and video streams.

3.2.5.1 Service stream type

Strong-interaction cloud VR services consist of two types of service streams: instruction streams and video streams.

1. Instruction streams are transmitted from terminals to clouds and mainly include motion information and operation instructions.

    Motion information mainly refers to the position and location information of VR headsets and gamepads. The motion capture system of a terminal periodically collects motion information because the users' head and hands are constantly moving. Terminals usually collect motion information frequently to ensure that it is accurate and up-to-date, even with constant movement. The motion information instructs the service platform how to perform rendering and coding, and the frame rate of the rendered and encoded video is lower than the frequency of motion information collection. Therefore, the original high-frequency motion information collected by the motion capture system needs to be further sampled and then transmitted to the service platform. In addition, this motion information can be sampled on terminals and then transmitted to the cloud. Alternatively, the terminals can transmit the original motion information, and the cloud can then perform sampling.

    Instructions mainly include button clicking and trigger pulling, which are usually random. Generally, VR terminals only start returning instructions when triggered by users.
2. Video streams are transmitted from the cloud to terminals.

    In weak-interaction cloud VR services, video sequences are sliced before being encapsulated into streaming media. In strong-interaction cloud VR services, video streams are encoded in real time and encapsulated and sent frame by frame without slicing.

3.2.5.2 Streaming protocols of
strong-interaction cloud VR services

Strong-interaction cloud VR services have high requirements on latency. Any excessive packet encapsulation and decapsulation will result in higher latency. Therefore, vendors mainly use TCP or UDP to send application data directly, depending on the features of different service streams.

1. Instruction stream
   UDP is preferred for transmitting frequently collected motion information because it is fast. Although UDP is less reliable than TCP and may result in packet loss, the frequent collection means that subsequent motion information can be received quickly to replace lost information. Furthermore, because motion information is coherent and regular, the cloud can predict the content of lost motion information by calculating the trajectory of what has already been collected.

   TCP is preferred for transmitting manual inputs of users, because such inputs are not frequently collected or linked to each other. If the input is lost, the cloud cannot respond, affecting user interaction experience. Therefore, a protocol that ensures reliable transmission is required.

2. Video stream
   Most vendors encapsulate and transmit video streams using TCP or UDP, or encapsulate them using RTP or a proprietary protocol and transmit them using TCP or UDP.

   • TCP-based transmission
     TCP has the advantage of highly reliable data transmission. It uses mechanisms such as sequence numbers, connection management, acknowledgments, retransmission on timeout, window control, traffic control, and congestion control to ensure that data is transmitted without errors, loss, or repetition and that it arrives in the correct sequence.

     When packets in a window are lost, the TCP protocol stack does not deliver the received packets to the application layer until the lost packets are successfully retransmitted. When packets arrive out of order, the TCP protocol stack reassembles them before delivering them to the application layer. The retransmission and reassembly processes increase end-to-end latency and may cause buffering.

   • UDP-based transmission
     The advantage of UDP is its high transmission speed, because it does not need to establish connections before data transmission and has no retransmission mechanism.

     Since UDP transmission is not as reliable as TCP, it provides high transmission performance on a stable and reliable network. When packet loss occurs, it relies on the retransmission mechanism of the upper-layer encapsulation protocol, which may create pixelation and affect user experience.

   • Direction of optimization for streaming protocols
     Vendors are currently proposing a Quick UDP Internet Connection (QUIC) protocol, and its standardization in the Internet Engineering Task Force (IETF), which has received much attention in the industry.

The QUIC protocol is implemented based on UDP and therefore has the same high speed. In addition, the QUIC protocol ensures the same reliability as TCP on the application layer.

– Fast

Low-latency connection: TCP is a connection-oriented protocol and requires a three-way handshake before a connection is created. UDP, however, is a connectionless protocol and does not need to allocate time for a handshake or connection establishment. Therefore, QUIC has lower latency than TCP.

Fast session reconnection: TCP uses 4-tuple parameters as session IDs, including the source IP address, source port number, destination IP address, and destination port number. When network switching occurs, sessions need to be re-established, whereas QUIC uses a unique session tag that does not change with network switching. As a result, a session can be quickly initiated without re-establishment.

Concurrent download based on session ID: As the session IDs of QUIC are unrelated to IP addresses, a plurality of network interfaces on devices can be used to simultaneously download data. Although different interfaces have different IP addresses, they use the same session ID. Consequently, data can be concurrently downloaded through these interfaces from the server, which speeds up data transmission.

Multiplexing: QUIC can concurrently send multiple data streams on a single connection, improving the transmission rate. In addition, QUIC is based on UDP that does not maintain packet order. Packet loss of one data stream does not affect the processing of other data streams.

– Reliable

Congestion control: QUIC has a congestion control mechanism at the application layer. It uses the same congestion control algorithm as TCP, but QUIC further improves the algorithm. For example, QUIC is more flexible in adjustment operations, such as algorithm start, handover, and stopping, so different congestion control algorithms are used to suit factors like services and latency. For strong-interaction cloud VR services, QUIC can adaptively select different congestion control algorithms based on the network latency to improve congestion control.

Packet loss correction mechanism: QUIC has a forward error correction (FEC) mechanism. It adds redundant data to each data packet and obtains other data packets by combining the original and redundant data. Small numbers of lost packets can be restored through other packets without the need for packet retransmission, ensuring data integrity and avoiding the latency that would accumulate through retransmission.

Chapter 4

Cloud VR Network Solution

This chapter focuses on improving virtual reality (VR) user experience. Based on the latest technical development trend and commercial cloud VR deployment experience, this chapter further analyzes the transport network requirements in different phases of cloud VR. In addition, it describes the cloud VR network transport solution and network evolution direction.

4.1 NETWORK METRIC REQUIREMENTS OF CLOUD VR SERVICES

The core objective of cloud VR network planning and deployment is to ensure a positive experience. Throughput and transmission latency are key network metrics. Figure 4.1 shows the relationship between key factors of cloud VR experience and network metrics. In most cases, cloud VR services require ultra-high bandwidth, ultra-low latency, and ultra-low packet loss rates on networks. The implementation principles, deployment positions, and transmission paths of weak- and strong-interaction cloud VR services are different, resulting in different network requirements. Consequently, the network metric requirements for the two types of services are separately defined.

4.1.1 Network metric requirements for weak-interaction cloud VR services

4K VR videos predominantly use full-view transmission, share content delivery network (CDN) resources with traditional 4K IPTV (Internet Protocol television), and use the same streaming protocol as 4K IPTV. As the resolution and bitrate of VR videos are increasing, field of view (FoV) transmission is gradually used to save network bandwidth.

1. Bandwidth metrics
   Video streams are not completely stable, and traffic bursts may occur. As evidenced in 4K IPTV testing, when the network bandwidth is higher than or equal to 1.5 times that of the average bitrate, smooth

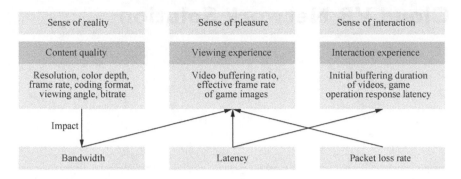

Figure 4.1 Relationship between key factors of cloud VR experience and network metrics.

Table 4.1 Network bandwidth requirements of weak-interaction cloud VR services

Metric	Comfortable-experience phase	Ideal-experience phase	Ultimate-experience phase
Typical panoramic resolution	8K	12K	24K or higher
Color depth	8 bits	10 bits	≥ 12 bits
Frame rate	30 FPS	60 FPS	≥ 60 FPS
Coding format	H.264/H.265	H.265/H.266	H.266
Bitrate (FoV transmission)	≥ 80 Mbit/s	≥ 280 Mbit/s	≥ 760 Mbit/s
Bandwidth (FoV transmission)	≥ 120 Mbit/s	≥ 420 Mbit/s	≥ 1140 Mbit/s

Note: Based on industry experience, the major factors involved are coding format, frame rate, and resolution. As the coding format develops from H.264 to H.265, and from H.265 to H.266, the compression ratio is expected to increase by 30%, respectively. This number is approximately 50% if the frame rate is doubled and approximately 15% if the resolution is doubled.

video playback can be ensured. Put simply, required network bandwidth = 1.5 × average bitrate.

Based on the bitrate calculation formula for weak-interaction cloud VR services described in Chapter 2, we can calculate required bandwidth values, as listed in Table 4.1.

2. Latency metrics

For weak-interaction cloud VR services, if the image loading time during playback or channel switching needs to be controlled to within 1s, the network latency must be controlled to within 20 ms. If there is no requirement on the image loading time, the network latency can be relaxed to a range between 30 and 40 ms, which is still acceptable. Table 4.2 lists the network round-trip time (RTT) requirements.

3. Packet loss metrics

After bandwidth and latency requirements are determined, packet loss requirements can be deduced according to the following Transmission Control Protocol (TCP) throughput formula.

Table 4.2 Network latency requirements of weak-interaction cloud VR services

Metric	Comfortable-experience phase	Ideal-experience phase	Ultimate-experience phase
Typical panoramic resolution	8K	12K	24K or higher
Network RTT	≤ 20 ms	≤ 20 ms	≤ 10 ms

Table 4.3 Packet loss rate requirements of weak-interaction cloud VR services

Metric	Comfortable-experience phase	Ideal-experience phase	Ultimate-experience phase
Typical panoramic resolution	8K	12K	24K or higher
Packet loss rate	$< 1 \times 10^{-5}$	$< 1 \times 10^{-6}$	$< 1 \times 10^{-6}$

$$\text{TCP throughput} \leq \min\left(\text{bandwidth}, \frac{\text{WindowSize}}{\text{RTT}}, \frac{\text{MSS}}{\text{RTT}} \times \frac{1}{\sqrt{\rho}}\right)$$

Note:
WindowSize: TCP window size
MSS: Maximum segment size
ρ: Packet loss rate on the network
   Table 4.3 lists the packet loss requirements of weak-interaction cloud VR services.

4.1.2 Network metric requirements of strong-interaction cloud VR services

In strong-interaction cloud VR service scenarios, the transmission network is responsible for connecting service platforms and cloud VR terminals. The network needs to transmit motion information and operation instructions upward and push streaming video data downward. This process encounters multiple challenges specifically related to bandwidth, latency, and packet loss.

   1. Bandwidth metrics
      When a user's operation or posture changes, new frames need to be pushed to them quickly, and this may cause traffic bursts. Therefore, an adequate margin of bandwidth is needed to accommodate such bursts. Considering the margin, network bandwidth needs to be approximately twice the average bitrate according to test data.
         Table 4.4 lists the details. The table was collated based on the bitrate calculation formula in Chapter 2.

Table 4.4 Network bandwidth requirements of strong-interaction cloud VR services

Metric	Comfortable-experience phase	Ideal-experience phase	Ultimate-experience phase
Typical content resolution (binocular)	4K	8K	16K or higher
Color depth	8 bits	10 bits	≥ 12 bits
Coding format	H.264/H.265	H.265/H.266	H.266
Frame rate	60 FPS	90 FPS	≥ 90 FPS
Bitrate	≥ 65 Mbit/s	≥ 270 Mbit/s	≥ 770 Mbit/s
Bandwidth	≥ 130 Mbit/s	≥ 540 Mbit/s	≥ 1.5 Gbit/s

2. Latency metrics

The network transmission latency can be divided into deterministic latency and undeterministic latency. The deterministic latency refers to optical fiber transmission latency and is, in most cases, determined by the deployment location of cloud servers. Undeterministic latency is predominantly caused by network congestion and air interface interference. If the transmission latency is too long, the black edge will increase, or the operation response will be obviously delayed, affecting user experience.

In the comfortable-experience phase of cloud VR, when the network RTT is controlled within 20 ms, there is a high probability that the black edges of mainstream strong-interaction VR applications (predominantly games) are within an acceptable range and no operation response delay will occur, as shown in Figure 4.2.

In addition, latency optimization involves not only adjustment of network architecture and cloud server deployment location, but also the selection of Wi-Fi devices. This differs from bandwidth issues that can be resolved by network expansion. These elements need to be properly designed and planned at the outset, as they are difficult to amend once deployed. Consequently, it is recommended that telecom operators construct and adjust networks one or two years in advance. This would be based on the network latency requirements of cloud VR services in the comfortable-experience phase, as shown in Figure 4.3 and Table 4.5.

3. Packet loss metrics

Packet loss may cause pixelation and buffering. According to test results, when the network RTT is within 15–20 ms, the packet loss rate must be less than 1×10^{-6} to ensure a comfortable experience, as shown in Table 4.6.

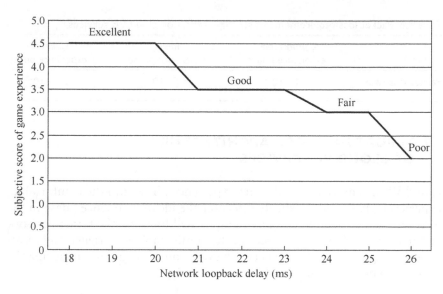

Figure 4.2 Subjective experience of VR games in different latency scenarios. Note: The scores in the figure are provided by test personnel based on subjective experience of the VR game *BlackShield: Upora Story.* The maximum score is 5.

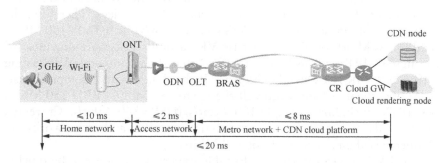

Figure 4.3 Network latency requirements in the comfortable-experience phase of cloud VR.

Table 4.5 Network latency requirements of strong-interaction cloud VR services

Metric	Comfortable-experience phase	Ideal-experience phase	Ultimate-experience phase
Network RTT (required value)	≤ 20 ms	≤ 10 ms	≤ 8 ms
Home Wi-Fi network	≤ 10 ms	≤ 7 ms	≤ 5 ms
Fixed access network	≤ 2 ms	≤ 2 ms	≤ 2 ms
Metro transport network	≤ 8 ms	≤ 1 ms	≤ 1 ms

Table 4.6 Packet loss requirements of strong-interaction cloud VR services

Metric	Comfortable-experience phase	Ideal-experience phase	Ultimate-experience phase
Packet loss rate	$< 1 \times 10^{-6}$	$< 1 \times 10^{-7}$	$< 1 \times 10^{-7}$

4.2 TARGET NETWORK ARCHITECTURE OF CLOUD VR SERVICES

Cloud VR has moved from the fair-experience phase into the comfortable-experience phase and is expected to enter the ideal-experience phase in the next few years. The following paragraphs will focus on the target network architecture of cloud VR services in the comfortable-experience and ideal-experience phases and future network evolution strategies for achieving the ultimate experience. For details, see Section 4.5.

4.2.1 Comfortable-experience phase

In the comfortable-experience phase, the single-channel bandwidth of cloud VR services must be 130 Mbit/s. Additionally, bandwidth must also be provided for 4K IPTV and high-speed Internet (HSI) services. Therefore, the user bandwidth must be 130 Mbit/s (VR)+50 Mbit/s (4K IPTV)+100 Mbit/s (HSI)=280 Mbit/s or higher. Because VR casting services are downloaded through 4K IPTV channels, it is required that clouds compress VR casting traffic to the 4K IPTV bandwidth level. If the clouds cannot compress casting traffic, the user bandwidth will change to 130 Mbit/s (VR)+130 Mbit/s (4K IPTV, including casting)+100 Mbit/s (HSI)=360 Mbit/s. Currently, most clouds do not compress casting service traffic, and so networks are planned based on a bandwidth of 360 Mbit/s.

Cloud VR services in the comfortable-experience phase can be quickly deployed by reusing the existing 4K IPTV transport network and optimizing some parts to reduce cost.

In conclusion, the target network architecture of cloud VR services in the comfortable-experience phase is "Home Wi-Fi network+4K IPTV transport network+reusing CDN/building cloud rendering nodes", as shown in Figure 4.4.

1. Home Wi-Fi network
   To meet the high-speed and low-latency access requirements of cloud VR services, home Wi-Fi networks often use high-performance dedicated Wi-Fi access points (APs), gigabit optical network terminals (ONTs), gigabit network cables, and corresponding intelligent networking services.

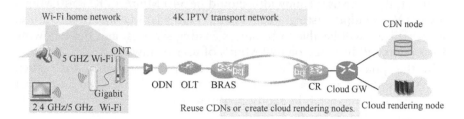

Figure 4.4 Target network architecture of cloud VR services in the comfortable-experience phase. Note: CR: core router; ODN: optical distribution network; OLT: optical line terminal; BRAS: broadband remote access server.

2. 4K IPTV transport network

To quickly deploy cloud VR services at a low cost, the existing 4K IPTV transport networks can be reused, with optimization in the following aspects for higher bandwidth and lower latency:

- Upgrade from Gigabit Passive Optical Network (GPON)/Ethernet Passive Optical Network (EPON) to 10G PON/EPON
- Expansion and upgrade of uplink optical line terminal (OLT) ports
- Expansion and upgrade of metro networks

3. Reusing CDNs and adding cloud rendering nodes

In the comfortable-experience phase, existing CDN resources can be reused to distribute cloud VR video content. Additionally, cloud rendering nodes can be added for strong-interaction cloud VR services. In most cases, CDNs or cloud rendering nodes need to be deployed on metro networks.

This architecture design has the following advantages:

- Maximizing the reuse of existing network resources, such as IP, optical, and fiber to the home (FTTH) access networks, which can be expanded when necessary
- Minimizing deployment difficulty: Cloud VR services can be carried over Internet access channels, avoiding the need to deploy another set of virtual local area networks (VLANs), IP addresses, and authentication accounts.

4.2.2 Ideal-experience phase

In the ideal-experience phase, the single-channel bandwidth of cloud VR services is 540 Mbit/s. After 4K IPTV and Internet access services are provisioned, the user bandwidth is 540 Mbit/s (VR)+50 Mbit/s (4K IPTV)+100 Mbit/s (HSI)=690 Mbit/s. VR casting services are downloaded through 4K IPTV channels. For this reason, it is required that clouds compress VR casting traffic to the 4K IPTV bandwidth level. If the clouds cannot compress casting traffic, the user bandwidth should be 540 Mbit/s (VR) + 540 Mbit/s (4K IPTV, including casting) + 100 Mbit/s (HSI) = 1.18 Gbit/s. In the future, most headsets will be able to compress casting services, and the following description will be based on 690 Mbit/s of user bandwidth.

In this phase, the bandwidth and latency requirements are higher. The Wi-Fi access and transport network technologies need to be further upgraded and enhanced. In addition, a new network architecture needs to be constructed to ensure both bandwidth and latency.

Based on this situation, the core concept of the cloud VR solution in the ideal-experience phase is "upgraded and enhanced home network" + "simplified IP architecture/all-optical transport network" + "network with guaranteed latency and bandwidth", as shown in Figure 4.5.

1. Upgraded and enhanced home network
   In this phase, home networks still use independent access points (APs). However, the Wi-Fi capability needs to be upgraded to achieve a rate greater than 540 Mbit/s and a latency less than 7 ms.
2. Simplified IP architecture/all-optical transport network
   To improve the transmission efficiency of transport networks, the layers and architecture of the traditional IP networks need to be simplified. To be specific, broadband remote access servers (BRASs) need to be directly connected to core routers (CRs), and OLTs need to be directly connected to BRASs. In the future, IPv4 will be gradually extended to IPv4/IPv6 dual-stack and then completely replaced by IPv6 to reduce network address translation (NAT) and further simplify the network architecture.

   All-optical networks provide ultra-large bandwidth and guaranteed deterministic low latency, meeting the ultimate experience requirements of cloud VR services. OLTs can be connected to optical transport networks (OTNs) or BRASs and are the nodes for determining whether service streams go to optical networks or IP networks. To meet different service level requirements of a plurality of services,

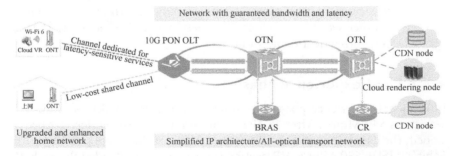

Figure 4.5 Target network architecture of cloud VR services in the ideal-experience phase.

OLTs need to support network slicing to transmit slices of different service levels on the same physical port.

3. Networks with guaranteed latency and bandwidth
Networks need to be restructured to achieve guaranteed bandwidth and latency.

4.2.3 It is recommended that CDN nodes and cloud rendering nodes be deployed on metro networks

According to the network metric requirements in the comfortable-experience phase of cloud VR, the latency from the metro network to the CDN node (streaming server for weak-interaction VR services)/rendering node (streaming server for strong-interaction VR services) must be less than or equal to 8 ms. For this to happen, the overall forwarding latency on the IP/OTN network must be less than or equal to 1 ms, the forwarding latency of the content network must be less than or equal to 1 ms, and the remaining 6 ms of latency budget is reserved for the transmission on optical fiber as well as queuing and buffering. Considering the impact of possible network congestion, it is recommended that the optical fiber distance be less than or equal to 200 km (unidirectional). This means that CDN nodes and cloud rendering nodes must be deployed in the metro network, as shown in Figure 4.6.

Since CDN nodes and cloud rendering nodes must be deployed on metro networks, the network architecture analysis will be focused on metro, access, and home networks in home broadband access scenarios, and focused on 5G network in mobile access scenarios.

4.2.4 Metro network

1. Comfortable-experience phase
In the comfortable-experience phase of cloud VR, telecom operators' 4K IPTV metro networks can be reused to implement fast provisioning and deployment, as shown in Figure 4.7.

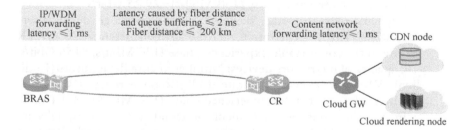

Figure 4.6 Metro network latency requirements for cloud VR in the comfortable-experience phase.

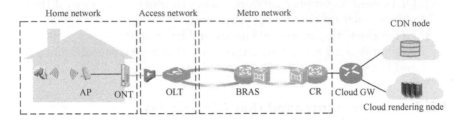

Figure 4.7 Network architecture of cloud VR services in the comfortable-experience phase: reusing the 4K IPTV metro network architecture.

Similar to the 4K IPTV metro network, the cloud VR metro network uses the following technologies:

- Flattened network to reduce unnecessary convergence: OLTs are directly connected to BRASs, reducing the number of IP network layers between BRASs to CRs or the number of hops between BRASs to CRs.
- Downward BRAS deployment: BRASs are deployed downward to simplify the deployment of virtual private LAN segments (VPLSs) and support flexible deployment of CDN/cloud rendering nodes. Latency is reduced as a result.

The network link usage is monitored in real time so that capacity expansion can be performed immediately when the load threshold required by cloud VR is exceeded. As a result, congestion and packet loss caused by traffic bursts are prevented.

In the comfortable-experience phase, the cloud VR deployment is small in scale because the number of users is limited. Assume that the user penetration rate is approximately 30% and the concurrency is expected to be lower than that of IPTV services. Assume that the concurrency on OLTs is 50%, on metro edges is 20%, and on metro cores is 10%. The capacity requirements of cloud VR on metro networks can be calculated as follows:

Capacity of OLT uplink ports: Number of OLT users (1,500)×VR user penetration rate (30%)×concurrency (50%)×VR bitrate in the comfortable-experience phase (130 Mbit/s)=29.25 Gbit/s

Capacity of metro edge devices: Number of edge device users (20,000)×VR user penetration rate (30%)×concurrency (20%)×VR bitrate in the comfortable-experience phase (130 Mbit/s)=156 Gbit/s

Capacity of metro core devices: Number of core device users (1 million)×VR user penetration rate (30%)×concurrency (10%)×VR bitrate in the comfortable-experience phase (130 Mbit/s)=3.9 Tbit/s

In addition, during deployment of cloud VR services, telecom operators should check whether the existing metro networks have the following problems:

- OLTs use the switch aggregation networking, which is complex and has a high convergence ratio.

- BRASs and OLTs are connected through GE links, which cannot address the increasing traffic.
- CRs and BRASs are connected through 10GE links, which cannot address the increasing traffic.

In most cases, metro networks may need to expand and upgrade to support cloud VR in the comfortable-experience phase. For that reason, capacity expansion needs to be properly planned to prevent congestion from affecting user experience.

OLT uplink ports must be upgraded to 4×10GE or 2×100GE.

Uplinks of metro edge devices must be upgraded to at least 2×100GE to connect to metro core devices.

Metro core devices must be upgraded to cluster platforms with a capacity of Tbit/s per slot.

2. Ideal-experience phase

In the ideal-experience phase, after cloud VR services are deployed on a large scale, the user penetration rate is at least 50%, and the concurrency reaches at least that of IPTV services. Assume that the concurrency on OLTs is 50%, on metro edges is 30%, and on metro cores is 20%. The capacity requirements of cloud VR on metro networks can be calculated as follows:

Capacity of OLT uplink ports: Number of OLT users $(1,500) \times$ VR user penetration rate $(50\%) \times$ Concurrency $(50\%) \times$ VR bitrate in the ideal-experience phase (540 Mbit/s)=202.5 Gbit/s

Capacity of metro edge devices: Number of edge device users $(20,000) \times$ VR user penetration rate $(50\%) \times$ Concurrency $(30\%) \times$ VR bitrate in the ideal-experience phase (540 Mbit/s)=1.62 Tbit/s

Capacity of metro core devices: Number of core device users (1 million) $\times$ VR user penetration rate $(50\%) \times$ Concurrency $(20\%) \times$ VR bitrate in the ideal-experience phase (540 Mbit/s) = 54 Tbit/s

Consequently, large-scale deployment of cloud VR in the ideal-experience phase requires high-capacity metro networks. As a result, boards/devices with higher rates and integration are required.

- The uplink ports of OLTs must be upgraded to at least 2×100GE.
- Uplinks of metro edge devices must be upgraded to Tbit/s capacity per slot to connect to metro core devices.
- Metro core devices must be upgraded to cluster platforms with a Tbit/s capacity per slot.

In addition to bandwidth, the latency on metro networks must be reduced to 6 ms (including the latency on CDNs). It is recommended that the overall forwarding latency on metro devices be less than 1 ms and the forwarding latency on CDNs be less than 1 ms. The remaining 4 ms of latency budget are reserved for transmission on optical fiber as well as queuing and caching.

4.2.5 Access network

4.2.5.1 Comfortable-experience phase

In the comfortable-experience phase, the access network latency must be less than or equal to 2 ms. Accordingly, copper cables and electrical cables must be replaced by the FTTH solution.

Currently, the mainstream FTTH modes are GPON and EPON. Since latency is not an issue, the focus is on bandwidth, as shown in Table 4.7.

The bandwidth required for cloud VR, 4K IPTV, and Internet access combined is 280 Mbit/s or higher. Compared with the available bandwidth listed in Table 4.7, it is clear that cloud VR services in the comfortable-experience phase can be provisioned only for a small number of EPON and GPON users.

Therefore, existing networks need to gradually upgrade to 10G PON as cloud VR users increase. To avoid bandwidth overload, the number of supported VR on GPONs should be evaluated using the following formula:

Number of supported users =

GPON port bandwidth × Capacity expansion thershold −

$$\frac{\text{Average rate of broadband users} \times \text{Split ratio} \times \text{Installation rate}}{\text{Average rate of VR users}}$$

The average rate of broadband users is evaluated based on the development of IPTV and HSI services as well as concurrency, as shown in Table 4.8.

Table 4.7 Bandwidth satisfaction achieved using different PONs in the comfortable-experience phase

PON	Capacity (Gbit/s^{-1})	Split ratio	Convergence ratio (%)	Available bandwidth (Mbit/s^{-1})	Satisfaction
EPON	1	1:64	50	31.25	Not satisfied (The number of users is limited.)
		1:32	50	62.50	Not satisfied (The number of users is limited.)
GPON	2.5	1:64	50	78.13	Not satisfied (The number of users is limited.)
		1:32	50	156.25	Not satisfied (The number of users is limited.)
10G EPON/	10	1:64	50	312.50	Satisfied
GPON		1:32	50	625.00	Satisfied

Note: Available bandwidth=Capacity/split ratio/convergence ratio.

Table 4.8 Prediction and evaluation of the average rate of broadband users

Category	Metric	2019	2020	2021
User prediction	Video user penetration rate	100%	100%	100%
VoD	Percentage of SD VoD services	20%	0	0
	Percentage of HD VoD services	30%	40%	30%
	Percentage of OTT 4K VoD services	50%	60%	70%
	Average bitrate of VoD users	13.0	15.2	16.7
	VoD concurrency	100%	100%	100%
	Average VoD rate	13.0	15.2	16.7
Internet access	Online rate of Internet access users	100%	100%	100%
service	Average rate of online Internet access users	7.0	11.0	16.8
Total bandwidth	Average rate of broadband users	20.0	26.2	33.5

Unit of bitrate and speed: Mbit/s.

Table 4.9 Prediction and evaluation of the average rate of VR users

Metric	2019	2020	2021
4K VR percentage of video services	45%	40%	35%
8K VR percentage of video services	5%	10%	15%
4K VR percentage of gaming services	45%	40%	35%
8K VR percentage of gaming services	5%	10%	15%
Average bitrate of VR users	45.0	50.0	55.0
VR user concurrency	80%	80%	80%
Average rate of VR users	36.0	40.0	44.0

Unit of bitrate and speed: Mbit/s.

The average rate of VR users is related to VR content bitrate, content proportion, and concurrency. Table 4.9 lists details about prediction and evaluation results.

The number of supported VR users on GPON ports from 2019 to 2021 is calculated based on telecom operators' network construction specifications. For example, the GPON capacity expansion threshold is 45%, the split ratio is 1:64, and the broadband service installation rate is 60%. See Table 4.10.

As shown in Table 4.10, GPON ports support limited cloud VR services. Communities with large penetration of cloud VR services need to be upgraded to 10G PON immediately.

To support the wide application of cloud VR, FTTH networks need to upgrade to 10G EPON/10G PON gradually. After the upgrade, even if the split ratio is 1:64 and the convergence ratio is 50%, each user can obtain a bandwidth of 312 Mbit/s, which is adequate to achieve comfortable-experience phase.

Table 4.10 Satisfaction of GPON ports in the ideal-experience phase

Year	GPON port bandwidth (Mbit/s⁻¹)	Capacity expansion threshold (%)	Average rate of broadband users (Mbit/s⁻¹)	Split ratio	Installation rate (%)	Average rate of VR users (Mbit/s⁻¹)	Number of users allowed for provisioning VR services
2019	2,300	45	20	1:64	60	36	7
2020	2,300	45	26.2	1:64	60	40	0
2021	2,300	45	33.5	1:64	60	44	0

Suggestions for the evolution from EPON and GPON to 10G EPON/10G PON are as follows:

1. Evolution from EPON to 10G EPON
   EPON and 10G EPON use the same upstream wavelengths and can share the same optical distribution network (ODN) in time division multiplexing (TDM) mode. Their downstream wavelengths do not overlap and can be received separately, as shown in Figure 4.8.

   There is no need to change the ODN during the evolution from EPON to 10G EPON. However, 10G EPON boards need to be added to OLTs, and existing EPON ONTs can be reused or replaced with 10G EPON ONTs if needed. Note that in 10G EPON and EPON hybrid scenarios, the upstream rates of EPON and 10G EPON are different. Consequently, the upstream bandwidth planning of users is complex, as shown in Figure 4.9.

2. Evolution from GPON to 10G PON
   The upstream wavelengths of GPON and 10G PON do not overlap, and they can share the same ODN through wavelength division multiplexing (WDM). In addition, their downstream wavelengths do not overlap and can be received separately, as shown in Figure 4.10. Because GPON and 10G PON are independent of each other, their bandwidth can be planned independently.

   There are two solutions for evolution from GPON to 10G PON.

   Solution 1: external wavelength division multiplexing 1r (WDM1r)

   The external WDM1r multiplexes the wavelengths on 10G PON and GPON ports and transmits the multiplexed wavelengths over the same backbone optical fiber. The original ONTs on GPON can still be used and need to be replaced with ONTs of 10G PON if needed. Deploying WDM1r will cause extra attenuation. For newly deployed GPON, it is recommended that a budget of 2–3 dBm be reserved. For PON ports that have been deployed on the live network, if the optical budget is insufficient, optical modules can be upgraded to high-power ones, as shown in Figure 4.11.

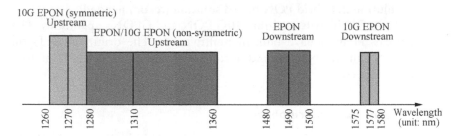

Figure 4.8 EPON/10G EPON wavelength range.

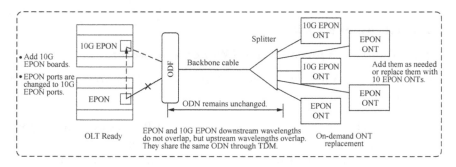

Figure 4.9 Suggestions for upgrading EPON to 10G EPON. Note: ODF is short for optical distribution frame.

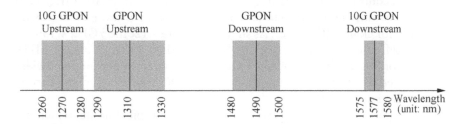

Figure 4.10 GPON/10G PON wavelength range.

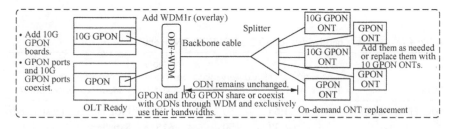

Figure 4.11 GPON/10G PON networking diagram.

Solution 2: hybrid PON board solution (recommended)

The PON boards integrate 10G PON and GPON capabilities. The optical modules have built-in multiplexers. The original ONTs on GPON can still be used and need to be replaced with ONTs of 10G PON if needed.

4.2.5.2 Ideal-experience phase

In the ideal-experience phase, the total access bandwidth of cloud VR, IPTV, and HSI services is 690 Mbit/s. EPON/GPON is far from suitable cloud VR services, and 10G EPON/GPON is required, as shown in Table 4.11.

4.2.6 Home network

4.2.6.1 Challenges faced by cloud VR home networks

To support cloud VR services, home networks need improvements in the following aspects:

1. The 5 GHz band is required to carry cloud VR services, and independent working channels need to be properly planned.

   The 2.4 GHz frequency band has a small number of channels that overlap. If the frequency bandwidth is 20 MHz, there are only three independent channels. The total frequency bandwidth is less than 80 MHz, which is not ideal for carrying cloud VR services.

   In contrast, the 5 GHz frequency band can provide a larger frequency bandwidth and more channels, and the planning is more flexible, suitable for cloud VR services. As shown in Figure 4.12, the 5 GHz Wi-Fi has four frequency bandwidths: 20 MHz, 40 MHz, 80 MHz, and 60 MHz. According to the test results, when the 80 MHz frequency bandwidth is used, the transmission rate can exceed 100 Mbit/s even under certain interference conditions.

   Figure 4.13 shows the Wi-Fi coverage of a typical home, which has three characteristics:
   - The 2.4 GHz frequency band has been overused and has severe interference.

Table 4.11 Available bandwidth for 10G EPON/GPON users

PON	Capacity (Gbit/s^{-1})	Split ratio	Convergence ratio (%)	Available bandwidth (Mbit/s^{-1})	Satisfaction in the ideal-experience phase
10G EPON/GPON	10	1:64	50	312	Not satisfied (restricted)
		1:32	50	625	Satisfied

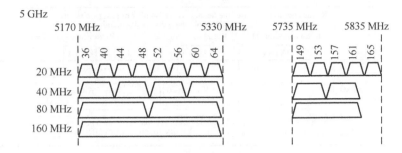

Figure 4.12 Four frequency bandwidths of 5 GHz Wi-Fi.

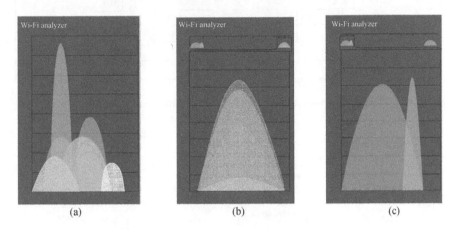

Figure 4.13 Wi-Fi coverage of a typical home. Note: Channels 52–64 share the frequency band with radars. Devices must support the DFS function for radar detection. (a) 2.4 GHz band, (b) 5 GHz high-frequency band, and (c) 5 GHz low-frequency band.

- 5 GHz high-frequency bands are also severely interfered because 5 GHz Wi-Fi routers have been widely used in homes and most of them work in high-frequency bands by default.
- 5 GHz low-frequency bands are seldom used and can be applied to carry cloud VR services if planned properly.

Interference causes contention and conflicts over air interfaces. Packets need to wait for a long time to be sent or need to be resent when a conflict occurs during transmission. This prolongs the packet transmission latency. If the latency exceeds the device tolerance duration or the number of retransmission attempts exceeds the threshold, slow Wi-Fi rate or even packet loss occurs, as shown in Figure 4.14.

In conclusion, 5 GHz low-frequency bands can be used to carry cloud VR services. However, to avoid conflicts, telecom operators need to provide detection and channel planning services.

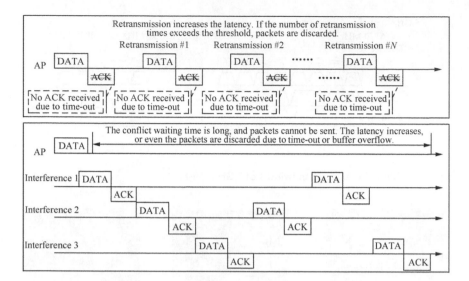

Figure 4.14 Latency and packet loss caused by interference.

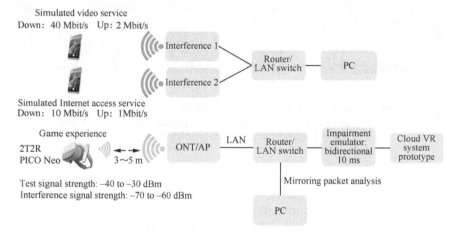

Figure 4.15 AP test networking.

2. The performance of 5 GHz Wi-Fi devices on the market varies. Ensure that high-performance devices are used.

   Many devices support 5 GHz Wi-Fi, but their prices and performance differ greatly. Huawei iLab has tested several common 5 GHz Wi-Fi products. Figure 4.15 shows the test networking.

   During the test, the following parameters are set for interference scenarios: traffic volume, signal strength, working channel, and number of interference sources.

The test objects are strong-interaction cloud VR services. The test focuses on user experience and air interface latency changes in different interference scenarios. The air interface latency can be obtained by analyzing the RTT of service packets captured through mirrored ports. The air interface latency should be within 7 ms.

Note: To ensure equitable test results, it is required that no unknown interference source exists in the test environment except the specified interference sources. Another requirement is that the Wi-Fi parameter settings are identical for each device under test.

Table 4.12 lists the test results, showing that the immunity to interference varies with products.

In the case of no interference, five models met the RTT requirement.

In the case of two channels of adjacent-channel interference, four models met the RTT requirement.

In the case of one channel of adjacent-channel interference and one channel of co-channel interference, only two models met the RTT requirement.

In the case of two channels of co-channel interference, only one model met the RTT requirement.

When 5 GHz Wi-Fi is widely used in the future, both adjacent-channel interference and co-channel interference will become unavoidable. As a result, Wi-Fi devices need to be strictly selected to ensure smooth experience of cloud VR services in typical interference scenarios that can be predicted in the next one or two years.

3. It is difficult to reuse existing ONTs to provide stable Wi-Fi.

In addition to Wi-Fi, the home networking mode also needs special focus, especially ONT deployment positions and network cable resources. This is described in two scenarios.

Table 4.12 Test results of common 5 GHz Wi-Fi products

Product model	No interference	Adjacent-channel interference (simulated video service)+adjacent-channel interference (simulated Internet access)	Co-channel interference (simulated video service)+adjacent-channel interference (simulated Internet access)	Co-channel interference (simulated video service)+co-channel interference (simulated Internet access)
Model 1	Passed	Failed	Failed	Failed
Model 2	Passed	Passed	Failed	Failed
Model 3	Passed	Passed	Failed	Failed
Model 4	Passed	Passed	Passed	Failed
Model 5	Passed	Passed	Passed	Passed

Note: Two channels of interference are designed to simulate Wi-Fi signals of neighbors. One channel carries video traffic, and the other carries Internet access traffic. Adjacent-channel interference and co-channel interference can also be simulated by changing the working channels.

- The ONT is placed in a weak-current box, and only one network cable is connected to the VR experience area.

  This scenario is common in new buildings. The weak-current box is usually located at a distance from the experience area, and the performance of Wi-Fi signals deteriorates after passing through walls. Consequently, this type of problem cannot be resolved by using ONTs with better Wi-Fi performance. Instead, high-performance Wi-Fi APs can be connected to ONTs. This can be done without changing the original networking and service access modes.

- ONTs are placed on desktops.

  Theoretically, problems in this scenario can be resolved by using ONTs with better Wi-Fi performance. Considering that the ONT replacement process is complex, high-performance Wi-Fi APs can be connected to the ONTs.

4.2.6.2 Suggestions on cloud VR home network planning

Three aspects need to be considered during home network deployment:

First, select an appropriate Wi-Fi frequency bandwidth and channel. It is recommended that the 80 MHz bandwidth and 2×2 multiple-input multiple-output (MIMO) be used. Additionally, it is recommended that the channel planning service be provided by telecom operators.

To ensure sufficient bandwidth, a proper 5G Wi-Fi frequency bandwidth needs to be selected. In addition, the limited channels must be properly planned. 5 GHz Wi-Fi supports four frequency bandwidths: 20 MHz, 40 MHz, 80 MHz, and 160 MHz, which support different rates. Currently, most VR terminals in the market support 2×2 MIMO. Figure 4.16 shows the maximum theoretical rates of different frequency bandwidths in different modulation and coding scheme (MCS) standards in the case of 2×2 MIMO.

MCS Index	Spatial Stream	Modulation Format	Coding Rate	Data Rate (Unit: Mbit/s)							
				20 MHz Channel		40 MHz Channel		80 MHz Channel		160 MHz Channel	
				800 ns GI	400 ns GI	800 ns GI	400 ns GI	800 ns GI	400 ns GI	800 ns GI	400 ns GI
0	2	BPSK	1/2	13	14.4	27	30	58.5	65	117	130
1	2	QPSK	1/2	26	28.9	54	60	117	130	234	260
2	2	QPSK	3/4	39	43.3	81	90	175.5	195	351	390
3	2	16-QAM	1/2	52	57.8	108	120	234	260	468	520
4	2	16-QAM	3/4	78	86.7	162	180	351	390	702	780
5	2	64-QAM	2/3	104	115.6	216	240	468	520	936	1040
6	2	64-QAM	3/4	117	130.3	243	270	526.5	585	1053	1170
7	2	64-QAM	5/6	130	144.4	270	300	585	650	1170	1300
8	2	256-QAM	3/4	156	173.3	324	360	702	780	1404	1560
9	2	256-QAM	5/6	N/A	N/A	360	400	780	866.7	1560	1733.4

Figure 4.16 Wi-Fi rates. Note: GI is short for guard interval.

When two channels of co-channel interference exist, the actual Wi-Fi rate is calculated in MCS6 mode. Considering a duty cycle of 50% and transmission loss of 40%, the actual data rate is MCS6 rate$\times$50%$\times$(1%$-$40%). That is, the rate supported by the 20 MHz frequency bandwidth is 39 Mbit/s, by the 40 MHz frequency bandwidth is 81 Mbit/s, by the 80 MHz frequency bandwidth is 175 Mbit/s, and by the 160 MHz frequency bandwidth is 350 Mbit/s. Currently, no terminal supports the 160 MHz frequency bandwidth. As a result, cloud VR services are carried using the 80 MHz frequency bandwidth.

5 GHz frequency band plans and available channels vary depending on specific countries and regions. For example, in Europe, the 80 MHz frequency bandwidth provides only four channels. The channel selection is too complex for users. As a result, door-to-door installation is needed to scan and select available Wi-Fi channels and gateway installation positions.

Second, select high-performance Wi-Fi gateways that have strong anti-interference capabilities and support radar channels and gigabit ports. The details are as follows:

- In the case of two to four channels of co-channel interference, the gateway air interfaces must support a latency less than 10 ms and a rate greater than 130 Mbit/s.
- The gateways must support radar frequency band setting and automatic radar detection. The 5 GHz frequency band has few available channels. For example, in Europe, only four channels are available, among which three are dynamic frequency selection (DFS) channels. To prevent co-channel interference, DFS channels must also be used. The Wi-Fi gateways running on DFS channels must support periodic DFS detection. This detects radar interference on the channels. If radar interference is detected, the Wi-Fi gateways need to switch to other channels.

Last, select a proper home network scheme and use high-performance APs to carry cloud VR services.

Cloud VR reuses existing 4K-ready networks, which also carry 4K IPTV and Internet access services. Since IPTV uses wired access, only Internet access and cloud VR services are competing for Wi-Fi bandwidth. To avoid interference, three deployment solutions are provided.

Solution 1: Use high-performance dedicated APs to carry cloud VR services. This solution can ensure high-quality experience and is recommended, as shown in Figure 4.17.

Solution 2: Reuse existing ONTs or home gateways (HGWs), which support only one 5 GHz frequency band. Cloud VR and Internet access services share the band, affecting VR service experience negatively. In addition, the existing ONTs/HGWs have poor performance and do not support radar channels. They have fewer available channels, which are prone to conflicts. Hence, this solution is not recommended.

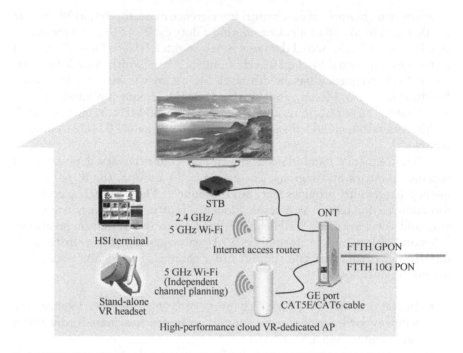

Figure 4.17 Adding APs to carry cloud VR services. Note: STB is short for set-top box.

Solution 3: Replace existing ONTs with high-performance tri-band Wi-Fi ONTs (two 5 GHz frequency bands and one 2.4 GHz frequency band). Currently, a large number of ONTs are deployed in weak-current boxes. Therefore, replacing ONTs cannot provide adequate rate for cloud VR services. As a result, this solution cannot be used currently.

This section describes the recommended deployment solution 1 in detail. The connection mode varies depending on ONT deployment locations, which can be classified into two scenarios.

Scenario 1: When ONTs are deployed in weak-current boxes, APs can be connected in either of the following modes.

When deployed in weak-current boxes, ONTs are connected to HGWs through a network cable. Internet access services are carried through the 5 GHz or 2.4 GHz Wi-Fi of the HGWs, and IPTV services through the ETH port of the HGWs. During cloud VR service deployment, new APs can be connected to the network in two modes, as shown in Figure 4.18.

Mode 1: APs are directly connected to HGWs through network cables.

The implementation is easy and does not require any change in networking. However, cloud VR traffic is forwarded to APs through HGWs, posing high requirements on HGW bandwidth. As a consequence, this mode is recommended when gigabit HGWs are available.

Mode 2: APs are connected between ONTs and HGWs in serial mode.

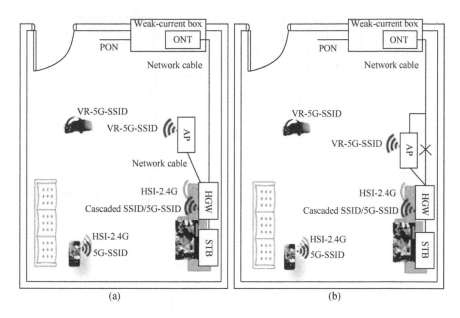

Figure 4.18 Adding dedicated APs for cloud VR (ONTs deployed in weak-current boxes).
(a) Mode 1: APs are directly connected to HGWs through network cables.
(b) Mode 2: APs are connected between ONTs and HGWs in serial mode.

In this access mode, the original home networking needs to be changed. Additionally, the Point-to-Point Protocol over Ethernet (PPPoE) dial-up mode needs to be deployed on ONTs. The implementation is complex. However, because new APs carry cloud VR traffic, HGWs are not impacted. Hence, this mode is suitable for 100 Mbit/s HGWs.

Scenario 2: ONTs are deployed on desktops, and APs are directly connected to the ONTs through network cables.

In this scenario, the ONTs carry Internet access traffic through 5 GHz and 2.4 GHz Wi-Fi and IPTV traffic through the ETH port. During deployment of cloud VR services, new APs used exclusively for these services can be connected to ONTs only through network cables, as shown in Figure 4.19.

In the ideal-experience phase of cloud VR, it is advised to reuse the networking mode used in the comfortable-experience phase, but dedicated high-performance APs are to carry cloud VR services. Furthermore, the Wi-Fi performance must ensure a rate higher than 540 Mbit/s and latency lower than 7 ms. As a result, Wi-Fi 6 is required.

Wi-Fi 6, also known as IEEE 802.11ax, has the following improvements over the 5 GHz 802.11ac standard:

- The orthogonal frequency division multiple access (OFDMA) is introduced to improve the bandwidth utilization.

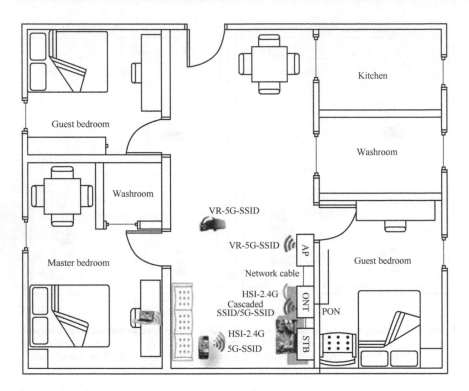

Figure 4.19 Adding dedicated APs for cloud VR (ONTs deployed on desktops).

- The 1024 quadrature amplitude modulation (QAM) is introduced to increase the physical rate by approximately 40%.
- Four times more subcarriers are supported, increasing the range of coverage.
- Multi-user multiple-input multiple-output (MU-MIMO) increases air interface efficiency and transmission efficiency in multi-user scenarios.

The 802.11ax standard can achieve a maximum air interface rate of 10 Gbit/s. Even when the bandwidth loss caused by overhead and signal attenuation is factored in, the actual data rate can still meet the requirements of different cloud VR experience phases.

4.2.7 5G network

On June 14, 2018, 3GPP officially approved the freezing of the standalone (SA) version of the 5G New Radio (NR) standard. This milestone paves the way for future trial and commercial use of 5G networks. 5G networks can provide 100 Mbit/s bandwidth anytime anywhere to meet HD video experience with 4K or higher VR resolution. The network latency of 5–8 ms will eliminate motion sickness.

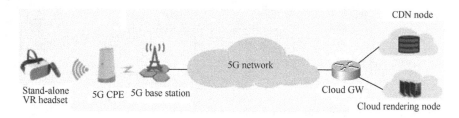

Figure 4.20 Networking of connecting 5G CPEs to the cloud VR platform.

However, the built-in Wi-Fi modules in current VR terminals may not support 5G. Consequently, converting 5G signals into Wi-Fi signals by using pieces of 5G CPE (customer premise equipment) is more common, as shown in Figure 4.20. Similar to home broadband access, this access mode is also susceptible to interference.

As 5G modules grow mature and cheaper, more VR terminals will be equipped with built-in 5G modules to render greater mobility and freedom.

4.3 CLOUD VR NETWORK TRANSMISSION SOLUTION

Cloud VR is regarded as the future of video services. Currently, OTT videos are carried over Internet access channels, and IPTV videos are carried over dedicated channels. Figure 4.21 shows a typical video transmission solution.

Metro side: Internet access services are generally carried by local IP networks, and IPTV services are carried by local IP networks or Layer 3 virtual private networks (L3VPNs).

Access side: Internet access and IPTV services are carried by independent VLANs to ensure service isolation. Currently, the mainstream solution is to carry IPTV services in dual-channel mode. Only a small number of telecom operators use the single-channel solution.

4.3.1 Dual-channel transmission

The set-top box (STB) is connected to the dedicated IPTV port of the ONT for independent dial-up using a dedicated IP address, as shown in Figure 4.22.

When cloud VR services are deployed, three transmission solutions are available, as shown in Figure 4.23.

Solution A: Reuse HSI channels to carry VR content.

Cloud VR terminals obtain IP addresses from ONTs and share the PPPoE channel with Internet access services, as shown in Figure 4.24.

This solution does not require any extra configurations and is therefore recommended. In this mode, VR multicast services are not provided by

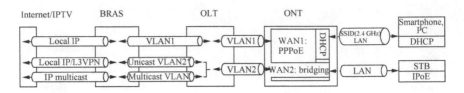

Figure 4.21 Typical video transmission solution.

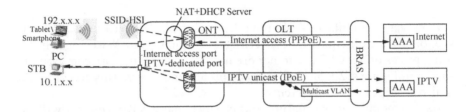

Figure 4.22 Dual-channel IPTV transmission.

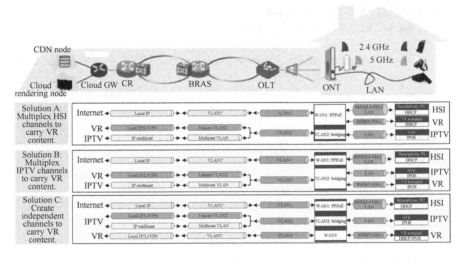

Figure 4.23 Cloud VR transmission solutions in the dual-channel scenario.

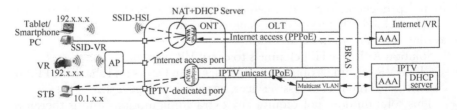

Figure 4.24 Reusing HSI channels to carry VR services.

default, and live VR services are delivered in VoD mode. If there are a large number of users in the future, multicast streams can be separated and pushed to the ONTs separately. This does not affect the PPPoE dial-up mode.

Advantage: Terminals can access the Internet using the Dynamic Host Configuration Protocol (DHCP) without manual configurations or major network changes.

Disadvantage: CDN resources must be deployed on the public network.

Solution B: Reuse IPTV channels to carry VR content.

The ONTs bind the dedicated cloud VR access ports of APs to the existing IPTV channels. Similar to STBs, cloud VR terminals perform IP over Ethernet (IPoE) dial-up authentication through IPTV channels, as shown in Figure 4.25.

To connect a cloud VR terminal, the IPoE account must be added to the authentication, authorization, accounting (AAA) server, and the terminal must support DHCP Option 60/61 for IPoE authentication. The process is complex and as a result, this solution is not recommended.

Advantage: Video CDN resources can be reused.

Disadvantage: Terminals need to customize the dial-up function similar to IPoE and be allocated with accounts. When IPTV services are carried over private networks, terminals cannot access public network resources.

Solution C: Create independent channels to carry VR content.

Based on the 4K IPTV transport solution, an IPoE logical channel is added to carry VR services. This requires a VR AP-dedicated port reserved on ONTs and bound to the wide area network (WAN) interface of the independent IPoE channel, as shown in Figure 4.26.

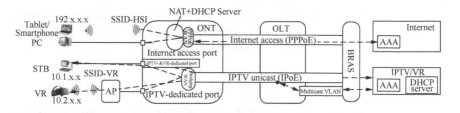

Figure 4.25 Reusing IPTV channels to carry VR content.

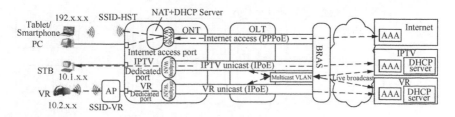

Figure 4.26 Creating independent channels to carry VR content.

The reconstruction involves planning of VLANs, IP addresses, and routing policies of the VR dedicated channels from ONTs to BRASs. This further involves addition of the AAA server and DHCP server for authenticating VR unicast channels. Finally, the process includes reconstruction of the operation support system (OSS) and service provisioning system. The reconstruction procedure is complex.

Advantage: Services can be properly isolated. The solution is suitable for developing mature services.

Disadvantage: Networks need to be changed significantly, and the reconstruction period is lengthy. The terminal dial-up access mode depends on the authentication scheme.

4.3.2 Single-channel transmission

The ONT is placed in the weak-current box. The ONT has only one IPTV port, which is connected to the HGW. As a result, the STB cannot be connected to the ONT and must share the Internet access channel. Even though cloud VR terminals and APs are added, they must also share the same channel, as shown in Figure 4.27.

In both dual-channel and single-channel scenarios, reusing is the fastest solution and requires the least end-to-end changes.

4.3.3 Casting transmission solution

The VR content displayed on a headset can be shared with others by casting it to a TV screen. To implement casting, cloud VR devices, STBs, and clouds need to exchange signaling and data.

Currently, there are predominantly two cloud VR casting solutions: cloud Extensible Messaging and Presence Protocol (XMPP) casting solution and local Digital Living Network Alliance (DLNA) casting solution, as shown in Figure 4.28.

1. Cloud XMPP casting solution
   In this solution, the cloud VR service platform synchronizes traffic to the IPTV system, and the STB fetches the casting traffic from the

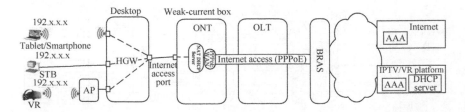

Figure 4.27 Cloud VR transmission in the single-channel scenario.

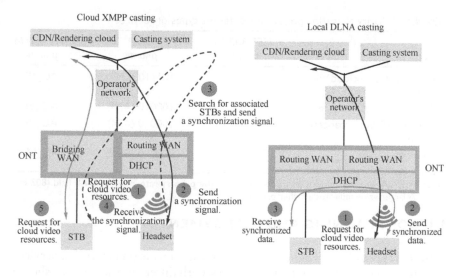

Figure 4.28 Comparison of VR casting solutions.

IPTV system. The STB traffic and cloud VR terminal traffic are independent of each other. Therefore, the network bandwidth must support two copies of VR traffic.

Advantage: STBs and cloud VR terminals only need to communicate with the cloud system, and they do not need to communicate with each other.

Disadvantage: The network needs to transmit two copies of VR content, one to the VR terminal and the other to the STP, increasing the traffic load on the network.

2. Local DLNA casting solution

Cloud VR terminals and STBs use the DLNA protocol to transmit casting traffic. As the Wi-Fi AP and VR terminal need to process two copies of traffic, the experience is poor in a test, and the terminal power consumption is high. In addition, the cloud VR terminal and STB are on the same subnet (that is, cloud VR is also transmitted through the IPTV channel). The IPTV services and Internet access services are carried on independent planes. Consequently, they are forwarded and isolated on ONTs and cannot interact with each other locally.

Advantage: The DLNA solution on terminals is mature and easy to implement.

Disadvantage: Wi-Fi APs and terminals need to process independent copies of traffic. The test experience is poor, and the terminal power consumption is high. The STBs and headsets need to directly communicate with each other locally.

Table 4.13 Priority allocation policies for different types of services

Service	IEEE 802.1p priority	DSCP priority	Wi-Fi WMM priority
Strong-interaction cloud VR service	5	101110 (EF)	AC_VI
IPTV/cloud VR VoD service	4	100010 (AF4)	AC_VI
IPTV/cloud VR live broadcast service	4	100010 (AF4)	AC_VI
HSI service	0	000000 (BE)	AC_BE

Note: For VLAN packets, priorities are marked using the primary rate interface (PRI) field (802.1p). A larger value indicates a higher priority.

4.4 QOS PLANNING AND DEPLOYMENT

Different types of services have differing requirements on networks. Services need to be classified to put them in queues with different priorities, as shown in Table 4.13.

For IPv4 packets, priorities are marked based on first several bits (Differentiated Services Code Point, DSCP) of the type of service (ToS) field. The higher the value, the higher the priority.

For Wi-Fi packets, priorities are marked based on Wi-Fi multimedia (WMM), and the priorities in descending order are AC_V0, AC VI, AC BE, and AC BK.

- Strong-interaction cloud VR services, such as cloud VR games, are highly interactive and latency sensitive, and consequently, they require high-priority assurance.
- For IPTV/cloud VR VoD services, the bandwidth of the self-operated VoD service is preferentially guaranteed.
- If IPTV/cloud VR live broadcast services use the multicast mode, they are sensitive to packet loss because once packet loss occurs, a large number of users will be affected. Therefore, the priority of these services must be the same as that of VR games. However, cloud VR live broadcast services are usually implemented in VoD mode. Hence, the priority must be the same as that of VoD services.
- HSI services require a basic bandwidth guarantee and need to be forwarded on a best-effort basis.

After the priorities are defined, the corresponding actions need to be performed on network nodes for the QoS to take effect. QoS actions include priority marking, committed access rate (CAR)/shaping, and scheduling. One or more of the three actions need to be deployed on different network nodes, as shown in Figure 4.29.

Figure 4.29 Typical E2E QoS deployment rules.

4.4.1 Priority marking

The process of setting different priorities for data packets is called priority marking. In most cases, service classification and priority marking are concurrently performed on edge nodes. A simple E2E traffic classification can implement priority scheduling of service packets, as shown in Figure 4.30.

- Downstream direction: Traffic can be classified and marked at the metro ingress, and ACL policies can be configured to identify matched traffic.
- Upstream direction: Traffic can be identified and marked on incoming ONT ports. The volume of upstream traffic of VR services is small. If the upstream Internet speed is adequate, traffic classification and marking are unnecessary.

4.4.2 CAR/shaping

In most cases, the BRASs can limit the upstream and downstream rates using CAR or traffic shaping. CAR does not require cache or scheduling, and no queuing latency is introduced. However, burst traffic may be transparently transmitted to downstream devices. Hence, CAR is applicable if downstream devices have a large cache. In traffic shaping mode, user traffic is shaped through queues, and burst traffic is limited to the 10 ms level, which has a small impact on downstream devices. However, traffic shaping introduces jitter. As a result, shaping is applicable if downstream devices have a small cache. In the cloud VR scenario, the CAR mode is recommended because it does not introduce jitter.

When Internet access channels are used to carry cloud VR services, contention for bandwidth may occur. To avoid this situation, common solutions including hierarchical quality of service (HQoS) and destination address accounting (DAA) are provided, as shown in Figure 4.31.

- The BRAS identifies VR service streams based on the server address list and user domain.
- DAA is configured on the BRAS to separately limit the rate of Internet access and cloud VR services and ensure that 200 Mbit/s of bandwidth

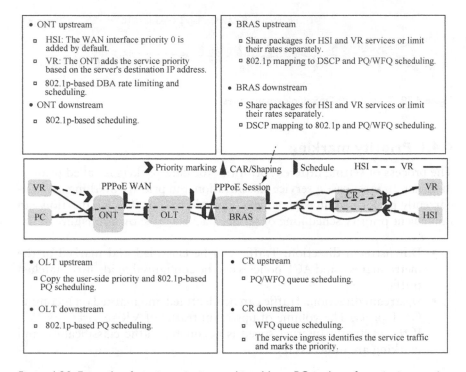

- ONT upstream
  - HSI: The WAN interface priority 0 is added by default.
  - VR: The ONT adds the service priority based on the server's destination IP address.
  - 802.1p-based DBA rate limiting and scheduling.
- ONT downstream
  - 802.1p-based scheduling.

- BRAS upstream
  - Share packages for HSI and VR services or limit their rates separately.
  - 802.1p mapping to DSCP and PQ/WFQ scheduling.
- BRAS downstream
  - Share packages for HSI and VR services or limit their rates separately.
  - DSCP mapping to 802.1p and PQ/WFQ scheduling.

Priority marking   CAR/Shaping   Schedule   HSI – – – VR ——

VR   PPPoE WAN   PPPoE Session   VR

PC   ONT   OLT   BRAS   CR   HSI

- OLT upstream
  - Copy the user-side priority and 802.1p-based PQ scheduling.
- OLT downstream
  - 802.1p-based PQ scheduling.

- CR upstream
  - PQ/WFQ queue scheduling.
- CR downstream
  - WFQ queue scheduling.
  - The service ingress identifies the service traffic and marks the priority.

Figure 4.30 Example of service priority marking. Note: PQ is short for priority queuing; WFQ is short for weighted fair queuing.

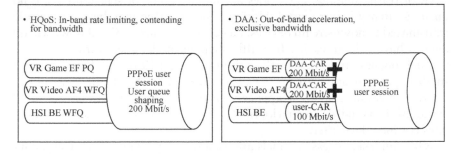

- HQoS: In-band rate limiting, contending for bandwidth

| VR Game EF PQ |
| VR Video AF4 WFQ |
| HSI BE WFQ |

PPPoE user session
User queue shaping
200 Mbit/s

- DAA: Out-of-band acceleration, exclusive bandwidth

VR Game EF	DAA-CAR 200 Mbit/s
VR Video AF4	DAA-CAR 200 Mbit/s
HSI BE	user-CAR 100 Mbit/s

PPPoE user session

Figure 4.31 Technological principles of HQoS and DAA.

is dedicated for VR services. The priorities of VR service packets are also changed (AF4 for VR videos and EF for VR games).

- The priority scheduling mode of the OLT Internet access traffic profile is changed from local priority to packet priority.
  - Local priority: When congestion occurs, the system performs queue scheduling based on the 802.1p priority specified in the traffic profile.

- Packet priority: When congestion occurs, the system performs queue scheduling based on packet priorities.
- On the Wi-Fi side of ONTs/APs, WMM performs air interface scheduling based on the DSCP priority of packets.

4.4.3 Scheduling deployment

The objective of scheduling is to prioritize VR and IPTV traffic while reserving some for HSI services. The scheduling policy may vary with network nodes.

1. Metro network equipment
   Because there are a large number of services on metro networks, the strict priority (SP)+weighted fair queuing (WFQ) scheduling mode is usually used. The SP scheduling mode is used for services that are mission-critical but small in traffic volume, such as voice, management, and live broadcast services. The WFQ scheduling mode is used for video, enterprise, and HSI services. In the WFQ mode, the weight setting for queues is critical and must be based on the traffic volume of each service. For example, if the multicast traffic of a site is 0.7 Gbit/s, the VoD traffic is 2.5 Gbit/s, and two devices are connected through a bonded link of $2 \times 10GE$, the multicast traffic accounts for 3.5% and the VoD traffic accounts for 12.5% of the total bandwidth. Considering the uneven hash-based traffic distribution on member links and possible traffic bursts, the recommended weight is 10% or higher for multicast queues and 25% or higher for VoD queues.
2. Access network OLTs
   If OLTs carry many services, SP+WFQ scheduling can be used as on metro networks. If only broadband services exist on OLTs, the default SP scheduling mode can be used to avoid complex planning and deployment. PON ports are planned based on the split ratio, and the reserved bandwidth is sufficient. Even if the SP scheduling mode is used, there is an extremely low probability that Internet traffic is starved for bandwidth due to bursts of other traffic.
3. Wi-Fi air interface
   If video services and common Internet access services share Wi-Fi channels, the WMM mechanism of the Wi-Fi standard is recommended to prioritize video services.

4.5 FUTURE NETWORK EVOLUTION STRATEGY OF CLOUD VR

With the improvement of screen resolution, chip performance, and content quality, VR videos will gradually evolve to the ultimate-experience phase

Table 4.14 Service latency requirements in the ultimate-experience phase of cloud VR

E2E network RTT	Home network	Fixed access network	Metro transport network
≤ 8 ms	≤ 5 ms	≤ 2 ms	≤ 1 ms

(full-view 12K or 24K). This requires a bandwidth higher than 1 Gbit/s and network RTT less than or equal to 8 ms, as shown in Table 4.14.

The evolution is detailed as follows:

- Home Wi-Fi technology: Gigabit capacity is required, and 802.11ax or 60 GHz Wi-Fi is recommended to further reduce interference and latency.
- Access technology: The access network needs to be upgraded to 25G/50GPON to achieve gigabit access for each user.
- Metro network: The network architecture is flattened, and WDM devices are moved down to central offices (COs).
- Deterministic low-latency transport network: Cloud rendering nodes are further moved to metro edges, and technologies such as network slicing and cloud-network synergy are used to ensure deterministic low latency.

4.5.1 Wi-Fi technology evolution: 60 GHz

Regardless of 2.4 GHz or 5 GHz Wi-Fi, even if channel adjustment is used, it is difficult to eliminate the interference of adjacent Wi-Fi signals, especially in densely populated areas. As shown in Figure 4.32, the 60 GHz band is 2.16 GHz wide and provides more spectrum, although the number of available frequencies may vary in different regions. In addition, 60 GHz Wi-Fi is only marginally affected by neighboring APs due to its poor wall penetration capability. Consequently, 60 GHz Wi-Fi is suitable for VR services that require limited mobility and involve heavy traffic.

Based on the current 802.11ad standard, wider channels are available to support a data transmission rate of up to 7 Gbit/s by using a low-power modulation scheme. The future 802.11ay standard is more advanced and supports a maximum of eight spatial streams using the advanced 8-Phase-shift keying (8-PSK) modulation mode. In addition, the 2.16 GHz frequency bandwidth can be extended to 4.32 GHz, 6.48 GHz, and even 8.64 GHz. Theoretically, the maximum rate can reach 275 Gbit/s.

4.5.2 Access technology evolution: 25G/50G/100G PON

The next-generation PON technology implements 25G PON by improving per-wavelength capacity. In addition, multiple 25G PON wavelengths can be combined to implement 50G/100G PON. When the convergence ratio

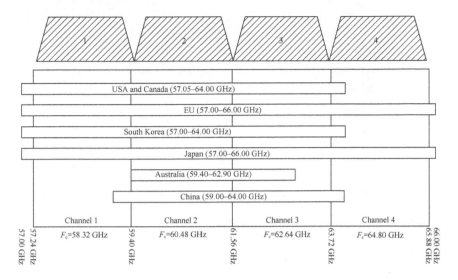

Figure 4.32 Free 60 GHz spectrum ranges in different countries.

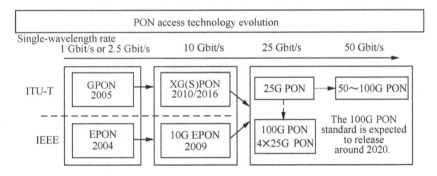

Figure 4.33 PON technology evolution.

is 50% and the split ratio is 1:32 or 1:64, 25G PON can provide 1 Gbit/s bandwidth for users. This meets the bandwidth requirements of cloud VR in the ultimate-experience phase, as shown in Figure 4.33.

4.5.3 Metro network evolution: flattened network architecture and WDM deployment at COs

The increasing popularity of cloud VR poses the following challenges to traditional metro networks:

- The capacity is inadequate for cloud VR services.
- The traditional design with high convergence ratio cannot cope with the high concurrency of cloud VR services.

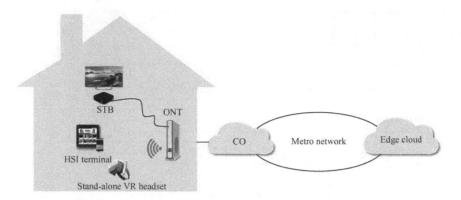

Figure 4.34 Flattened metro network architecture.

- The latency fluctuation and packet loss rate of traditional networks cannot ensure the quality of cloud VR services.

To address these challenges, a flattened metro network architecture is required. Specifically, OTN devices need to be moved downward to COs and rendering nodes to edge clouds, building networks with ultra-large capacity, ultra-low latency, and zero packet loss, as shown in Figure 4.34.

4.5.4 Cloud–network synergy with deterministic low latency

Deterministic latency/bandwidth networks predominantly use three technologies: edge rendering, network slicing, and cloud–network synergy, as shown in Figure 4.35.

1. Edge rendering
   Edge rendering indicates that network edge devices provide certain computing and storage capabilities to implement real-time distribution of cloud VR services and reduce latency.
2. Network slicing
   The bandwidth of a traditional transport network is shared by multiple services. It is difficult to avoid service traffic conflicts and ensure the latency of sensitive services. FlexE is an interface technology used to implement service isolation and network slicing on transport networks. In March 2016, the Optical Internetworking Forum (OIF) officially released the first-generation FlexE standard that supports a 100 Gbit/s rate. This is defined as an intermediate layer between Ethernet layer 2 and layer 1. The standard aims to provide on-demand bandwidth on user-side interfaces and isolate interfaces to reduce latency, as shown in Figure 4.36.

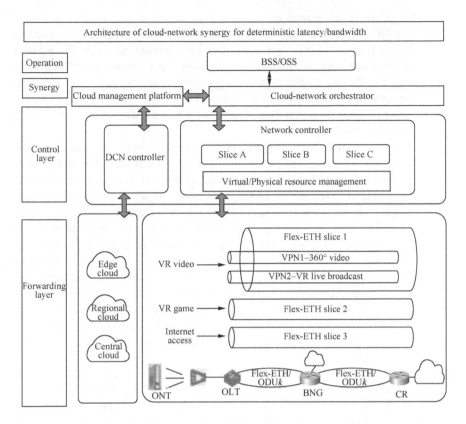

Figure 4.35 Architecture of cloud–network synergy for deterministic latency/bandwidth. Note: BSS is short for business support system. ODU*k* is short for optical channel data unit. BNG is short for broadband network gateway.

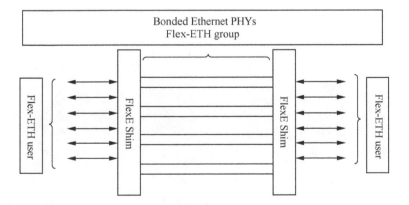

Figure 4.36 Overall architecture of FlexE.

3. Cloud–network synergy

It is difficult to allocate an independent FlexE to each user in advance, due to limited FlexE slice resources on network devices. To achieve optimal resource utilization, the cloud–network synergy technology is used to allocate physical pipes only when users actually use services, implementing dynamic on-demand resource allocation. The cloud–network synergy technology offers on-demand, dynamic, end-to-end, and open features.

- On-demand: Networks can allocate resources on demand based on cloud VR service requirements, such as bandwidth, latency, packet loss rate, and jitter. Networks can also scale in or out resources as required based on the change of cloud VR service volume.
- Dynamic: Static resource planning is prone to resource waste due to high-bandwidth needs of cloud VR. The best way to avoid resource waste is by performing end-to-end computing in seconds when a cloud VR service session occurs, dynamically allocating and scheduling resources through each device node, and releasing resources immediately when the service is terminated.
- End-to-end: The congestion on any node on the path may affect the entire cloud VR service. This being the case, end-to-end management and computing are required to ensure transmission quality on each node.
- Open: Cloud–network synergy can be used not only for operator-operated services, but also for OTT services, promoting the development of cloud VR services. Cloud–network synergy should provide friendly, clearly defined, and comprehensive interfaces for OTTs to customize network quality for services such as cloud VR.

Chapter 5

Cloud VR Terminals

As cloud virtual reality (VR) terminals provide users with entry to the virtual world, the quality of these terminals plays an important role in user experience. Compared with traditional video and game services, cloud VR services have revolutionary service experience modes, such as full immersion and cloud interaction. As a result, various factors affect user experience, including terminal weight, definition, comfort, freedom of interaction, network transmission performance, heat dissipation, and power consumption.

With the powerful computing capability of cloud rendering servers, cloud VR can greatly reduce the hardware requirements of terminals while ensuring stable transmission of video streams. This feature equips cloud VR terminals with unparalleled advantages compared to traditional VR terminals, such as lighter weight and lower costs, facilitating the popularization of VR.

5.1 CLOUD VR TERMINAL FORMS

5.1.1 Working principles of VR terminals

Chapter 1 elaborates on the development history of VR. After decades of technological advancement and iteration, the VR industry has made breakthroughs in numerous key technical fields, and VR terminals have evolved from bulky to light and from tedious to convenient. Major vendors have gradually launched VR terminals since 2016, increasing the public's reception of VR.

The interaction between users and VR terminals involves three important phases: information input, processing, and output, as shown in Figure 5.1.

The main body of a VR terminal is the headset, which is a display equipped with a closed mask near the user's eyes. VR headsets display images in the direction that users face. Because these images are isolated from the real world, users feel as if they are in virtual spaces. Figure 5.2 shows the basic components of a VR headset.

Processor: Generates images and computes positioning information based on sensor data. It is the core component for presenting computing data to users' virtual environments. Different from traditional videos and games,

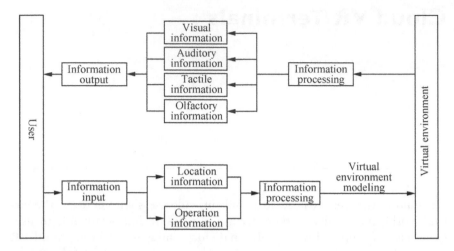

Figure 5.1 Working principles of VR terminals.

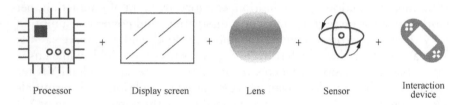

Processor   Display screen   Lens   Sensor   Interaction device

Figure 5.2 Basic components of a VR headset.

VR applications need to present images based on interaction and position, which requires high computing speeds. Therefore, processor chip performance is crucial.

Display screen: One or two high-performance display screens are used to present images to users, and resolution is key to image definition. A higher screen resolution requires a higher image resolution and processor performance. In addition, display screens must have a high refresh rate to ensure smooth motion images.

Lens: By refracting light, the lens draws images on the screen close to the user's retina, enabling them to easily see virtual images through the screen. Currently, mainstream VR terminals use Fresnel lenses.

Sensor: Sensors are the information input core of VR terminals. A sensor is composed of a series of monitoring apparatuses, such as an accelerometer, a gyroscope, and an optical sensor, which is configured to sense information such as user location, movement direction, speed, and environment.

Interaction device: The interaction device implements interaction between a user and the virtual world through action tracking and key control, allowing users to operate and control objects in the virtual world and further enhance their immersion.

5.1.2 Classification and comparison of VR terminals

VR terminals are generally classified into three types based on their forms: smartphone VR headsets, standalone VR headsets, and tethered VR headsets. Figure 5.3 shows VR terminal categories and typical devices within each category.

The following section describes the differences between these VR terminals.

5.1.2.1 Smartphone VR headset

Device form: It consists of a smartphone and VR glasses and serves as an entry-level VR product.

Working principle: The smartphone provides the processor, screen, and sensor, and the VR glasses provide the optical lenses required to convert the panoramic content on the smartphone screen into immersive three-dimensional (3D) images, as shown in Figure 5.4.

Smartphone VR headset experience depends on screen resolution and processor speed. Most VR glasses (such as Google Cardboard) only provide convex lenses for image conversion. Some VR glasses (such as Samsung Gear VR) provide additional gyro sensors, and the bottom layer of the smartphone systems is optimized for VR, further improving user experience.

Advantage

This type of VR headset is both inexpensive and portable. Most smartphone VR headsets have no hardware compatibility requirements

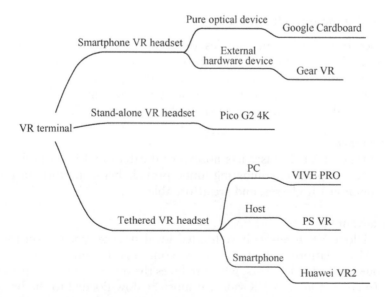

Figure 5.3 VR terminal categories.

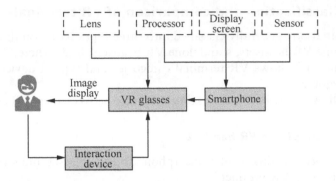

Figure 5.4 Implementation principles of smartphone VR headsets.

except for Samsung Gear VR, which only works with specific Samsung smartphone models. Users can experience VR services once they install VR-based apps on their smartphones.

Disadvantage
Limited by the performance and screen resolution of smartphones, the definition, immersion, and interaction quality of images cannot provide an optimal experience.

Typical devices
Google Cardboard and Samsung Gear VR

5.1.2.2 Standalone VR headset

Device form: As the name implies, the computing, display, and control of virtual images run independently on a standalone device.
Working principle: The standalone VR headset provides a display screen, lens, sensor, and processor and can perform computing, input, output, and display independently, as shown in Figure 5.5.

Advantage
This type of VR headset has no external cables and is portable. They have independent computing units, provide better performance than common VR glasses, and are affordable.

Disadvantage
Standalone VR headsets have limited local storage space. Over the top (OTT) platforms often excessively compress the online video bitrate due to bandwidth costs, which reduces the quality of user experience. To enjoy a lossless VR video, it must be downloaded to the headset,

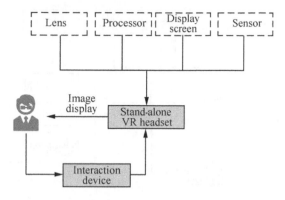

Figure 5.5 Implementation principles of standalone VR headsets.

which may not have adequate storage space to store the video. For example, a 3-minute 4K VR video requires 900 MB storage space, a 3-minute 8K VR video requires 1.8 GB storage space, and a VR game requires a significant amount of GB storage space, far beyond the storage capacity of standalone VR headsets.

Standalone VR headsets' local processors offer limited computing capabilities. Due to the size and weight limit, standalone VR headsets' local processors have a lower performance than that of PC VR. Therefore, most standalone VR headsets have limited content because they can only run simple weak-interaction applications.

The battery life is poor. The battery and processor of standalone VR headsets are integrated, posing higher requirements on quality, battery endurance, heat dissipation, and safety.

Typical devices
Oculus Quest, VIVE Focus Plus, Pico G2 4K, Deepoon P1 PRO, Skyworth V901.

5.1.2.3 Tethered VR headset

Device form: The VR headset connects to a high-performance PC, host, or smartphone through a cable for computing and rendering.

Working principle: VR applications are rendered and coded on the PC, host, or smartphone and then transmitted to the VR headset for display through a data cable (such as high-definition multimedia interface (HDMI), DisplayPort (DP), or universal serial bus (USB) cable), as shown in Figure 5.6.

Tethered VR headsets are classified into PC VR headset (connected to PCs) and split VR headset (connected to hosts or smartphones) that function like standalone VR headsets using the split design.

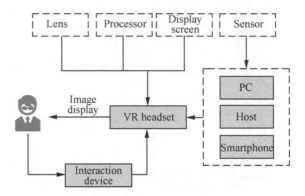

Figure 5.6 Implementation principles of tethered VR headsets.

Advantage

PC VR: Based on the powerful computing capability of high-performance PCs, the products implement local real-time image rendering, coding, and transmission, maximizing image quality and ensuring low-latency transmission. They can provide users with high-quality, highly interactive, and highly immersive experiences.

Split VR headset: The working principles of split VR headsets are similar to those of standalone VR headsets. The only difference is that the computing unit has been separated from the VR headset and placed on the host box or smartphone. This form not only has the same advantages as those of standalone VR headsets, but also reduces the weight of VR headsets. With the development of 5G networks and the popularization of 5G smartphones, split VR headsets are undoubtedly the best VR device form.

Disadvantage

PC VR: A PC equipped with a high-performance graphics card may cost thousands of dollars, and the cable restricts user movement. Even a portable backpack is still too heavy. If outside-in 6DoF (degrees of freedom) motion tracking is involved, the installation and commissioning of locators is intimidatingly complex.

Split VR headset: Similar to standalone VR headsets, the computing and rendering capabilities of split VR headsets depend on host boxes and smartphones, and their performance is lower than that of PCs. In addition, most vendors bundle headsets with their smartphones or host boxes and content platforms.

Typical device

PC VR: VIVE PRO, Oculus Rift, and Deepoon E3

Split VR headset: Huawei VRGlass, PS VR, and 3Glasses X1

Table 5.1 Classification and comparison of VR terminals

Terminal type	Price	Weight	Definition	Interaction	Freedom	Experience evaluation
Standalone VR headset	Medium	Medium	High	Medium	High	Medium
PC VR	High	Large	High	High	Low	High
Split VR headset	Medium	Small	High	Medium	High	Medium
Smartphone VR headset	Low	Small	Low	Low	High	Low

Table 5.1 lists the comparison results of the preceding VR terminals.

The comparison results indicate that smartphone VR headsets and split VR headsets will define the future of VR terminals. Split VR headsets can be considered a split version of standalone VR headsets. As shown in Figure 5.7, the market scale of standalone VR headsets was estimated to reach 42.7% in 2019, which is a 16.1% increase compared with 26.6% in 2018, and 64.6% by 2023.

The following conclusions can be drawn based on the development trend of the VR terminal market scale:

1. PC VR is expensive, and the upgrade cycle is long. Therefore, PC VR is not well received by consumers and is usually used in industries.
2. VR glasses are affordable but have become a thing of the past due to the poor experience delivered.
3. With the emergence of cost-effective standalone VR headsets such as Oculus Go (Xiaomi) and PICO G2 in 2018, users can enjoy excellent immersive experiences at low prices. In addition, the application of the 6DoF positioning and tracking technology greatly enriches the application scenarios of standalone VR headsets. For that reason, standalone VR headsets have become the optimal choice.

5.1.3 Cloud VR terminal selection

The cloud VR solution utilizes powerful cloud computing and rendering capabilities to reduce hardware requirements on terminals. From a solution architecture perspective, cloud VR and traditional VR terminals have the same three forms.

1. Smartphone VR headset
   Smartphones access the cloud VR service platform through 5G or Wi-Fi networks.
2. Standalone VR headset
   Standalone VR headsets access the cloud VR service platform through 5G or Wi-Fi networks.

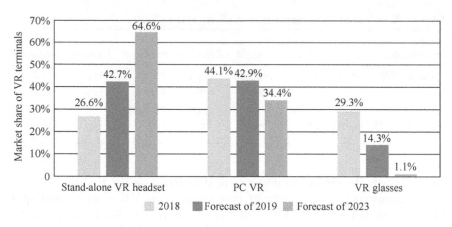

Figure 5.7 Market share of VR terminals (International Data Corporation, IDC).

3. Tethered VR headset

The VR headset connects to a PC, host, or smartphone through an HDMI or USB cable and then connects to the cloud VR service platform through an optical fiber or wireless network.

According to the VR terminal forms described in Section 5.1.2, future cloud VR terminals should be cordless and lightweight. Therefore, smartphone VR headsets, standalone VR headsets, and split VR headsets will be the mainstream forms of cloud VR terminals. Smartphone VR headsets helped millions of users try out VR due to its low cost and the prevalence of smartphones. However, only standalone VR headsets and split VR headsets can provide optimal experiences.

Figure 5.8 shows the working principles of cloud VR terminals. Most processing components have migrated to the cloud. Image computing, rendering, and coding are performed on the cloud, and images are transmitted to cloud VR terminals as video streams through a high-bandwidth and low-latency network. The terminals only require on-board processing functions for decoding video streams and local image rendering and for displaying images to users.

Table 5.2 lists the technical specifications of mainstream standalone VR headsets in 2019.

Unlike traditional VR terminals, cloud VR terminals separate computing from display. The main factor that affects user experience is latency, including latency in cloud computing, rendering, network transmission, terminal image decompression, and video processing. Therefore, the key technical difficulties of cloud VR terminals lie in solving the motion sickness caused by high latency and the image quality deterioration caused by image compression, decompression, packet loss, and jitter during transmission. With

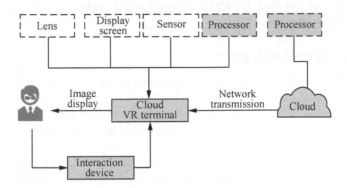

Figure 5.8 Implementation principles of cloud VR terminals.

Table 5.2 Technical specifications of mainstream standalone VR headsets in 2019

Module category	Component	Specifications
Screen	Material type	LCD or OLED with quick response
	Resolution	Binocular 3K–4K
	Refresh rate	≥ 70 Hz
Optics	Lens type	Fresnel lens
	FoV	≥ 100°
	Adjustment function	Self-adaptive pupil distance, adjustable focal length, or goggle design
	Eye protection mode	Anti-blue-ray design
Freedom	Helmet	6DoF
	Handle	3DoF/6DoF
Wireless transmission	Wi-Fi	802.11a/b/g/n/ac 2.4 GHz/5 GHz, 2×2 MIMO
	5G	Not supported
Processor	CPU	Qualcomm: Snapdragon 835; Samsung: Exynos 8895
Storage	Memory	≥ 4 GB
	Flash memory	≥ 32 GB; microSD card capacity ≥ 128 GB
Endurance	Battery capacity	≥ 3,500 mAh
Weight	Entire device (excluding the headset)	≤ 350 g

the breakthrough of end-to-end technologies in the VR industry, cloud VR terminals will keep pace with traditional VR terminals in terms of display and interaction technologies and develop toward lighter, higher resolution, as well as larger field of view (FoV).

5.2 DEVELOPMENT STATUS OF KEY CLOUD VR TERMINAL TECHNOLOGIES

5.2.1 Chip technology

Cloud VR terminals need to access networks through 5G or Wi-Fi and perform image decoding, as well as local rendering, on video streams received from the cloud. These functions require the chips of cloud VR terminals to have powerful processing capabilities to ensure low latency and high-quality experiences.

Mobile VR devices will be the mainstream form of cloud VR terminals. All the functions of smartphone VR headsets and phone-based split VR headsets depend on smartphones' chips. Following the explosive growth of the standalone VR headset market over the last two years, major mobile chip vendors have begun to launch mobile chip solutions for standalone VR headsets.

For example, Qualcomm, a leading mobile chip company, has released the Snapdragon 835 and XR1 chips, which are derived from the Snapdragon 835 chip and dedicated to the XR computing platform. These chips have been widely used in multiple types of standalone VR headsets. On December 6, 2019, Qualcomm released the XR2 chip, a derivative of Snapdragon 865. The GPU and CPU performance of the XR2 chip is twice that of the XR1 chip. In addition, the XR2 chip supports 8K 60 FPS (frames per second) video decoding and 3K resolution per eye. Furthermore, the XR2 chip integrates technologies such as 5G, AI, visual processing, interaction, and audio to better meet immersive XR requirements.

The terminal chips of standalone VR headsets offer the same core functions and technologies as smartphone chips. Table 5.3 lists the core technical parameters of mobile chips, using the Qualcomm Snapdragon 855 as an example.

In 2019, the mobile chips in most standalone VR headsets supported 4K 60 FPS video decoding. Some chips, such as the Samsung Exynos 8895, support 8K maximum decoding capability. This particular chip was used in the Skyworth VR headset V901 and was the only chip to feature in a standalone VR headset and support 8K hardware decoding in 2019. Snapdragon 855 and higher-end chips (including XR2) also support 8K hardware decoding but have not been used in standalone VR headsets. If standalone VR headsets do not have the 8K hardware decoding capability, they can use the 8K player as an alternative.

Table 5.4 lists the mainstream mobile VR chips and cloud VR terminals in 2019.

5.2.2 Display technology

Sight is our most important sense through which we perceive the world. As such, display is the most important output in a VR headset. Figure 5.9 shows experiment data about color psychology: sight accounts for 87% of human visual, auditory, tactile, olfactory, and taste sensations.

Table 5.3 Core parameters of mobile chips (Snapdragon 855)

Function	Specifications
Long Term Evolution (LTE)	LTE Frequency Division Duplex (FDD), LTE Time Division Duplex (TDD) (including Citizens Broadband Radio Service (CBRS)), License Assisted Access (LAA), and LTE broadcast
5G	5G technology: 5G NR 5G spectrum: mmWave, sub-6 GHz 5G mm Wave specifications: 800 MHz bandwidth, 8 carriers, 2×2 MIMO 5G sub-6 GHz specifications: 100 MHz bandwidth, 4×4 MIMO
Wi-Fi	Wi-Fi standards: 802.11ad, 802.11ay, 802.11ax-ready, 802.11ac Wave 2, 802.11a/b/g, and 802.11n Wi-Fi frequency band: 2.4 GHz, 5 GHz, and 60 GHz
RF	Qualcomm®RF front-end (RFFE) solution
CPU	Clock frequency: up to 2.84 GHz CPU core: Qualcomm®Kryo™ 485 CPU, Octa-core CPU CPU architecture: 64-bit
GPU	Qualcomm®Adreno™ 640 GPU 8K 360 VR video playback Maximum color depth of 10 bits, Rec 2020 color gamut Video coding: H.265 (HEVC), HDR10+, HLG, HDR10, H.264 (AVC), VP8, and VP9
Memory	Memory frequency: 2,133 MHz Memory type: 4×16 bits, LPDDR4x
Positioning technology	BeiDou, Galileo, GLONASS, dual-band GNSS, GPS, QZSS, SBAS
Bluetooth	Version: 5.0 Transmission rate: 2 Mbit/s
Audio	Audio technology: Qualcomm True Wireless™ technology, Qualcomm® broadcasting audio technology, Qualcomm Aqstic™ audio technology, and Qualcomm®aptX™ audio technology
USB	USB 3.1, USB-C

Data source: Official Qualcomm website.

Display information can include color, brightness, contrast, angle, resolution, and depth. Our preference for visuals is evolving with the medium, and flat displays are not enough. Users crave more immersive VR displays.

5.2.2.1 Resolution

Research shows that our eyes cannot see the individual pixels on the display, and will not experience the screen-door effect when pixels per degree (PPD) is greater than 60. PPD is calculated based on the angle of view and the number of pixels on the display. It is the result of the following formula:

$$PPD = px / FoV$$

Table 5.4 Mainstream mobile VR chips and cloud VR terminals in 2019

Vendor	Model	Hardware decoding capability	Cloud VR terminal
Qualcomm	Snapdragon 821	4K	Oculus GO (Mi VR Standalone)
	Snapdragon 835	4K	VIVE FOCUS PLUS, Oculus Quest, and Pico G2 4K
	Snapdragon XR1	4K	Deepoon P1 PRO and 3Glasses X1
	Snapdragon 855	8K	Smartphone VR headset
	Snapdragon XR2	8K	Not applied on standalone VR headsets
Samsung	Exynos 7420	4K	Deepoon M2 PRO
	Exynos 8895	8K	Skyworth VR S8000 and V901
Allwinner Technology	VR9	6K	Deepoon P1

Data source: public data.

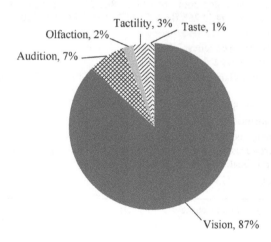

Figure 5.9 Five senses.

FoV indicates the display extent that can be seen and is represented as either a vertical or horizontal angle. px indicates the number of pixels within this angle.

Smartphones and TVs are the most popular flat display devices. In most cases, the distance between a smartphone screen and our eyes is about 30 cm, and the distance between a TV screen and our eyes is about 2.5 m. Table 5.5 lists relevant data for two typical display devices.

Most mainstream 6-inch and 2.5K smartphones can reach a PPD of 102, and 55-inch 4K TVs can reach a PPD of 148, meeting the PPD requirement for VR terminals and surpassing the limit our eyes can perceive.

Table 5.5 Typical FoV for mobile phones and TVs

Terminal type	Typical size (1 inch=2.54 cm)	Watching distance (m)	Horizontal FoV	Typical resolution	Horizontal PPD
Smartphone	6 inch	0.3	25°	2.5K (2,560×1,440)	102
TV	55 inch	2.5	27.5°	4K (3,840×2,160)	148

The principles behind VR are very different. It provides users with a new immersive 3D experience that flat displays cannot provide.

There are two core components for visual output in VR: the lens and the VR display. A convex lens gives depth to the image, which is usually placed before the focal point of the lens. The image must not be placed on the focal point of the lens; otherwise no image will be generated. If the object is placed after the focal point, the object is displayed as a normal image. When the image is placed past the focal point, but less than 2×focal lengths away, the image is displayed upside-down and enlarged. A VR display works much like a magnifying glass. We see a magnified version of the virtual environment on the display (Figure 5.10).

With this display in mind, VR imposes higher requirements on the screen refresh rate, latency, FoV, and resolution.

If the screen refresh rate is too low and the latency is too high, users will feel dizzy. Entry-level VR requires a screen refresh rate greater than 60 Hz and a response latency less than 5 ms. The refresh rates of most VR headsets range from 90 to 120 Hz, and their latency is within 3 ms.

Since VR offers an immersive experience, FoV is a key factor. The normal FoV of human eyes is about 110°. If the FoV of a VR headset is less than that, black edges will appear around the image and severely affect the visual experience. FoV currently has little impact on the VR experience as most VR headsets now have an FoV of 100° or more, and some can even reach 200°.

The most prominent issue facing VR today is definition. A low definition will cause a screen-door effect, and individual pixels will be visible. There are two main reasons for unclear VR images.

- VR content needs to be evenly distributed in a 360° space, but our eyes can only see images within a restricted FoV which can make it look like part of the image is missing.
- The full FoV may be covered by the VR image, but the pixels allocated for every 1° of FoV (PPD) are smaller than those of commonly displayed images.

The VR headset screen comes in a compact form factor. To achieve such a high resolution on small screens poses high technical requirements. The screen resolution of current VR terminals can reach 3K–4K and at most 8K. However, the visual experience is equivalent to standard definition TV.

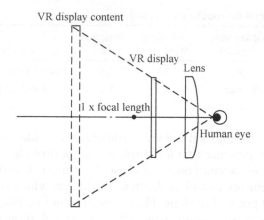

Figure 5.10 VR display principle.

Table 5.6 Equivalent comparison between VR images and traditional TV images under different resolutions

Binocular resolution of VR display screens	PPD	VR resolution	Equivalent TV experience resolution
2K (2,160×1,200)	10	4K	240P
4K (3,840×2,160)	21	8K	480P
8K (7,680×3,840)	32	12K	720p
16K (15,360×7,680)	64	24K	4K

Table 5.6 lists the equivalent comparison between VR content and traditional TV images under different resolutions.

As shown in the preceding table, the PPD of screens with 8K content and 4K resolution is only 21. However, our eyes can still see individual pixels up until 60 PPD. 24K displays with 24K content and 16K resolution are the development goal of VR. This would give a visual experience equivalent to the effect of traditional 4K TV images.

5.2.2.2 Display materials

The current mainstream PC VR headsets and standalone VR headsets use two types of display materials: organic light-emitting diode (OLED) and liquid crystal display (LCD).

1. OLED
   The OLED display uses a very thin organic coating and a glass or plastic substrate. When an electric current passes through, the organic coating emits light, and no backlight material or color filter is required. The advantages of the OLED display are that it does not require

backlight and is thinner, brighter in color, and consumes less power. However, burn-in is common, eye damage is possible, the manufacturing process is relatively immature, and yield is low.

OLED is classified into active matrix OLED (AMOLED) and passive matrix OLED (PMOLED) based on the driving mode. AMOLED features high efficiency and low power consumption and can easily implement high brightness, high resolution, and a high color range. In addition, it is easier to improve integration and decrease the size of components in AMOLED displays, making them more common in smartphones and also preferable in the display of VR headsets.

2. LCD
   LCD displays consist of two parallel glass plates with materials such as the liquid crystal layer, polarizer, and color filter layer filled in between. It requires a backlight as it does not emit any light. After years of development, LCD technology is mature, and their prices are relatively cheap. As long as they are in good condition, no obvious color cast will appear, even after years of use. They do, however, consume a lot of power.

OLED displays have long been considered more suitable for displays placed close to the eyes due to advantages such as low persistence, low power consumption, and rich colors. Most high-end PC VR terminals such as HTC VIVE and Oculus Rift use AMOLED displays. Standalone VR headsets usually use LCD displays due to factors such as cost and weak local processing.

As of 2019, most of the AMOLED screens used for VR terminals are provided by Samsung. In addition, OLED screens have been in short supply because of their low yield. The cost of OLED screens remains high, and LCD displays are developing much faster than expected. It is easier to increase the pixel density on LCD displays, and LCD displays have lower prices, so the market share for LCD displays in VR terminals has been growing.

French market research institute Yole Développement estimated that LCD displays would occupy an increasing market share in the VR terminal market, and OLED displays would continue to be used in high-end VR terminals. Figure 5.11 shows the prediction of the penetration rate of display materials in the VR market. It was estimated that the penetration rate of LCD displays in VR terminals was to reach 71% by 2023. Table 5.7 lists the VR terminal display parameters released by mainstream vendors in 2019.

5.2.3 Perception and interaction

VR terminal perception and interaction improve a user's immersion in the virtual world through sensory channels, such as location tracking, immersive sound fields, gesture interaction, eyeball tracking, tactile feedback, and olfactory feedback.

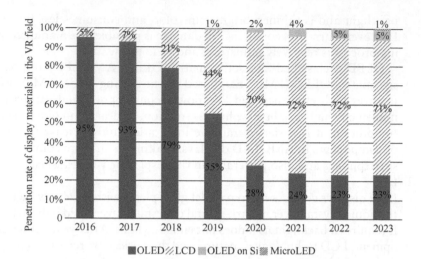

Figure 5.11 Penetration rate prediction of display materials in the VR market (data source: Yole Développement).

Table 5.7 VR terminal display specifications released by mainstream vendors in 2019

Vendor	Model	Form	Display Materials	Resolution	FoV	Refresh Rate
HTC	Vive Cosmos	PC VR	LCD	2880×1700	110°	90 Hz
	Vive Focus Plus	Standalone VR headset	OLED	2880×1600	110°	75 Hz
Oculus	Rift S	PC VR	LCD	2560×1440	Slightly greater than 110°	80 Hz
	Quest	Standalone VR headset	OLED	3200×1440	Approx. 100°	72 Hz
Deepoon	P1 Pro 4K	Standalone VR headset	LCD	3840×2160	100°	90 Hz
Valve	Valve Index	PC VR	LCD	2880×1600	135°	120 Hz
PICO	Pico G2 4K	Standalone VR headset	LCD	3840×2160	101°	75 Hz
3Glasses	3Glasses X1	Split VR headset	LCD	2400×1200	105°	Unknown
Skyworth VR	V901	Standalone VR headset	LCD	3840×2160	105°	75 Hz
iQIYI	Qiyu2S	Standalone VR headset	LCD	3840×2160	101°	72 Hz
Huawei	VR Glass	Split VR headset	LCD	3200×1600	90°	70 Hz (smartphone) 90 Hz (computer)

5.2.3.1 Location tracking

Location tracking is an important way for users to transfer information to virtual environments through VR terminals. The industry invested in this technology early and it is now mature and common in VR.

There are two mainstream VR location tracking solutions.

- Outside-in: An external tracking device, such as a camera or light tower, marks a VR terminal worn by a user (including a headset or an auxiliary device) to track the VR terminal.
- Inside-out: The VR terminal detects the change of the external environment and calculates the user's motion and position in reverse.

Optical and laser-based outside-in location tracking technology was applied to products and widely used in offline experience stores in 2017. From 2018 to 2019, VR terminal vendors such as Pico, HTC, and Oculus released next-generation standalone VR terminals with inside-out location tracking, starting a gradual replacement of outside-in technology as the mainstream technology for VR location tracking. VR terminals with inside-out 6DoF head interaction and 6DoF handle interaction have become the dominant trend in the development of VR location tracking. Table 5.8 compares the location tracking technologies used by such VR terminals in 2019. Regardless of which location tracking technology is used, the standard inertial measurement unit (IMU) is used for basic auxiliary positioning to determine the movement location and angle.

5.2.3.2 Gesture recognition

Hand-held controllers are the mainstream method for VR interaction, and this includes both 3DoF and 6DoF interaction. While these peripherals offer an exciting level of interactivity, the ability to use our actual hands for interaction (such as drawing, writing, and capturing) without external devices could further enhance the immersive experience of the VR environment.

The company Leap Motion secured an early start in this field, using computer vision technology to design a gesture recognition sensor. The sensor has two built-in infrared cameras, which can capture palm motions in the real world from different angles, generate palm motion information, and transmit this data to applications. The sensor can be installed on a VR terminal as an accessory to provide gesture recognition for the cloud VR terminal.

More and more VR terminal vendors are trying to add gesture recognition to controllers. For example, two cloud VR terminals released in 2019, Oculus Rift S and Valve Index, have gesture sensing functions to sense the bending of fingers and the holding of objects, adding more refined interaction to their controllers.

Table 5.8 Comparison of mainstream location tracking technologies used by current VR products

Vendor	Model	Form	Released in	Head tracking solution	Handle tracking solution	Overall assessment
HTC	VIVE	PCVR	2016	Outside-in	Laser positioning	High positioning precision, low latency, large positioning space, poor stability and durability due to mechanical scanning, and complex operations because of external positioning devices.
	VIVE Pro	PCVR	2018	Outside-in	Laser positioning	Larger positioning space compared with the VIVE.
	VIVE Focus Plus	Standalone VR headset	2019	Inside-out	Ultrasonic	High degree of freedom, no need for external devices, slightly delayed positioning, and drift after a period of use.
HTC	VIVE Cosmos	PCVR	2019	Inside-out	Computer vision+ active visible light	High degree of freedom, no need for external devices, poor positioning precision, poor anti-interference, and highly reliant on ambient light.
Valve	Index	PCVR	2019	Outside-in	Laser positioning	High positioning precision, low latency, and large positioning space require external positioning devices and involve complex operations.
Sony	PSVR	PCVR	2016	Outside-in	Computer vision+ active visible light	Small positioning space, poor positioning precision, poor anti-interference performance, highly reliant on ambient light.
Oculus	Rift CV1	PCVR	2016	Outside-in	Infrared positioning	High positioning precision and low latency but a small positioning space.
	Rift S	PCVR	2019	Inside-out	Computer vision	High positioning precision and low latency.
	Quest	Standalone VR headset	2019	Inside-out	Computer vision	High positioning precision and low latency.

(Continued)

Table 5.8 (Continued) Comparison of mainstream location tracking technologies used by current VR products

Vendor	Model	Form	Released in	Head tracking solution	Handle tracking solution	Overall assessment
Microsoft	Windows MR headsets of Lenovo, Dell, and Samsung	PCVR	2017	Inside-out	Computer vision + active visible light	High DoF, no need for external devices, poor positioning precision, poor anti-interference, and highly reliant on ambient light.
Pico	NEO	Standalone VR headset	2017	Inside-out	Ultrasonic	High degree of freedom, no need for external devices, low power consumption, and obvious latency and drift in positioning.
	NEO2	Standalone VR headset	2020	Inside-out	Computer vision + electromagnetic	High degree of freedom, no need for external devices, and improved positioning latency and precision compared with first-generation products.
Nolo	Nolo CV1	Positioning accessory	2018	Outside-in	Ultrasonic + laser + radio positioning	Works flexibly with multiple VR terminals that have 6DoF head interaction and 3DoF hand interaction. Positioning has latency and drift. The positioning space is 180° in front of a user, and dead zones appear when the user turns around.

5.2.3.3 *Voice interaction*

A large number of images, text, and functions on the user interface (UI) are a problem for TVs and smartphones and also cause issues for users. The same is true for users accessing a VR application platform. Voice instructions can feel more natural and convenient, and they work in any direction.

Speech recognition is not a new technology. Many VR terminals already support this function, such as the Deepoon P1 Pro VR and the iQIYI VR iQUT.

5.2.3.4 *Eye tracking*

Eye tracking tries to model and simulate eye motions by sensing eye movement. Eye tracking technology was first used in medicine and has since been applied commercially on PCs and smartphones. With the development of the VR industry, eye tracking technology can also bring more natural and comfortable interaction to VR applications. Therefore, the technology is highly relevant to VR.

Eye tracking technology has a high entry bar. Few companies are researching this technology, but its application in the VR field has attracted much attention. FOVE in Japan is the first VR headset to integrate eye tracking technology. Other vendors include SMI in Germany, Tobbi in Sweden, and 7Invensun and Shanghai Qingtech in China.

Figure 5.12 shows a 7Invensun product that combines Droolon F1 (an eye tracking accessory) and VIVE Cosmos (VR terminal). The product captures user eye data in real time, including eye direction, pupils, and eyelids, and provides the data to VR hardware vendors or VR content developers.

Eye tracking technology not only introduces more natural interactions without the need for controllers, but can also be used for foveated rendering to render display images where the user is looking in high definition and render peripheral images in lower resolution. Foveated rendering can reduce pressure on the GPU and reduce rendering latency. The resulting frame rate increase could also reduce dizziness. This technology can be used in the cloud VR solution to reduce the pressure on cloud rendering and transmission bandwidth.

Figure 5.12 Application of eye tracking accessories to VR terminals (7Invensun).

5.2.3.5 Immersive sound field

Hearing is an important sense second only to our vision and plays an increasingly important role in VR immersion. Dummy head recording (DHR) can truly simulate the human ear's response to sound localization and frequency. This technology produces three-dimensional data with fixed content and direction. Users often have to move their head when experiencing VR content, and the sound source should change to match. This provides better stereo immersion. A head-related transfer function (HRTF) is required to ensure visual and auditory consistency, so as to implement a realistic sound direction and distance effect, and simulate sound atmospheres and phenomenon, including reflection, blocking, isolation, and reverberation. Dolby Laboratories, Facebook, and Google have all built immersive VR experiences that meet these auditory and acoustic requirements.

HRTF uses a simulated head or real-time model, powerful computing software, and a headset equipped with a location tracking device to establish a sound data model, so that users can experience vivid sound when moving their heads. Figure 5.13 shows the schematic workflow of the HRTF when a user experiences a VR application. When the user's head moves, the HRTF calculates the sound source to provide the user with sound at the corresponding angle.

HRTF differs from individual physiological and anatomical structure. Different auricle shapes and interaural level difference (ILD) introduce

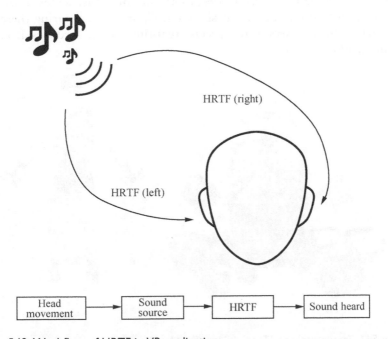

Figure 5.13 Workflow of HRTF in VR applications.

different HRTF data. Therefore, the Swedish audio giant Dirac released the Dynamic 3D Audio solution for AR/VR to optimize HRTF.

Sound output devices for VR terminals include mainly speakers and headsets. For users who want an immersive VR experience, it is better to use headsets that isolate external noise. Most users do not have such high requirements and consider it unnecessary to wear a headset while also wearing a VR headset. This makes it necessary for VR terminals to include speakers. Appropriately designed speakers can deliver a satisfying 3D audio experience to users. For example, the P1 panoramic sound IMAX VR headset released by Deepoon in August 2018 is equipped with two external panoramic sound speakers on both sides of the VR headset, close to the front edge of users' ears. These give users immersive sound even in noisy environments.

5.2.3.6 Tactile feedback

The industry recognizes that tactile feedback can improve VR immersion. Initial tactile feedback for VR requires the cooperation of VR controllers, and all mainstream VR terminal vendors (Oculus, Sony, and HTC) use controllers with vibration feedback. With these, they can provide vibration as feedback to actions (such as shooting) in strong-interaction VR games.

Other applications of tactile feedback include tactile gloves and vests. For example, the tactile package TactSuit launched by bHaptics, a Korean tactile feedback research and development company, contains wearable devices such as vests, masks, gloves, footwear, and wrist wraps, providing 70 vibration feedback points, as shown in Figure 5.14. Wearing these tactile devices allows users to feel precise real-time tactile feedback from the virtual world.

Figure 5.14 Tactile package "TactSuit" launched by bHaptics.

5.2.3.7 Olfactory feedback

In addition to visual, auditory, and tactile feedback, olfactory feedback is applied to enhance user experience though smell. One example is the Splayer XVR launched by Hangzhou Smell Kingdom Technology Co., Ltd. in China. The player is an external digital olfactory device designed and manufactured for existing VR devices that lack olfactory feedback. The device primarily consists of gas power, precision control, and power supply components, an indicator, a material box mechanism, and a wing locking mechanism. It can precisely deliver smells as instructed via Bluetooth and is installed at the bottom of a VR terminal as an external device (see Figure 5.15).

Smell Kingdom used the VR smell player to perform fire drills as early as 2017. Users were able to smell smoke, burning plastic, and kerosene in simulated environments, creating a more realistic scenario for the fire drill. The device is shown in Figure 5.16.

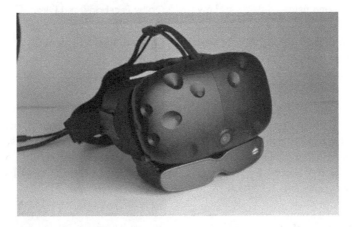

Figure 5.15 Smell player (Smell Kingdom).

Figure 5.16 Fire drill using a smell player.

Table 5.9 Perception and interaction technologies

Category	Subcategory	Maturity	Typical vendor
Head location tracking	Outside-in	High	Valve, HTC, and Oculus
	Inside-out	High	HTC, Oculus, and Pico
Hand location tracking	Laser	High	Valve and HTC
	Infrared light	High	Oculus
	Visible light	Medium	Sony
	Ultrasonic	Medium	Japan TDK (acquired Chirp Microsystems, whose technology is used by both HTC and Pico)
	Computer vision	High	Microsoft and Oculus
Gesture recognition		Medium	Leapmotion and uSens
Voice interaction		High	iFLYTEK and Unisound
Eye tracking		Medium	Tobbi, SMI, Qixin, and 7Invensun
Immersive sound field		Low	Dolby, Facebook, and Dirac
Tactile feedback		Medium	Oculus, VRgluv, and bHaptics
Olfactory feedback		Low	FeelReal, Smell Kingdom
Brainwave interaction		Low	Neurable

Our pursuit of immersive VR is never-ending and is developing toward interaction with more senses. In addition to the mainstream perception and interaction technologies just mentioned, many vendors are researching technologies involving walking and brainwave interaction. Table 5.9 summarizes the maturity of perceptual interaction technologies and lists some of their vendors.

5.2.4 Network transmission

Cloud VR content is transmitted to terminals as video streams for display, placing high requirements on the access network bandwidth.

PC VR connects to the cloud VR service platform through a wired home network. The performance of gigabit Ethernet can meet the service requirements of cloud VR.

Standalone VR headsets, split VR headsets, and smartphone VR headsets require wireless network transmission. There are two solutions for using these devices: 5G wireless technology and high-performance indoor Wi-Fi.

5.2.4.1 5G wireless technology

Cloud VR places high requirements on network bandwidth and latency, which current 4G networks cannot meet. With its higher bandwidth and lower latency (as shown in Table 5.10), 5G technology is indispensable to the development of the VR industry. The advent of the new 5G era has

Table 5.10 Performance comparison between 5G and 4G

Item	Theoretical peak download rate (Gbit/s^{-1})	Single-user experience rate (Mbit/s^{-1})	Round-trip latency (ms)	Connections per square kilometer	Area traffic density (Mbit/s^{-1} m^{-2})
4G	1	10	10	100,000	0.1
5G	10	100	1	1,000,000	10

raised expectations for the convergence of 5G and VR, resulting in mass use of VR.

The commercial use of 5G networks will promote the wide use of 5G smartphones. For example, the three major operators in South Korea started to provision 5G services to the public in April 2019. Many smartphone vendors in China have already launched 5G smartphones, and it is foreseeable that 5G smartphones will grow in popularity in the near future. Users can experience cloud VR through VR headsets and 5G smartphones from anywhere at any time.

5.2.4.2 High-performance indoor Wi-Fi

With fiber to the home (FTTH), cloud VR terminals can be connected through Wi-Fi. VR terminals and APs have supported 802.11ac in the 6 GHz band since 2019 to carry cloud VR services in the fair-experience phase.

Wi-Fi technologies are experiencing upgrades. In October 2018, the Wi-Fi Alliance released Wi-Fi 6, which is based on the 802.11ax standard. Compared with the 802.11ac standard, Wi-Fi 6 has a higher transmission rate and reduced latency and leverages MU-MIMO and OFDMA technologies, enabling optimal concurrent services for multiple devices. However, no VR terminal supported Wi-Fi 6 until 2019. Furthermore, few wireless routers support Wi-Fi 6. VR terminals that support Wi-Fi 6 are expected to enter the market in 2020.

5.2.4.3 Summary

5G makes it possible for massive VR consumption, particularly among mobile users, whereas high-performance indoor Wi-Fi will be preferred by home cloud VR users.

5.2.5 Head motion rendering

As described in Section 2.4.3, the required MTP (motion to photon) latency cannot be achieved if cloud VR rendering and terminal refreshing are performed sequentially. Therefore, a more viable solution is for both the cloud and the terminals to carry out asynchronous processing. (Section 2.4.3

explains the process of terminal–cloud asynchronous rendering.) This section focuses on the head motion rendering technologies of cloud VR terminals in the terminal–cloud asynchronous rendering process, including asynchronous time warp (ATW), asynchronous space warp (ASW), and reprojection.

5.2.5.1 ATW

ATW technology was first used by Oculus in Gear VR headsets. This technology transforms VR image content based on a user's head movement to reduce the MTP latency.

1. What is TW?
   TW is short for time warp. Time warp corrects an image frame that is rendered before the user moves their head. It obtains an accurate image frame for the current head position, thereby reducing perceived latency. TW can also be applied in VR to increase the frame rate.
2. What is ATW?
   ATW completes TW on another thread that is in parallel with rendering. Before each vertical synchronization (V-Sync), the ATW thread performs TW based on the latest rendered image frame to generate a new image for display.
3. Why ATW is used?
   To display accurate images, VR terminals need to promptly refresh the displayed images within each vertical synchronization period. However, if the rendering period is too long, frame loss may occur. In this case, users can become disoriented as multiple images can appear simultaneously. Moreover, if the user moves their head during this period, the images may appear displaced. This can worsen if the frame rate and refresh rate are low or the user moves their head too fast.

   ATW technology can resolve this issue. If the render thread does not render a new image within a vertical synchronization period, the TW thread interrupts the render thread and twists the previously rendered image. Although the image frame may not be completely accurate, the TW thread adjusts the image based on head movement to eliminate image distortion. In cloud VR, the rendering is migrated to the cloud. As a result, cloud VR terminals only need to perform ATW processing based on the images rendered on the cloud.

   Figure 5.17 shows the process of ATW in terminal–cloud asynchronous rendering. For further details about ATW, visit Oculus' official blog. In cloud VR, rendering is performed on the cloud instead of by a GPU. The cloud rendering system renders the images (L1 and R1) of the left and right eyes and pushes them to the cloud VR terminal. The terminal inserts an ATW process before displaying the images. The images that are rendered within the first V-Sync period can be directly

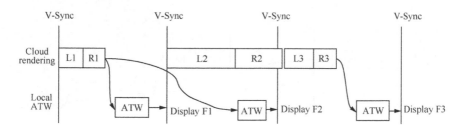

Figure 5.17 ATW process in terminal–cloud asynchronous rendering.

displayed. However, the images within the second V-Sync period are not rendered in time, meaning no processing is performed and thus the images cannot be transmitted to the terminals in time, causing image distortion. The ATW of the terminals can predict and display the next image frame based on both the previous frame and head movement to ensure that images remain smooth.

5.2.5.2 ASW

ATW technology is not perfect. It only considers head movement, not head tilt, and therefore it is most suitable for 3DoF VR. Additionally, when an image has moving objects, ATW may not function properly because it is limited to warping a rendered image without considering the positioning or movement of an object within an image. The object will remain in its original position even after the image has been warped, resulting in distortion when it is updated. For this reason, Oculus improved ATW technology and consequently launched the advanced ASW.

The ASW predetermines a moving object by using two generated image frames and generates a new frame based on the previous frame. By inserting the frames computed by the ASW into every two original frames, a 45 FPS application can be displayed at a rate of 90 FPS.

Similarly, as shown in Figure 5.18, the ASW rendering is also performed on the cloud in cloud VR. In the second and fourth V-Sync periods shown in the figure, the displayed frames are derived from two consecutive frames rendered in the cloud based on the predicted movement of the object and depth information.

ASW does not replace ATW but rather acts as backup. For example, if a head tilt motion occurs or frames are continuously lost, the ATW and ASW complement each other and cover all visual motions, including head movement, head tilt, object movement, and depth information, ensuring smooth image display.

According to Oculus' official blog, ASW's frame prediction and computing are not perfect for some images, which may cause disorientation among users. The following are typical examples:

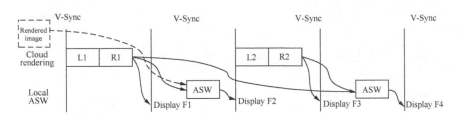

Figure 5.18 ASW process in terminal–cloud asynchronous rendering.

- Quick lighting changes. In scenes that feature frequent light flashing, light movement, and fade-in and fade-out, the ASW struggles to track fast changes in lighting. As a result, images may become distorted.
- Block removal. After the object in an image moves, another image is required to fill in the area blocked by the object. However, the ASW is unable to distinguish which content needs to be filled. In this case, the subsequent image is enlarged to fill in the area, ghosting the image.
- Fast object movement. A typical example is when an object quickly moves along an iron gate, the ASW struggles to determine the movement direction of the object.
- Difficulty in tracking a quick head-locking element. Some applications use head-locking elements, such as menus and video images. If the applications attempt to process these elements by themselves without leveraging the locking layer provided by the Oculus SDK, image jitter may occur when the locked elements move too fast.

5.2.5.3 Reprojection

In addition to the ATW and ASW technologies launched by Oculus, platforms such as Valve, Steam, and PS VR also adopt the following two technologies:

- Interleaved reprojection: When the rendering capability is only 45 FPS, the application can run at half framerate and reproject every other frame, giving the impression of 90 FPS movement. The disadvantage is that movement and animation may cause ghosting.
- Asynchronous reprojection: Similar to asynchronous time warping, asynchronous reprojection is based on the previous image and sensor data, eliminating ghosting and resulting in smoother images.

Oculus' ATW and ASW technologies are widely used in mainstream standalone VR headsets. Unfortunately, regardless of which technology is applied, achieving perfect images in all situations is a difficult feat. Through further innovation, VR terminals will provide a smoother VR experience.

5.3 INTERCONNECTION BETWEEN CLOUD VR TERMINALS AND THE CLOUD PLATFORM

5.3.1 Cloud platform interconnection requirements

In addition to the native functions of VR terminals, such as location tracking, motion capture, video stream decoding, and image refreshing, cloud VR terminals need to connect to the cloud platform and the underlying hardware. Figure 5.19 shows the interconnection between cloud VR terminals and the cloud platform, assuming that the management systems for weak-interaction and strong-interaction cloud VR services are integrated.

After a user logs in to a cloud VR terminal, they must enter the service management system for authentication. If authentication is successful, the platform delivers VR services to the cloud VR terminal.

Moreover, the cloud VR terminal needs to connect to modules in the service management system, such as the system upgrade module and casting service module to support online system upgrade and casting.

To summarize, in order to connect to the cloud platform, cloud VR terminals may need function adaptation, authentication, application integration, system upgrade, and casting, as described in Table 5.11.

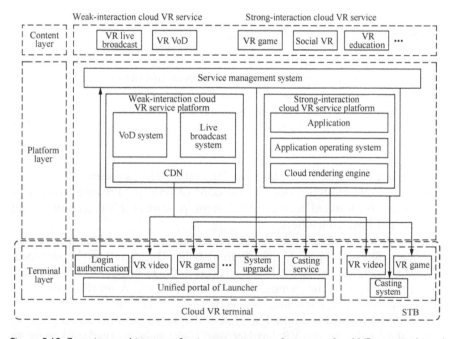

Figure 5.19 Function architecture for interconnection between cloud VR terminals and the cloud platform.

Table 5.11 Requirements for cloud VR terminal function adaptation

Function category	Sub-category	Function description
System function customization	System function customization	Customize functions based on user requirements on terminal systems
Access entry customization	Home screen customization	Customize home screen UIs based on user requirements
Login authentication	Guest access	Allow users to access limited content without login
	Authorized login	Allow authorized users to access limited content
		Bind with the STB to use the casting function
	User center	Manage user login operations and login status
Cloud VR application integration	VR application integration	Integrate cloud VR applications
Casting service	Casting information transfer	Connect to the casting module of the service management system to transmit casting information
System upgrade	System upgrade	Connect to the upgrade module of the service management system to implement online upgrade

5.3.2 System function customization

A cloud VR platform requires some control over connected terminals in order to, for example, restrict accessible content and the installation of apps from other sources, prevent malicious system tampering, and implement customized startup processes, as shown in Table 5.12.

Figure 5.20 shows the typical startup process of a customized cloud VR terminal.

- Bootsplash: The bootsplash can be customized as required.
- Controller configuration/button control prompt: Provides controller configuration and head control button prompts for VR terminals that do not have controllers.
- Network connection check: If the terminal is connected to the network, this step is skipped. If the terminal is not connected to the network, the terminal displays a list of available Wi-Fi hotspots or a message indicating that the terminal is not connected yet. After the connection is successful, the terminal proceeds to the next step.
- Safety protocol prompt: The system displays warnings about possible safety risks during VR headset use. Users need to read and agree to the information before accessing the home screen.

Table 5.12 Management and control of cloud VR terminals

Function module	Function requirement
Application center	Prohibit users from installing external applications
File management	Allow users to browse images and videos locally but prohibit them from using app installation files
Factory setting	Allow users to roll back to the factory version of customized cloud VR terminals
Notification of network faults	Display customized messages when network faults occur
Cache clearing	Allow users to clear the cache to ensure smooth running of VR terminals
Startup process	Customize the startup process and related messages based on user requirements

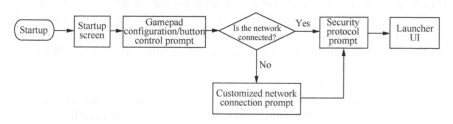

Figure 5.20 Typical startup process of a customized cloud VR terminal.

5.3.3 Login authentication

Login authentication prevents unauthorized access and protects platform content.

If a cloud VR platform is operated by a telecom operator, users can use existing broadband accounts so that operators can manage multiple services, such as mobile video, IPTV, and cloud VR, in a unified manner.

On current VR terminals, users need to enter accounts or passwords by using a controller that is supplied with the VR headset. If no controller is provided, users need to move their head to input text, which is complex and troublesome. To resolve this problem, a unified account (such as an existing mobile number) can be used for login. For example, a mobile app that uses a unified account can be used to perform authorized login, or a verification code can be sent to a user's phone to complete login. The user can view their login status by visiting settings on the cloud VR terminal. After the authentication succeeds, users can access authorized content.

5.3.4 UI customization

The UI of cloud VR terminals can be customized. The home screen will display various VR content, as well as basic settings such as file management, connections, user center and cache clearing. The main page should be user friendly, as follows:

- The UI should be simple and clear.
- The UI background should be visually beautiful and immersive.
- Basic icons, such as battery level and the back button, should comply with standard design and be easy to understand.
- Icons in the virtual environment should be positioned at a suitable and comfortable distance from the user's eyes.
- Customizable design should enable, for example, background and application icons to be customized by users (Figure 5.21).

5.3.5 Application integration

The home screen is loaded after a user accesses the cloud VR platform, and various cloud VR applications are displayed on the home screen. Cloud VR terminals also need to integrate the cloud VR applications. Weak-interaction and strong-interaction cloud VR applications involve different modules.

1. Weak-interaction cloud VR applications

   After a user attempts to open a weak-interaction cloud VR application on a cloud VR terminal, the VR service platform verifies whether a user has access or not. If verification is successful, the platform returns the program list. After the user selects the desired content, the VR service platform allocates the corresponding CDN node based on

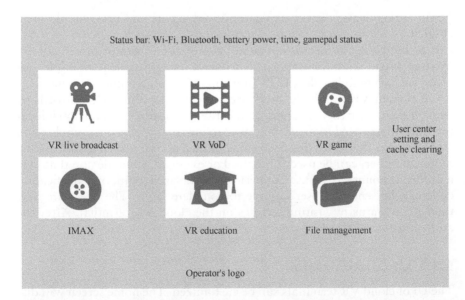

Figure 5.21 Typical UI design diagram of operators' cloud VR terminals.

the user's IP address and region and delivers the video streams to the user's terminal.

2. Strong-interaction cloud VR applications

After a user attempts to open a strong-interaction cloud VR application on a cloud VR terminal, the VR service platform verifies whether a user has access or not. If verification is successful, the platform returns the program list. After the user selects the desired content, the cloud rendering system allocates a VM and starts the application and renders, codes, and pushes application images based on the control information sent by the cloud VR terminal.

5.3.6 Casting

For PC VR, the terminal is connected to the monitor, and content is displayed on both the VR headset and PC monitor. For standalone VR headsets or smartphone VR headsets, the content can be viewed only by their users. To share the content with others, the casting function is needed.

Currently, there are two mainstream casting modes: local casting and cloud casting. In local casting mode, cloud VR terminals directly compress and code the content displayed on headsets and push the content to the TV STB for playback. In cloud casting mode, the cloud casting system synchronizes messages between cloud VR terminals and STBs. The STBs pull streams from CDN or cloud rendering nodes.

5.3.6.1 Local casting

Currently, Digital Living Network Alliance (DLNA) is a typical local casting mode. However, this mode has many restrictions compared with the cloud casting mode.

- Viewing quality is difficult to maintain. Both the content downloaded to the cloud VR terminal and the content cast to the STB is transmitted via Wi-Fi. The Wi-Fi capacity may not be adequate for the doubled traffic, resulting in poor viewing quality.
- The implementation is difficult. Cloud VR terminals and STBs must be on the same LAN. In reality, however, cloud VR and IPTV services are carried on different network planes.
- Higher power consumption halves the battery life of VR terminals due to extra coding and streaming.

Consequently, the cloud casting mode is most suitable for current cloud VR services to ensure a stable viewing experience without changing the existing network.

5.3.6.2 Cloud casting

In the cloud casting mode, a casting system needs to be established on the cloud. This system then searches for user accounts to pair the cloud VR terminal with the STB. This requires neither the direction communication between the cloud VR terminal and STB nor extra Wi-Fi bandwidth. In the cloud casting mode, two copies of traffic need to be transmitted concurrently – one for the cloud VR terminal and another for the STB. Figure 5.22 shows the process of cloud casting.

1. The cloud VR terminal sends a casting request.
2. After receiving the request, the cloud casting system queries the user account, finds the corresponding STB, and sends a casting signal. During the casting process of a weak-interaction cloud VR application, the cloud VR terminal needs to periodically synchronize video playback information (such as playback progress and head movement information) to the STB through the cloud casting system to ensure that the video playback images on the STB are the same as those on the cloud VR terminal.
3. The STB receives the casting signal sent by the cloud casting system.
4. The STB requests resources from the CDN node or cloud rendering node.
5. After receiving the request, the CDN node or cloud rendering node pushes casting streams to the STB.

5.3.6.3 Evolution of casting solutions

The cloud casting mode will place a greater burden on network bandwidth and cloud system performance due to the doubled VR traffic and extra signaling, particularly in the case of high concurrency.

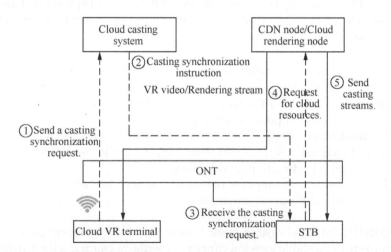

Figure 5.22 Process of cloud casting.

As such, the casting function needs to be implemented by ONTs on home networks to reduce the transmission pressure on clouds and networks (as shown in Figure 5.23).

This does not require extra network or Wi-Fi resources and minimizes latency.

5.3.7 System upgrade

Terminals can be updated through the cloud VR service management system. To reduce pressure on terminals and the cloud, incremental upgrade packages are most suitable (Figure 5.24).

Cloud VR uses powerful cloud computing and rendering capabilities to reduce the hardware requirements on terminals and improve user experience. With quality networks and continuous advancement of key terminal technologies, such as chip decoding, display, perception interaction, wireless network transmission, and head motion rendering, cloud VR will provide users with an optimal experience.

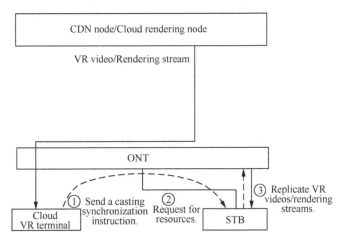

Figure 5.23 Improved casting process.

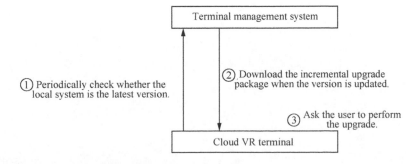

Figure 5.24 Cloud VR terminal upgrade process.

Chapter 6

Research on Cloud VR Service Experience

This chapter delves into the key technical solutions and user requirements for cloud virtual reality (VR). It intends to serve as a reference for standardizing service experience and product performance for an open and thriving industry.

6.1 ANALYSIS AND MODELING

Recently, an in-depth study of the cloud VR industry was conducted, covering over 30,000 users samples[18] obtained through interviews and surveys.

The research applied the Kano model to organize more than 300 pieces of data and summarizes the key requirements of cloud VR users (as shown in Figure 6.1).

The Kano model was originally created in 1984 by Noriaki Kano, a professor at Tokyo University of Science. This model categorizes user requirements as follows:

- Basic: These are requirements that users often take for granted. When these requirements are not met, users will become very dissatisfied. However, when these requirements are met (for example, good image quality and smooth playback and no latency, motion sickness, black edges, or distortion), users are usually unaware of them.
- Expected: These requirements are less demanding than basic requirements. They are expected by users, but not mandatory, and can include casting and sharing and high visual and sound quality.
- Delight: These requirements are also not mandatory, but are unexpected, and improve the VR immersiveness. They may include sensory immersion such as smell and temperature.

The basic and expected requirement categories will form the basis for cloud VR research and performance evaluation. In order to deliver these requirements, the physical network must meet certain standards.

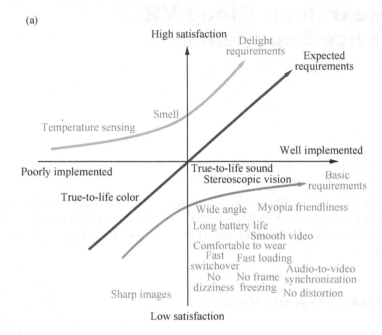

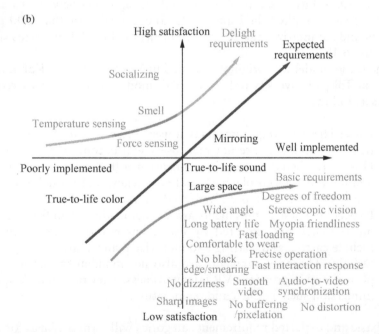

Figure 6.1 Key requirements for cloud VR user experience. (a) Weak interaction (panoramic video) and (b) strong interaction (games and education).

We can classify the requirements for cloud VR user experience into immersive and interactive VR. These two categories can be further divided into four dimensions: content, display, operation, and response quality. Figure 2.2 in Chapter 2 shows the cloud VR user experience requirement model.

- Immersive VR focuses on users' audiovisual experience during VR playback. This may include sensory immersion such as smell, force, and temperature. The level of immersiveness depends on VR headset and network quality.
- Interactive VR refers to the user being physically present in the virtual world. Accurate positioning and fast feedback are required to ensure that the displayed content matches the movement of users.

6.1.1 Definition and breakdown of immersive VR requirements

We can divide the requirements for immersive VR into content and display quality. Content quality includes image definition, smoothness, color fidelity, and stereoscopic effect, while display quality depends on whether audio and visual signals are in sync and whether image distortion, pixelation, or buffering occurs.

6.1.1.1 Definition

Most cloud VR users suffer from low definition displays. The number and quality of pixels determine the image definition within the user's view, which is affected by factors such as content resolution, terminal screen resolution, decoding capability, and field of view (FoV).

- The definition of panoramic videos is mainly confined by low content resolution.
- Low definition of rendered images is caused by low terminal screen resolution.
- Bitrate determines the average number of bits per pixel. Therefore, within a user's visual range, a higher bitrate indicates higher definition.
- When the resolution is insufficient, a wider FoV does not lead to better image quality. A larger FoV means smaller PPD and lower definition, which can lead to the screen-door effect. Table 6.1 lists the standard FoV ranges of cloud VR terminals in each phase.

Most VR videos are panoramic. During playback, a VR terminal first projects all pixels onto the inside of a sphere and then displays content within a user's FoV, as shown in Figure 6.2.

Table 6.1 Mainstream FoV of cloud VR terminals in each phase

Development stage	FoV of mainstream VR terminals
Comfortable-experience phase	100°–110°
Ideal-experience phase	120°
Ultimate-experience phase	≥ 140°

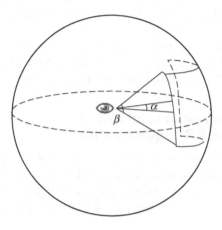

Figure 6.2 Spherical projection of panoramic videos.

In general, panoramic videos have an aspect ratio of 2:1. In standard 4K panoramic videos, the resolution is approximately 3,840×1,920. Suppose that the FoV is 90°, and the resolution of the image displayed on the screen is only 960×960 or 10–11 PPD, this is equivalent to watching a 240P video. 8K resolution places higher requirements on the screen resolution of terminals. For details, see Table 6.2.

6.1.1.2 Smoothness

Smoothness of video and rendering services (for example, gaming) is determined by frame rate. For video services, frame rate is determined by content source. Research shows that 24 FPS is the threshold for smooth videos, and a lower frame rate will affect users. Almost all VR videos can deliver 24 FPS. Unlike animated video images, game images are completely dependent on graphics card (graphics processing unit, GPU) rendering. This means that there are no animated objects in the images. Therefore, to deliver the same level of smoothness as videos, games require a higher rendering frame rate. Moreover, smoothness is related to the terminal screen's refresh rate. Refresh rate refers to the number of times a terminal can draw a new image on its screen from the GUP in one second. Figure 6.3 shows images at different frame rates.

Table 6.2 Requirements on the screen resolution of VR terminals

VR full-view video definition	VR single-eye definition	Equivalent TV definition
4K	1K	240P
8K	2K	480P
16K	4K	960P

Note: 960P indicates 1,280×960.

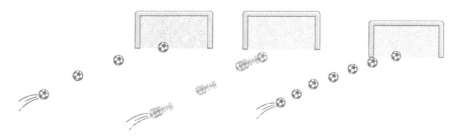

Figure 6.3 Images at different frame rates.

6.1.1.3 Color fidelity

More bits per pixel (BPP) of a color depth leads to a wider variety of colors and shades which results in higher-quality images. However, image definition precedes color fidelity. Improving the color depth without improving definition will have no significant effect. In the comfortable-experience phase of cloud VR, a color depth of 8 BPP for videos can meet user requirements. As definition improves, users may require a color depth of 10 BPP or even 12 BPP.

6.1.1.4 Stereo effect

VR applications often generate virtual three-dimensional (3D) spaces. Generally, stereoscopic vision is produced by the fusion of two slightly different views of a scene on each eye, while stereophonic sound is achieved by controlling the number of microphones during recording and the number of speakers during playback. Figure 6.4 shows the stereo effect.

6.1.1.5 Audio-to-video synchronization

When processing multimedia content, a video player needs to separate video data from audio data to achieve independent decoding and rendering. If the audio is out-of-sync with video, users' experience will be bad. To prevent such an issue, a synchronization mechanism needs to be introduced. Figure 6.5 shows the working principle of a video player.

Figure 6.4 Stereo effect.

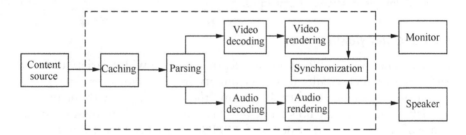

Figure 6.5 Working principle of a video player.

6.1.1.6 Image distortion

There are two monocular FoVs with a viewable area of 200°–220°. The overlap area of two monocular FoVs is known as a binocular FoV, in which a binocular parallax is generated to produce a stereoscopic vision. In most cases, a binocular FoV is 120°, as shown in Figure 6.6.

In order to display realistic and immersive images, most VR headsets expand the FoV through the lenses. However, as no rendering is performed on the image, this will lead to pincushion distortion, as shown in Figure 6.7.

The general fix is to use barrel anti-distortion on the source image to make the view appear normal, as in Figure 6.8.

6.1.1.7 Pixelation/buffering

Video data loss during network transmission is the main cause of pixelation and buffering in cloud VR services.

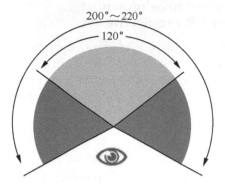

Figure 6.6 FoV of a person.

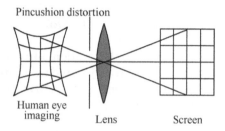

Figure 6.7 Distortion principles of VR images.

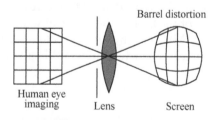

Figure 6.8 Anti-distortion principles of VR images.

Video on demand (VoD) services are usually carried over Transmission Control Protocol (TCP), which is more prone to latency. When the data download rate is slower than the video playback speed (bitrate), buffering occurs.

Multicast video and rendering services are carried over User Datagram Protocol (UDP), which is less prone to latency but more prone to packet loss. Packet loss may cause buffering or pixelation, depending on the mechanisms used by decoders to process frame data loss. If the decoder freezes the image until the next complete I-frame arrives, buffering occurs. If the decoder ignores the lost frame, pixelation occurs.

6.1.2 Definition and breakdown of interactive VR requirements

Interactive VR requirements are divided into operation and response quality. Operation quality refers to degrees of freedom (DoF), accuracy, comfort, battery life, and usability. Response quality concerns issues such as dizziness, lag, loading time, black edges and smearing, user operation response, and image quality switching.

6.1.2.1 DoF

DoF describes the six basic motions of an object. These six motions fall into translations and rotations.

- Translation: A body can translate in 3DoF: forward/back, up/down, and left/right.
- Rotation: A body can also rotate with 3DoF: roll, pitch, and yaw.

Currently, 3DoF terminals support only rotation, offering users 360° views. In contrast, 6DoF terminals support rotation and translation, allowing users to roam free in a virtual environment, particularly in strong-interaction services. Figure 6.9 shows 3DoF and 6DoF.

6.1.2.2 Precision

A virtual world is a simulation of the physical world. Providing accurate mapping and response in the virtual world requires accurate location and movement information of the user in the physical world. Currently, an inertial measurement unit (IMU, which usually includes a gyroscope, accelerometer, and magnetometer) is widely used in VR headsets to track rotations.

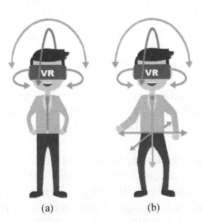

(a)　　　　　(b)

Figure 6.9 DoF. (a) 3DoF and (b) 6DoF.

Table 6.3 Comparison of tracking technologies

Item	Outside-in tracking	Inside-out tracking
Motion capture precision	High	Slightly lower
Processing latency	Relatively low	Relatively high
External sensor	Required	Not required
Movement range	Restricted by sensor coverage	Unlimited
Terminal cost	Reasonable	High
Occlusion	Susceptible	Not susceptible

Other technologies used to measure movements include lasers, infra-red light, ultrasonic sound waves, and positioning technologies based on image recognition (IRB). Some of these spatial positioning technologies require external sensors. Such technologies are referred to as an outside-in tracking, which is mature and highly precise, but can only be used in a fixed area.

There are also inside-out tracking technologies, which do not require any external sensors. The headsets use a built-in time-of-flight (TOF) camera to detect environment change and then use algorithms to calculate its own motion track. This poses higher requirements on terminal processing performance and has a lower positioning accuracy. However, it supports a wider range of activities and is less affected by obstacles. It is therefore suitable for mobile scenarios.

Table 6.3 compares these tracking technologies.

6.1.2.3 Comfort

VR headsets must be comfortable. Therefore, the headset design must consider weight, size, heat dissipation, seal, and breathability.

6.1.2.4 Battery life

The analysis of user habits shows that IMAX and gaming are the most popular service scenarios of cloud VR. An IMAX movie is about 2–3 hours long. The average duration per use in gaming is about 1 hour. The batteries of VR terminals are usually not removable. Therefore, the battery life of headsets, handles, and position trackers is a major usage bottleneck.

6.1.2.5 Usability

To meet the requirements of users with vision problems, most VR devices either allow users to wear glasses within a headset or have a built-in object distance adjustment function, which adjusts the distance between the display and eyes to accommodate up to 600° of nearsightedness with the naked eye.

6.1.2.6 Dizziness

For details, see Section 2.1.2.

6.1.2.7 Lag

The virtual reality system needs to quickly reflect the location and actions of users in the physical world. If processing is too slow, the interaction experience will be poor.

For details, see Chapter 2.

6.1.2.8 Loading time

Loading time refers to the time a cloud VR video or game takes to load. For VR videos, users prefer an initial loading time of less than 3 seconds.

As for VR games, the loading time usually takes between 30 and 60 seconds. Unlike PC VR games that are stored and loaded locally, cloud VR games need to allocate rendering server resources, code and decode videos, and transmit streams. However, the increased latency is mere milliseconds and has little impact on the loading time that is measured in seconds. What requires attention is the increased loading duration in strong-interaction cloud VR services caused by insufficient platform resources in high concurrency.

6.1.2.9 Black edges and smearing

For details, see Section 2.4.3.

6.1.2.10 Operation response time

Based on experience with online first-person shooters, a latency within 100 ms is acceptable. In addition to cloud rendering and streaming, motion capturing and display rendering can affect the operation response time.

6.1.2.11 Image switching

In the tile-wise streaming (TWS) FoV transmission solution, a video source file is divided into multiple tiles, each of which corresponds to a different HD AoV (high-definition angle of view). After the terminal sends head movement information to the cloud, the cloud transmits high-quality tile images, along with low-quality full-view images back to the terminal. The terminal uses the low-quality full-view images first until the high-quality images arrive and then replaces and stitches the two together. If the high-quality images take too long to display (more than 200 ms), users will see the content shift from blurry to clear, which affects the overall experience.

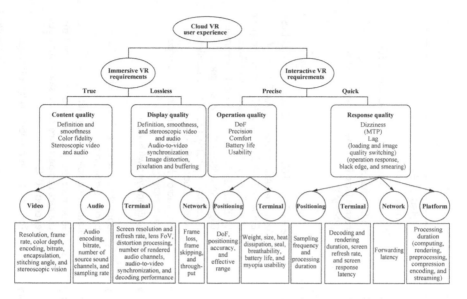

Figure 6.10 Mapping between cloud VR user experience requirements and evaluation items.

6.2 EVALUATION BASELINE

Section 6.1 describes the key requirements of cloud VR user experience. These can be broken down into functional components and modules, as shown in Figure 6.10.

Numerous studies on evaluation methods have been conducted in the VR industry.

Currently, strong-interaction cloud VR services usually adopt asynchronous rendering between the terminal and cloud, whereas cloud VR video services adopt full-view video transmission and FoV video transmission. For details about how these three solutions are implemented, see Chapter 2.

6.2.1 Evaluation items

6.2.1.1 Terminal and cloud asynchronous rendering

Table 6.4 lists the evaluation criteria of this solution.

6.2.1.2 Full-view video transmission

Table 6.5 lists the evaluation criteria of this solution.

6.2.1.3 FoV video transmission

Table 6.6 lists the evaluation criteria of this solution.

Table 6.4 Terminal and cloud asynchronous rendering evaluation criteria

Component	Module	Item	Mandatory/optional	Suggestion
Terminal	Screen	Screen resolution	Mandatory	≥ 1,440×1,600×2
		Screen refresh rate	Mandatory	≥ 90 Hz
		Screen type	Optional	Thin film transistor (TFT)-LCD/OLED
		Screen size	Optional	≥ 3.5 inches×2
	Lens	Lens material	Optional	Fresnel lens, Poly(methyl methacrylate) (PMMA)
		FoV	Mandatory	100°–120°
	Video	Decoding type	Mandatory	H.264
		Decoding performance	Mandatory	≥ 4,096×2,160 at 60 FPS, 100 Mbit/s@H.264
	Audio	Decoding type	Mandatory	Advanced Audio Coding (AAC)/AAC+/ Enhanced AAC Plus (eAAC+), MP3, Adaptive Multi-Rate (AMR)/ Adaptive Multi-Rate Wideband (AMR-WB), Musical Instrument Digital Interface (MIDI), Pulse-code modulation (PCM), OGG, Free Lossless Audio Codec (FLAC)
		Number of rendering channels	Mandatory	Dual audio channels, built-in dual stereo speakers
		Audio-to-video synchronization	Mandatory	Audio in sync with video
	Correction	Distortion correction	Mandatory	Supported. The image has no pincushion or barrel distortion
	Comfort	Headset type	Optional	Standalone/Split VR headset
		Headset heat dissipation	Mandatory	Good heat dissipation performance, and the contact temperature of the skin does not exceed 40°C
		Headset seal	Mandatory	Good seal with no obvious light leakage

(Continued)

Table 6.4 (Continued) Terminal and cloud asynchronous rendering evaluation criteria

Component	Module	Item	Mandatory/optional	Suggestion
		Headset breathability	Mandatory	Good breathability, and normal breathing is not affected
		Headset weight (including battery)	Mandatory	≤ 500 g
	Battery life	Battery capacity	Optional	3,500–4,000 mAh
		Battery life (while watching video)	Mandatory	≥ 2.5 hours
	Usability	Eye comfort mode	Optional	Low blue light certification
		Myopia usability	Mandatory	Allows users to wear glasses, or supports focusing
	Performance	MTP (motion to photon) latency	Mandatory	≤ 20 ms
		Terminal decoding latency	Mandatory	≤ 15 ms
		Motion rendering latency	Mandatory	≤ 5.5 ms
		Screen refresh latency	Mandatory	≤ 11 ms (90 FPS)
		Screen response latency	Mandatory	≤ 5 ms
	Communication	Wi-Fi	Mandatory	Supports 2×2 MIMO and 802.11ac@5 GHz.
	System	System	Optional	Android
		Version	Optional	7.1–8.1
	Hardware	CPU	Optional	Qualcomm 835/Samsung Exynos 8895
		Memory	Optional	4G RAM, LPDDR4X, 1866M
		Storage	Optional	64 GB UFS2.1, supporting 256 GB microSD card

(Continued)

Table 6.4 (Continued) Terminal and cloud asynchronous rendering evaluation criteria

Component	Module	Item	Mandatory/optional	Suggestion
Positioning suite	Positioning	DoF (headset)	Mandatory	6DoF
		DoF (handle)	Mandatory	6DoF
		Positioning (headset)	Optional	Ultrasonic/laser/infrared combined positioning
		Positioning (handle)	Optional	Ultrasonic/laser/infrared combined positioning
		Positioning precision (headset)	Mandatory	≤ 2 mm
		Positioning precision (handle)	Mandatory	≤ 2 mm
		Position sampling frequency (headset)	Mandatory	≥ 120 Hz
		Position sampling frequency (handle)	Mandatory	≥ 120 Hz
		Pose sampling mode (headset)	Optional	6-axis/9-axis pose sensor
		Pose sampling mode (handle)	Optional	6-axis/9-axis pose sensor
		Pose sampling precision (headset)	Mandatory	0.0001
		Pose sampling precision (handle)	Mandatory	0.0001
		Pose sampling frequency (headset)	Mandatory	≥ 400 Hz
		Pose sampling frequency (handle)	Mandatory	≥ 100 Hz
		Range	Mandatory	FoV 100°, 5 m radius

(Continued)

Table 6.4 (Continued) Terminal and cloud asynchronous rendering evaluation criteria

Component	Module	Item	Mandatory/optional	Suggestion
Signal processing		Handle connection mode	Optional	2.4 GHz Wi-Fi/Bluetooth
		Signal transmission latency (handle)	Mandatory	≤ 3 ms
		Signal processing latency	Mandatory	≤ 2 ms
	Battery life	Capacity (base station)	Optional	1,800 mAh
		Capacity (handle)	Optional	1,000 mAh
		Battery life (base station)	Mandatory	≥ 7 hours
		Battery life (handle)	Mandatory	≥ 2.5 hours
Network	Performance	Packet loss rate	Mandatory	≤ 1 × 10^{-6}
		Forwarding latency	Mandatory	≤ 20 ms
		Transmission bandwidth	Mandatory	≥ 80 Mbit/s
Platform	Video coding	Resolution	Mandatory	≥ 1,440 × 1,600 × 2
		Bitrate	Mandatory	≥ 40 Mbit/s
		Frame rate	Mandatory	≥ 50 FPS
		Coding format	Mandatory	H.264
		Color depth	Mandatory	≥ 8 bits
		FoV	Mandatory	≥ 100°–120°
		Stereoscopic vision	Mandatory	3D
	Audio coding	Bitrate	Optional	128 kbit/s
		Coding format	Optional	AAC
		Number of source audio channels	Optional	Dual audio channels
		Sampling rate	Optional	48 kHz

(Continued)

Table 6.4 (Continued) Terminal and cloud asynchronous rendering evaluation criteria

Component	Module	Item	Mandatory/optional	Suggestion
	Performance	Platform processing latency	Mandatory	≤ 30 ms
		Computing & rendering latency	Optional	≤ 11 ms
		Preprocessing latency	Optional	≤ 2 ms
		Compression coding latency	Optional	≤ 15 ms
		Streaming latency	Optional	≤ 2 ms
	Function	User and system resource scheduling	Mandatory	System resources can be locked and released
		Service program release and management	Mandatory	The go-live/go-offline and typesetting of application content can be controlled
		Rendering coding parameter adjustment	Mandatory	Parameters such as coding compression can be dynamically set and adjusted
		System reliability protection	Mandatory	The application server supports link protection, and the database supports two-node cluster backup
		User status monitoring	Mandatory	User online duration, resource consumption, and user experience can be viewed
		Platform performance monitoring	Mandatory	There are alarms for resource overload, system programs, or user operations
		Screen display	Mandatory	Screen mirroring through an STB is supported
	Encapsulation	Encapsulation protocol	Optional	TCP/UDP. Firewall traversal is required for UDP

(Continued)

Table 6.4 (Continued) Terminal and cloud asynchronous rendering evaluation criteria

Component	Module	Item	Mandatory/optional	Suggestion
Hardware		CPU	Optional	22 cores, 2.6 GHz or higher
		Memory	Optional	60 GB
		Network adapter	Optional	10G
		Graphics card	Optional	NVIDIA Tesla M60/Tesla V100
		System	Optional	Windows 7/Windows 10
		Virtual platform	Optional	Fusion sphere 6.2/VMware sphere 6.7
Service	Experience	Program loading wait duration	Mandatory	≤ 60 seconds
		MTP latency threshold-crossing	Mandatory	Every time MTP latency exceeds 20 ms, an MTP latency threshold-crossing event is logged
		Black edge threshold-crossing	Mandatory	Every time the black edge exceeds 5°, a black edge threshold-crossing event is logged
		Pixelation	Mandatory	Statistics on lost packets and frame types for each frame during decoding are collected
		Buffering	Mandatory	If the interval between displayed adjacent effective frames exceeds 50 ms, a buffering event is logged

Table 6.5 Evaluation criteria of full-view video transmission

Component	Module	Item	Mandatory/optional	Suggestion
Terminal	Screen	Screen resolution	Mandatory	$\geq 1,440 \times 1,600 \times 2$
		Screen refresh rate	Mandatory	≥ 90 Hz
		Screen type	Optional	TFT-LCD/OLED
		Screen size	Optional	≥ 3.5 inches$\times 2$
	Lens	Lens material	Optional	Fresnel lens, PMMA
		FoV	Mandatory	$100°-120°$
	Video	Decoding type	Mandatory	H.264 and H.265
		Decoding performance	Mandatory	$\geq 4,096 \times 2,160$ at 60 FPS, 100 Mbit/s H.264 (4K H.264) $\geq 7,680 \times 3,840$ at 30 FPS, 200 Mbit/s H.265 (8K H.265)
	Audio	Decoding type	Mandatory	AAC/AAC+/eAAC+, MP3, AMR/AMR-WB, MIDI, PCM, OGG, FLAC
		Number of rendered channels	Mandatory	Dual audio channels, built-in dual stereo speakers
		Audio-to-video synchronization	Mandatory	Subjective synchronization without obvious time difference
	Positioning	DoF (headset)	Mandatory	3DoF
		DoF (handle)	Optional	3DoF
		Pose sampling mode (headset)	Mandatory	6-axis/9-axis pose sensor
		Pose sampling mode (handle)	Optional	6-axis/9-axis pose sensor
		Pose sampling precision (headset)	Mandatory	≤ 0.0001
		Pose sampling precision (handle)	Optional	≤ 0.0001

(Continued)

Table 6.5 (Continued) Evaluation criteria of full-view video transmission

Component	Module	Item	Mandatory/optional	Suggestion
		Pose sampling frequency (headset)	Mandatory	≥ 400 Hz
		Pose sampling frequency (handle)	Optional	≥ 100 Hz
	Correction	Distortion correction	Mandatory	Supported, without pincushion distortion
	Comfort	Headset type	Optional	Standalone/Split VR headset
		Headset heat dissipation	Mandatory	Good heat dissipation performance, and the contact temperature of the skin does not exceed 40°C
		Headset seal	Mandatory	Good seal with no obvious light leakage.
		Headset breathability	Mandatory	Good breathability, and normal breathing is not affected
		Headset weight (including battery)	Mandatory	≤ 500 g
	Battery life	Battery capacity	Optional	3,500–4,000 mAh
		Battery life (while watching video)	Mandatory	≥ 2.5h
	Usability	Eye comfort mode	Optional	Low blue light certification
		Myopia usability	Mandatory	Allows users to wear glasses or supports focusing
	Performance	MTP latency	Mandatory	≤ 20 ms
		Terminal decoding latency	Mandatory	≤ 15 ms
		Motion rendering latency	Mandatory	≤ 5.5 ms
		Screen refresh latency	Mandatory	≤ 11 ms (90 FPS)
		Screen response latency	Mandatory	≤ 5 ms

(Continued)

Table 6.5 (Continued) Evaluation criteria of full-view video transmission

Component	Module	Item	Mandatory/optional	Suggestion
Communication	System	Wi-Fi	Mandatory	Supports 2×2 MIMO and 802.11ac@5 GHz.
		System	Optional	Android
		Version	Optional	7.1–8.1
	Hardware	CPU	Optional	Qualcomm 835 (4K)/Samsung Exynos 8895 (4K–8K)
		Memory	Optional	4G RAM, LPDDR4X, 1866M
		Storage	Optional	64 GB UFS2.1, supporting 256 GB microSD card
Network	Performance	Packet loss rate	Mandatory	$\leq 9 \times 10^{-5}$ (4K@H.264) $\leq 1.7 \times 10^{-5}$ (8K@H.265)
		Forwarding latency	Mandatory	≤ 20 ms
		Transmission bandwidth	Mandatory	≥ 60 Mbit/s (4K@H.264) ≥ 120–180 Mbit/s (8K@H.265)
Content	Video coding	Resolution	Mandatory	$3,840 \times 1,920$ (4K@H.264) $7,680 \times 3,840$ (8K@H.265)
		Bitrate	Mandatory	≥ 40 Mbit/s (4K@H.264) ≥ 80–120 Mbit/s (8K@H.265)
		Frame rate	Mandatory	≥ 30 FPS
		Coding format	Mandatory	4K@H.264, 8K@H.265
		Color depth	Mandatory	≥ 8 bits
		Stitching angle	Optional	$180°$–$360°$
		Stereoscopic vision	Optional	3D/2D

(Continued)

Table 6.5 (Continued) Evaluation criteria of full-view video transmission

Component	Module	Item	Mandatory/optional	Suggestion
	Audio coding	Bitrate	Optional	128 kbit/s
		Code	Optional	AAC
		Number of source audio channels	Optional	Dual audio channels
		Sampling rate	Optional	48 kHz
	Encapsulation	Encapsulation protocol	Mandatory	HLS over TCP
Service	Experience	Video loading wait duration	Mandatory	≤ 2 seconds
		MTP latency threshold-crossing	Mandatory	Every time MTP latency exceeds 20 ms, an MTP latency threshold-crossing event is logged
		Buffering	Mandatory	If the playback buffer is empty, a buffering event is logged

Table 6.6 Evaluation criteria of FoV video transmission

Component	Module	Item	Mandatory/optional	Suggestion
Terminal	Screen	Screen resolution	Mandatory	≥ 1,440×1,600×2
		Screen refresh rate	Mandatory	≥ 90 Hz
		Screen type	Optional	TFT-LCD/OLED
		Screen size	Optional	≥ 3.5 inches×2
	Lens	Lens material	Optional	Fresnel lens, PMMA
		FoV	Mandatory	100°–120°
	Video	Decoding type	Mandatory	H.264 and H.265
		Decoding performance	Mandatory	≥ 4,096×2,160 at 60 FPS, 100 Mbit/s H.264 (4K H.264) ≥ 7,680×3,840 at 30 FPS, 200 Mbit/s H.265 (8K H.265)
	Audio	Decoding type	Mandatory	AAC/AAC+/eAAC+, MP3, AMR/AMR-WB, MIDI, PCM, OGG, FLAC
		Number of rendered channels	Mandatory	Dual audio channels, built-in dual stereo speakers
		Audio-to-video synchronization	Mandatory	Subjective synchronization without obvious time difference
	Positioning	DoF (headset)	Mandatory	3DoF
		DoF (handle)	Optional	3DoF
		Pose sampling mode (headset)	Mandatory	6-axis/9-axis pose sensor
		Pose sampling mode (handle)	Optional	6-axis/9-axis pose sensor
		Pose sampling precision (headset)	Mandatory	≤ 0.0001

(Continued)

Table 6.6 (Continued) Evaluation criteria of FoV video transmission

Component	Module	Item	Mandatory/optional	Suggestion
		Pose sampling precision (handle)	Optional	≤ 0.0001
		Pose sampling frequency (headset)	Mandatory	≥ 400 Hz
		Pose sampling frequency (handle)	Optional	≥ 100 Hz
	Correction	Distortion correction	Mandatory	Supported, without pincushion distortion
	Comfort	Headset type	Optional	Stand-alone/split VR headset
		Headset heat dissipation	Mandatory	Good heat dissipation performance, and the contact temperature of the skin does not exceed 40°C
		Headset seal	Mandatory	Good seal with no obvious light leakage.
		Headset breathability	Mandatory	Good breathability, and normal breathing is not affected
		Headset weight (including battery)	Mandatory	≤ 500 g
	Battery life	Battery capacity	Optional	3,500–4,000 mAh
		Battery life (while watching video)	Mandatory	≥ 2.5 hours
	Usability	Eye comfort mode	Optional	Low blue light certification
		Myopia usability	Mandatory	Allows users to wear glasses or supports focusing
	Performance	MTP latency	Mandatory	≤ 20 ms
		Terminal decoding latency	Mandatory	≤ 15 ms
		Motion rendering latency	Mandatory	≤ 5.5 ms
		Screen refresh latency	Mandatory	≤ 11 ms (90 FPS)
		Screen response latency	Mandatory	≤ 5 ms

(Continued)

Table 6.6 (Continued) Evaluation criteria of FoV video transmission

Component	Module	Item	Mandatory/optional	Suggestion
Communication System	Wi-Fi		Mandatory	Supports 2×2 MIMO and 802.11 ac@5 GHz.
	System		Optional	Android
	Version		Optional	7.1–8.1
	Hardware	CPU	Optional	Qualcomm 835 (4K)/Samsung Exynos 8895 (4K–8K)
		Memory	Optional	4G RAM, LPDDR4X, 1866M
		Storage	Optional	64 GB UFS2.1, supporting 256 GB microSD card
Network	Performance	Packet loss rate	Mandatory	$\leq 9 \times 10^{-5}$ (4K@H.264) $\leq 1.7 \times 10^{-5}$ (8K@H.265)
		Forwarding latency	Mandatory	≤ 20 ms
		Transmission bandwidth	Mandatory	≥ 60 Mbit/s (4K@H.264) ≥ 120–180 Mbit/s (8K@H.265)
Content	Video coding	Resolution	Mandatory	3,840×1,920 (4K@H.264) 7,680×3,840 (8K@H.265)
		Bitrate	Mandatory	≥ 40 Mbit/s (4K@H.264) ≥ 80–120 Mbit/s (8K@H.265)
		Frame rate	Mandatory	≥ 30 FPS
		Coding format	Mandatory	4K@H.264, 8K@H.265
		Color depth	Mandatory	≥ 8 bits
		Stitching angle	Optional	180°–360°
		Stereoscopic vision	Optional	3D/2D
	Audio coding	Bitrate	Optional	128 kbit/s

(Continued)

Table 6.6 (Continued) Evaluation criteria of FoV video transmission

Component	Module	Item	Mandatory/optional	Suggestion
		Code	Optional	AAC
		Number of source audio channels	Optional	Dual audio channels
		Sampling rate	Optional	48 kHz
	Encapsulation	Encapsulation protocol	Mandatory	HLS over TCP
Service	Experience	Video loading wait duration	Mandatory	≤ 2 seconds
		MTP latency threshold-crossing	Mandatory	Every time MTP latency exceeds 20 ms, an MTP latency threshold-crossing event is logged
		Buffering	Mandatory	If the playback buffer is empty, a buffering event is logged

6.2.2 Evaluation methods

6.2.2.1 Terminal and cloud asynchronous rendering

During cloud rendering and streaming, a terminal submits instructions to the cloud, and the cloud performs rendering, coding, and streaming. The terminal then receives and decodes the streams. This is an extra process of cloud VR relative to local VR during service processing and the major cause of black edges, smearing, and lag.

Latency is measured through timestamping. When the terminal sends an instruction, timestamp T_1 is added. When the platform receives the instruction, timestamp T_1' is added. After the platform processes the data, timestamp T_2' is added to the frames sent out. When receiving frames, the terminal records timestamp T_2 and parses the timestamps T_2', T_1', and T_1. After decoding the frame data, the terminal records timestamp T_3, calculates the latency values, and records the result in a log (Figure 6.11).

- Cloud rendering and streaming latency $= T_3 - T_1$
- Cloud rendering processing latency $= T_2' - T_1'$
- Terminal decoding latency $= T_3 - T_2$
- Network transmission latency $= T_2 - T_1 - (T_2' - T_1')$

Note: The instruction sent by the terminal to the platform contains FoV information to the precision of 10^{-4}. This information is reserved in the entire cloud rendering and streaming process, being used as the unified identifier of the instruction and the corresponding video frame in a complete strong-interaction process.

Buffering: If buffering occurs during a game, the image is suddenly suspended and is restored to normal after a period of time. In the cloud VR solution, the main cause of this problem is packet loss and network latency. In the terminal–cloud asynchronous rendering solution, in addition to the basic frames generated by the cloud rendering, the terminal performs local frame compensation by using asynchronous time warping (ATW) technology to maintain or improve the display frame rate. However, only basic frames

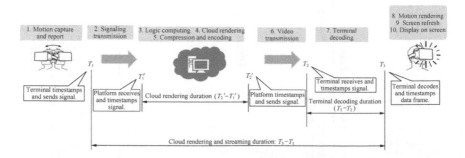

Figure 6.11 Service probe design for cloud rendering and streaming.

generated by cloud rendering are considered effective frames. During the actual experience, severe buffering occurs due to insufficient effective frames received by the terminal over a certain period of time. The terminal can predict and display only the latest effective frames. Inserted intermediate frames are highly similar to effective frames. This means that inserted frames cannot solve the problem of buffering. If the display interval between adjacent effective frames exceeds a specified period (for example, 50 ms), we can reasonably conclude that buffering has occurred during the game experience. The interval between displayed adjacent effective frames is the duration of a single buffering event. Figure 6.12 shows the buffering probe design for game services.

Pixelation: In cloud VR services transmitted using UDP, packet loss can cause pixelation. The pixelation type depends on the type of lost frames. Loss of I-frame data affects the decoding of the entire group of pictures (GoP), whereas loss of P-frame data affects all the subsequent P-frames until the GoP ends. The loss of an I-frame has a greater impact than the loss of a P-frame. In the actual tests, lost frames are measured, and their types are considered for calculation of pixelation duration. Figure 6.13 shows a GoP.

Black edge: Local asynchronous warping can only perform prediction based on the current image and cannot generate images out of nothing. Therefore, when a user rotates their head quickly, the area beyond the original field of view is displayed as a black edge or smear.

Theoretically, this problem can be resolved by performing super FoV rendering on the cloud. However, the actual effect is determined by head rotation speed and latency of cloud rendering and streaming. The effectiveness is uncertain and needs to be monitored. Based on the implementation principle, the black edge is actually the difference between the input user angle information and the angle of the warped frames during asynchronous warping. The black edge angle is calculated as follows:

Black edge angle = Head angle after ATW – angle in effective frames –

(super FoV – terminal FoV)/2

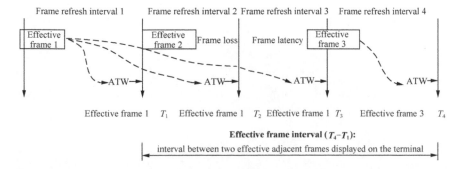

Figure 6.12 Buffering probe design for game services.

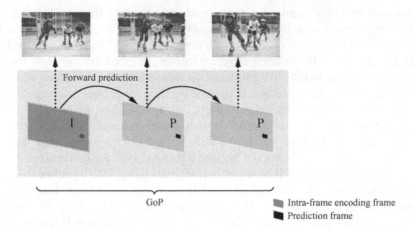

GoP

▨ Intra-frame encoding frame
■ Prediction frame

Figure 6.13 GoP decoding.

6.2.2.2 Full-view video transmission

Buffering: When the download rate (throughput) is smaller than the playback rate (bitrate), there is not enough data in the buffer for playback. Therefore, the volume of the remaining data in the buffer can be monitored to determine whether buffering occurs.

6.2.2.3 FoV video transmission

Image quality switching: Similar to adding timestamps during cloud rendering and streaming, the terminal side needs to record T_1 (sending time of the tile request) and T_2 (the time when all tiles are stitched, decoded, and sent to headset for display). $T_2 - T_1$ is the time it takes to switch image qualities. The terminal's motion capture and rendering display latencies are ignored, because they are fixed by product specifications. Figure 6.14 shows the image quality switching duration ($T_2 - T_1$).

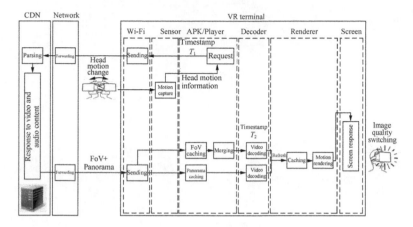

Figure 6.14 Image quality switching duration ($T_2 - T_1$).

Chapter 7

Cloud VR Business Practices

Owing to its immersive and interactive features, cloud virtual reality (VR) has burst onto the internet scene. This technology has been growing in popularity with operators because of its cloud–network integration and added business value. Cloud VR is ready for commercialization, driving the next generation of video services.

Despite its popularity, cloud VR is still at an early stage. Its development requires not only operators providing premium networks, but also cooperation among the whole VR ecosystem. Many VR vendors are concerned about how to promote cloud–network integration with operators while building their own business value.

This chapter summarizes existing cloud VR cases to offer a platform for cloud VR business practices and promote its wide commercial use.

7.1 CLOUD VR BRINGS MARKET OPPORTUNITIES TO OPERATORS

7.1.1 Current status of the cloud VR industry

The VR industry chain covers a wide range of areas, including hardware, software, and content applications, each with their own established ecosystem.[11]

Hardware: Figure 7.1 shows the hardware ecosystem of the VR industry. VR hardware mainly comprises chips, display screens, sensors, and optical components that are integrated into the terminals, as well as positional tracking, gesture recognition, and voice recognition peripherals. Along with leading VR terminal vendors such as Oculus and HTC, more and more upstream and downstream enterprises are entering this area.

Software: Figure 7.2 shows the software ecosystem of the VR industry. VR software mainly comprises operating systems, user interfaces (UIs), middleware, software development kits (SDKs), and three-dimensional (3D) engines for VR content development. Currently, VR content is still highly dependent on specific development platforms, and there is no unified standard for the different interfaces between platforms and terminals.

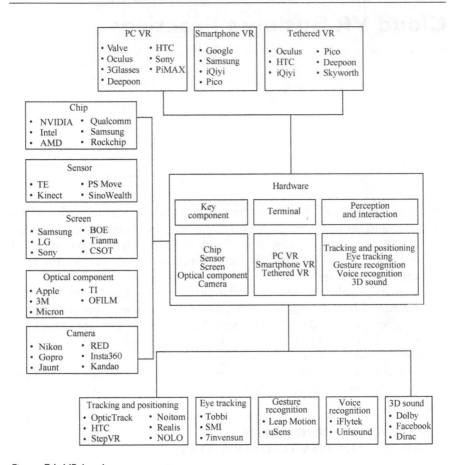

Figure 7.1 VR hardware ecosystem.

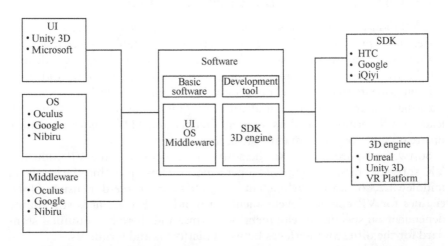

Figure 7.2 VR software ecosystem.

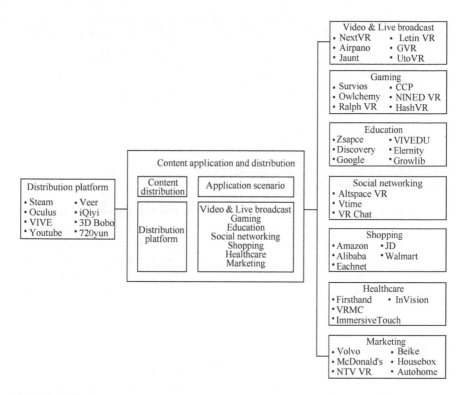

Figure 7.3 VR content ecosystem.

Content: Covering content production and distribution. Figure 7.3 shows the content ecosystem of the VR industry. Among the various 2B and 2C scenarios where VR is used, major investment has been into video, live broadcast, and gaming from the 2C area, as well as education, healthcare, and marketing in the 2B field.

Although the traditional VR industry is relatively mature, many problems still exist, particularly expensive terminals, no unified platform, and lack of copyright protection. Hopefully, with the rapid development of cloud computing and network transmission technologies, cloud VR can attract greater attention. In July 2018, China Mobile Fujian, together with Huawei, Letin VR, and Cyber Cloud, released the world's first home cloud VR service, promoting the penetration of the VR industry. In addition to China's policy to develop a cloud VR platform for service distribution and aggregation, there have been efforts to facilitate the formulation of cloud VR standards, which signifies a significant move from technical practices to commercial use.

As telecom operators, network solution providers, and cloud network services providers unite, the cloud VR industry chain takes shape, as shown in Figure 7.4.

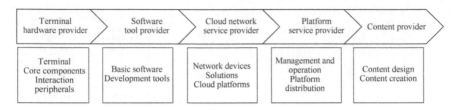

Figure 7.4 Cloud VR industry chain.

7.1.2 Operators have advantages in developing cloud VR

The formation of the industry chain has boosted the development of terminals, enrichment of contents, and maturity of network transmission and cloud computing technologies. Despite all the preconditions of cloud VR solution commercialization, there remains a lack of aggregation platforms and leaders. Telecom operators have unique advantages in networks, platforms, and user resources, labeling them as potential leaders for wide adoption of cloud VR services.

7.1.2.1 Network advantages

Traditional VR applications have high requirements on local hosts, such as large storage space and high-performance rendering and computing capabilities for strong-interaction applications. With cloud VR solutions, storage, rendering, and computing can be done on the cloud. Additionally, premium user experience can be ensured with high-bandwidth and low-latency network transmission, which can be provided by operators.

Ovum reported that by August 2019, more than 234 operators worldwide had released gigabit broadband services, and over 20 of them had released 10GE services. Furthermore, 5G networks are picking up momentum. Operators in South Korea, Switzerland, the UK, and China have started constructing and rolling out 5G networks.

China has witnessed rapid network development in recent years. According to the statistics released by China's Ministry of Industry and Information Technology (MIIT), 4G users in China had reached 1.269 billion by the end of October 2019, which was below 100 million by the end of 2014 (as shown in Figure 7.5). Meanwhile, China is aggressively accelerating 5G deployment. In June 2019, the MIIT issued 5G licenses to China Telecom, China Mobile, China Unicom, and China Broadcasting Network, ushering in a booming period for 5G base station construction.

Concerning fiber broadband networks, by the end of October 2019, the number of fiber to the home (FTTH/O) users in China had reached 416 million, accounting for 92% of the total number of fixed broadband users. Broadband users also enjoy increasingly higher bandwidth rates. 370 million

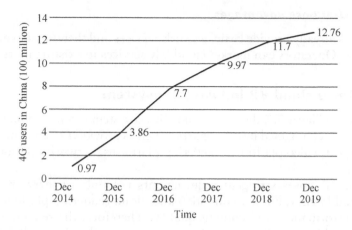

Figure 7.5 Growth trend of 4G users in China from 2014 to 2019.

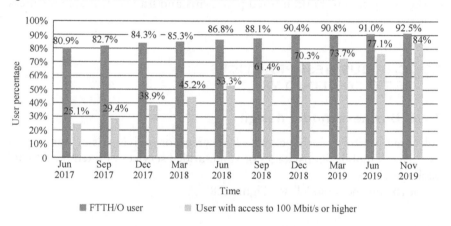

Figure 7.6 Development trend of fiber broadband networks from 2017 to 2019.

users experience rates of at least 100 Mbit/s, accounting for 81.8% of the total number of broadband users, as shown in Figure 7.6. Fixed broadband has now entered the gigabit era. The number of gigabit fixed broadband home users in China has reached 641,000.

7.1.2.2 Platform advantages

Internet Protocol television (IPTV) has become a mainstream TV product for home broadband users. Operators can expand the existing IPTV video platform to include cloud VR services and build a cloud VR rendering platform to provide cloud VR services.

Furthermore, operators can reuse the existing operation management platform to perform authentication, billing, and content management for cloud VR services.

7.1.2.3 User base advantages

Operators already provide basic network services and therefore have a large user base. Operators can market cloud VR services to existing users.

7.1.3 Telco cloud VR industry ecosystem

As shown in Figure 7.7, the telco cloud VR ecosystem is centered on telecom operators, accompanied by other parties such as providers of content, operation support, video platforms, rendering platforms, network solutions, and terminals.

Cloud VR poses stringent requirements not only on network bandwidth and latency, but also on video and cloud rendering platforms, terminal performance, and content quality. Therefore, the telco cloud VR industry, which is still in its early stage, requires the close collaboration of the ecosystem to build unified platforms and find sustainable business models.

7.2 2C/2H BUSINESS PRACTICES OF TELCO CLOUD VR

7.2.1 Business model design

Telecom operators provide cloud VR services for individuals or home users as a part of mobile 5G packages or value-added services of fixed broadband packages.

For the business model, see Figure 7.8.

7.2.1.1 VR content providers

1. Responsibilities
   Provide copyrighted VR content and give permission to operators for importing content into the cloud VR platform.
2. Qualification requirements
   Be legally certified to develop software and provide high-quality VR content.
3. Compliance requirements
   Currently, there is no unified standard or clear regulation for VR content. However, to ensure the quality and compliance of VR content, it must be reviewed and regulated.
   The compliance review covers technical compliance, regulatory compliance, and accuracy.
   a. Technical compliance
       Developers need to comply with at least the operators' requirements, and operators need to review the technical parameters, including

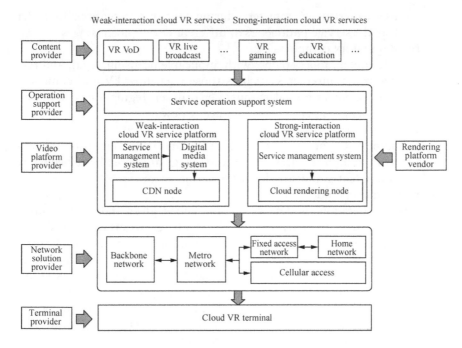

Figure 7.7 Telco cloud VR industry ecosystem.

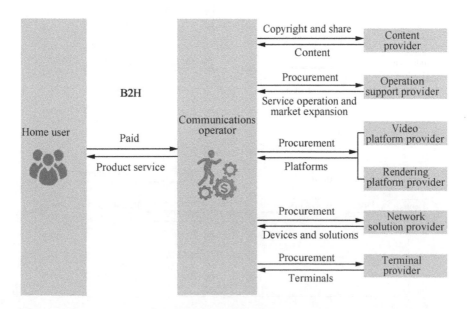

Figure 7.8 Business model of cloud VR 2C/2H services.

user experience parameters, during content aggregation. Table 2.1 lists the service parameters at different development stages.

b. Regulatory compliance

VR content must comply with applicable licensing, legal, and regulatory requirements, such as those regarding TV and game services. Content providers must perform self-regulation review, and the operators perform compliance review.

c. Accuracy

Some VR content, such as education and vocational training content, contains subject matter knowledge and must be reviewed by competent authorities for information accuracy.

4. Cooperation mode

Two cooperation modes are recommended given most VR content manufacturers are startups, and cloud VR services is an extension of operators' services. 1. Large-sized content manufacturers or platform providers can act as operators' content providers and sign long-term financial agreements. 2. For small-sized content startups or studios, whose content production is very limited, operators can select premium content and obtain the relevant copyrights. Small-sized content developers can also sell or reauthorize copyrights to large-sized ones and gain a proportion of revenue from operators.

Figure 7.9 shows the process of cooperation between operators and VR content providers.

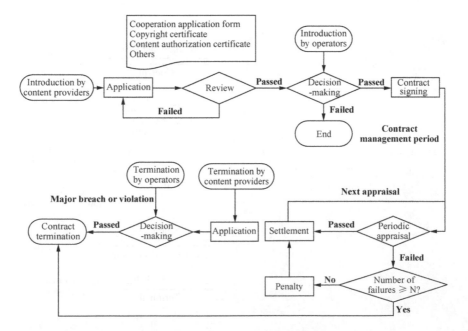

Figure 7.9 Introduction of and cooperation with VR content developers.

a. Ingestion

An operator can source content for its cloud VR content platform while allowing content providers to request for uploading content to the platform. In the latter case, the content providers need to provide application forms and supporting documents, such as copyright and content authorization certificates.

Content quality affects users' willingness to pay and the sustainable development of VR services. Therefore, how to keep introducing premium content and maintain the competitiveness of the platform is the key for operators. Operators can also enrich the content of the platform through cross-platform cooperation, provider competitions, partnership recruitment, and original content.

b. Cooperation management

After contract signing, operators can establish a periodic appraisal mechanism to manage VR content providers from the aspects of VR content quality, content updates, daily support, and compliance. Any breaches will be penalized, and consistent breaches will lead to termination.

If VR content providers choose to exit an agreement, they can apply to terminate the contract in advance. Operators can also terminate the contract if a major breach or violation is caused by VR content providers.

c. Fee settlement

Flexibility depends on the willingness of both parties. Generally, there are three modes.

- Royalty-free. Operators need to invest one-off costs, which may lead to financial loss if the number of subscribers cannot be achieved.
- Revenue sharing. This mode requires zero investment from operators but does not guarantee the benefits for VR content providers.
- Minimum guarantee and revenue sharing. This is between royalty-free and revenue sharing, offering flexibility.

7.2.1.2 Operation support providers

1. Responsibilities
   VR content aggregation and compliance check, O&M of cloud VR services, billing package design, market planning, and market expansion.
2. Qualification requirements
   Experienced in service operation and familiarity with the VR industry and cloud VR solutions.
3. Cooperation mode
   Operation support providers offer their services to operators for a periodical fee based on the labor input.

7.2.1.3 Video platform providers/rendering platform providers

1. Responsibilities
   Responsible for the establishment and O&M of the weak-interaction and strong-interaction cloud VR service platforms. The weak-interaction cloud VR service platform includes the cloud VR live broadcast and video on demand (VoD) systems. O&M includes content management, ingestion, transcoding, slicing, and transmission to content delivery network (CDN) nodes for distribution. While the strong-interaction cloud VR service platform covers service management as well as rendering, coding, and streaming of applications.
2. Qualification requirements
   Familiarity with the VR industry and cloud VR solutions and ability to construct video platforms, CDN nodes, and cloud rendering nodes.
3. Cooperation mode
   Both the weak-interaction and strong-interaction cloud VR service platforms include hardware devices and software platforms. Two cooperation modes are available. In one mode, the software platform is provided by the video platform providers/rendering platform providers, and the hardware devices are purchased by operators. In the other mode, both the hardware devices and software platform are provided by video platform providers/rendering platform providers. The software platform fee includes the development and O&M fee.

7.2.1.4 Network solution providers

1. Responsibilities
   Provision of technical support and equipment for end-to-end metro, access, home, and 5G network solutions.
2. Qualification requirements
   Familiarity with the architecture of the end-to-end cloud VR network solution and ability to deliver software and hardware.
3. Cooperation mode
   Network solution providers must plan throughout the cloud VR project. As shown in Figure 7.10, network solution providers assume different responsibilities in different phases during project initiation, planning, implementation, delivery, and O&M. Operators directly purchase software, hardware solutions, and services from network solution providers.

7.2.2 User package design

7.2.2.1 Current status of VR content billing

1. Online VR platforms
   Initially, the willingness among Chinese netizens to pay for VR services was low. Most VR videos on the current content platforms of

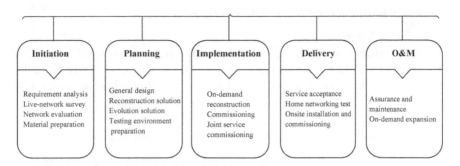

Figure 7.10 Roles of network solution providers in different phases.

mainstream VR terminals are free. Some high-quality VR videos will be packaged into applications that can be downloaded after payment.

Thanks to the improved awareness of intellectual property protection, Chinese netizens are more willing to pay for premium content. According to Intelligence Research Group, the paid network video market scale in China has increased year by year since 2013 and is expected to reach USD 9 billion by 2020.

Currently, mainstream VR content platforms, such as Steam VR and VIVEPORT, have developed mature billing methods. In April 2019, VIVEPORT launched the unlimited VR subscription service, which will be available for USD 8 a month or USD 70 for a year.

The cloud VR platform helps enrich VR content and popularize VR services. With a higher willingness to pay, there is huge market potential for online VR.

2. Physical VR stores

   Physical VR stores are usually located around crowded places. They provide users with VR games and movies that are billed by the following three modes.

   - Pay-per-use: On average, light casual games can be played for 5–10 minutes per time, while large story-driven games or multiplayer games can be played for about 30 minutes per time. Billing varies according to the location, duration, time, and demand in different cities.
   - Package billing: Multiple contents are packaged for a set fee, which is usually higher than that in the pay-per-use mode but allows users to experience more content types for a longer time.
   - VIP card: Offering discounts for long-term users.

   In general, physical VR stores mainly offer an expensive gaming experience. On the contrary, cloud VR 2C/2H services can bring VR games to individuals or families, not necessarily in VR stores. Additionally, they can bring a greater variety of VR content to family members of different ages. Affordable devices and reasonable package prices are bound to attract a large number of users and promote the popularization of VR.

7.2.2.2 Cloud VR service package design

1. Cloud VR service sales

   Operators can bundle cloud VR services into 5G or fixed broadband services and charge prices according to the service level. Early discounts can quickly attract 5G or broadband users. The following paragraphs take LG U+ and China Mobile Fujian as examples.

   Example 1: 5G VR services of South Korean operator LG U+

   In April 2019, LG U+ launched 5G services, followed by a range of VR and augmented reality (AR) content, including Pro Baseball, Golf,

Table 7.1 5G packages of LG U+

Package category	Tariff (USD)	Traffic	U+VR service tariff
5G Super Platinum	91	Unlimited traffic No rate limit, with an additional 50 GB shared data plan for homes and 100 GB shared data plan (applicable to packages sold before December 31, 2019)	USD 4/month for most content, excluding some premium content which requires extra payment
5G Platinum	83	Unlimited traffic No rate limit, with an additional 100 GB shared data plan (applicable to packages sold before December 31, 2019)	Only LG U+ 5G users can use the U+VR app for free in the promotional period until December 31, 2019
5G Premium	75	Unlimited traffic No rate limit, with an additional 100 GB shared data plan (applicable to packages sold before December 31, 2019)	
5G Special	67	Unlimited traffic No rate limit, with an additional 50 GB shared data plan (applicable to packages sold before December 31, 2019)	
5G Standard	60	150 GB data. The rate is limited to 5 Mbit/s when data usage exceeds the threshold.	
5G Light	44	9 GB data. The rate is limited to 1 Mbit/s when data usage exceeds the threshold.	
5G Light Youth	36	8 GB data. The rate is limited to 1 Mbit/s when data usage exceeds the threshold.	

Note: The data was published on LG U+ official website in September 2019.

Idol Live, AR Live, and VR live. Table 7.1 lists the packages and sales strategy for U+VR (a cloud VR app of LG U+).

As shown in the preceding table, 5G packages are charged based on levels of data usage. U+VR is sold as a value-added service for 5G users, and the application is installed on 5G mobile phones by default. During the promotional stage, the application can remain free while providing a certain data discount. Following the promotional stage, the operator will charge for data plans and content fees.

Example 2: China mobile Fujian's home broadband cloud VR service

In July 2018, China Mobile Fujian released the home cloud VR service to upgrade fixed broadband services.

The cloud VR service is bundled with the 500 Mbit/s fixed broadband plan. Users can subscribe to the cloud VR service only after they have purchased the 500 Mbit/s broadband plan. During the promotional stage, 500 Mbit/s broadband, cloud VR terminals, set-top boxes (STBs), routers, and cloud VR service packages are available in one discounted package to boost the marketability of the 500 Mbit/s broadband service. After the promotional stage, operators will charge for fixed broadband and cloud VR content fees.

2. Cloud VR content packages
   The production cost of cloud VR is much higher than that of traditional videos and games. Therefore, it is crucial to attract paying users through premium content and properly designed packages, as shown in Table 7.2.

   Cloud VR packages must be designed and content curated for different user groups to attract more subscribers.

7.3 B2B2C BUSINESS PRACTICES OF TELCO CLOUD VR

7.3.1 Business model design

In this B2B2C model, operators provide cloud VR services to government/enterprise customers that offer these services to their users.

Figure 7.11 shows the B2B2C business model.

7.3.1.1 Operators vs government/enterprise customers

Operators can provide cloud VR services for government/enterprise customers in two ways.

1. Lump sum subscription
   Funded non-profit organizations such as government agencies, schools, and community support subscribe to cloud VR platform services on a

Table 7.2 Cloud VR content packages

Package category	Package description	Billing mode
Free service package	This package is applicable to users who have not yet subscribed to any packages or cancelled their subscription. A small amount of free content can be provided to encourage customers to sign up to a second subscription. Package design: • A small amount of VR video content (less than or equal to 5% of the total number of VR video content items) is free. • All VR video content can be viewed for 5–10 seconds for free. • 1–2 VR casual games can be played for 1 minute for free.	Free
Basic service package	This package is applicable to mainstream consumption groups. It provides a certain proportion of premium content (for example, 50% to 60%) based on the subscription type. Basic service packages can include all services or offer services by type, such as VR video, VR gaming, and VR education.	By month/quarter/year
One-off VoD package	This package is applicable to VR live broadcasts (such as concerts and sports events) and some premium VR applications.	By time
VIP package	This package offers free access to all content except some live broadcast content and premium content that requires extra charge.	By month/quarter/year

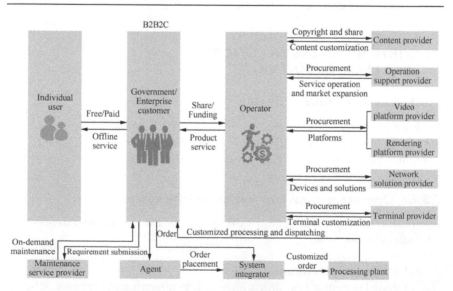

Figure 7.11 Cloud VR business model for industry verticals.

lump sum basis and then purchase network services from operators on a monthly or yearly basis.

Enterprises can also enjoy one-off subscriptions and determine billing methods for individual users, becoming self-reliant.

2. Joint marketing

To share the benefits and risks, operators and enterprises can collectively determine the billing mode and pricing, while enterprises can collect consumption information of individual users by leveraging the operator's charging system. The revenue is then shared between the two parties on a monthly basis.

7.3.1.2 Special requirements of cloud VR services in enterprise application

Compared with home services, cloud VR is more demanding in content, terminal peripherals, and scenario design in enterprise application.

1. Content

The home screen must be customized for different industries. It may be a VR classroom in the education industry or a virtual operating table.

2. Peripherals

Peripherals also need to be customized. For example, in vocational training scenarios, the controller may need to simulate professional equipment such as a wrench, fire extinguisher, or blow torch.

3. System integrators

A system integrator is like the general contractor and is responsible for surveying the requirements and design solutions for government/enterprise customers.

4. Factories

Cloud VR requires different settings to suit different scenarios, especially in stores and experience centers. Therefore, system integrators need to design the settings and decorations and find factories to make the materials.

5. Agents

Agents are entrusted by system integrators to provide VR services and expand the market.

6. Repair service providers

Provide maintenance and repair services for government/enterprise customers. This may involve the suppliers of VR terminals and peripherals.

7.3.2 Cloud VR live broadcast practices

On April 26, 2019, the 2018–2019 Chinese Basketball Association (CBA) finals took place in Guangdong, China. China Mobile Guangdong, together

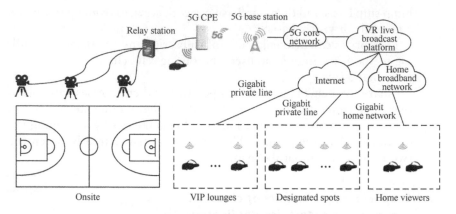

Figure 7.12 Cloud VR live broadcast of the CBA finals.

with Huawei and GVR, streamed the game over 5G and gigabit broadband. Figure 7.12 shows more details.

This solution used a 5G base station and pieces of 5G CPE (customer premise equipment) to transmit collected videos to the cloud VR platform at a bitrate of 30–50 Mbit/s. The live streams were then sent from the cloud VR live broadcast platform to VIP lounges in the stadium, designated spots, and home viewers at a rate no lower than 30 Mbit/s.

Through 5G and gigabit networks, high bitrate and low latency were achievable. Furthermore, VR social interaction such as voice chat and waving were achieved. During the entire live broadcast, the transmission was seamless, and the latency was in fact lower than the TV's live broadcast, offering a much better overall experience. Users could enjoy the live broadcast of the game in various places, such as VR stores, bars, VR cinemas, and fan clubs, either through 5G, fixed home broadband or private lines. The convergence of VR live broadcast and VR social networking makes the VR live broadcast experience more immersive and gripping. According to the feedback from viewers who watched the game in designated spots, nearly 94% of them are willing to buy 5G and gigabit network services to enjoy VR live broadcast, while 48.8% of viewers are willing to spend more than USD 5 for such content.

This case confirms that implementing cloud VR broadcast through 5G and gigabit broadband is feasible. Operators can offer regular VR live broadcasts to complement their existing VR content and services, boosting not only their own sales but also the marketability of 5G and gigabit broadband.

Figure 7.13 shows the responsibilities of each party in the sports VR ecosystem and the business model.

Telecom operators can coordinate with industry partners and profit in the following ways.

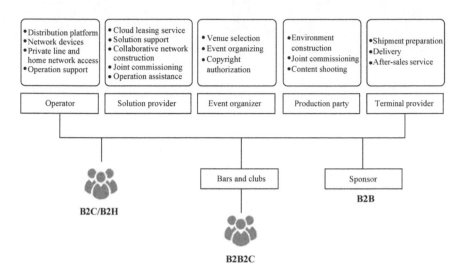

Figure 7.13 Cloud VR live broadcast business model.

- B2C/B2H: Provide dedicated VR live broadcast packages for sports enthusiasts that include 5G or home broadband services.
- B2B2C: Provide VR live broadcast services at VR centers, bars, and fan clubs through gigabit private lines and 5G networks.
- B2B: Charge sponsorship fees by playing ads during live VR streaming.

It can be inferred from Figure 7.13 that if operators want to stream a sports event, they have to pay for the following fees:

- Copyright fee: Paid to the event organizer
- Content shooting fee: Paid to the production party
- Marketing fee: Paid for marketing expenses
- Distribution platform fee: Revenue shared by the distributor.

Profit can be calculated as follows:

VR live broadcast profit = (Subscription fee × Number of users + Sponsorship fee) × (1 − Distribution platform fee) − Copyright fee − Content production fee − Marketing fee

The live event streaming solution and business model can also be used for streaming music concerts, fan meetings, exhibitions, and news events.

Cloud VR is still in its early stages. To achieve success, the cloud VR ecosystem requires mutual collaboration to drive the industry to the next level.

Chapter 8

Future of Cloud VR

As described in Chapter 1, cloud virtual reality (VR) has a wide range of application scenarios, including consumer-oriented scenarios such as IMAX, 360° VR video and live broadcast, game, and music. Cloud VR also covers industry scenarios such as education, healthcare, manufacturing, and tourism. Consumers can wear VR headsets to watch 360° VR immersive videos or play VR games. Schools can use VR-immersive teaching methods, while hospitals can use VR to simulate operations. In addition, VR shopping and apartment hunting are developed.

The future of cloud VR will see it converge with 5G, gigabit broadband, artificial intelligence, IoT, and big data technologies, to become widely applied in more fields.

Although cloud VR has paved a way for the popularization of VR, there is still a long way to go to reach the ultimate phase. This involves improving terminal experience, creating high-quality content, innovating applications and business models, as well as ensuring cloud and networks run optimally, providing huge potential for market development. For example, artists and entertainment creators can use VR as a new medium to explore and introduce creative content such as VR videos, games, live broadcasts, and art. Technology development teams can focus on improving terminals and VR definition, developing screen and chip technologies, and inventing more advanced VR peripherals to create more immersive VR. Professionals in vertical industries can develop highly compatible applications based on the requirements of the industry, meaning that VR technology can better meet business needs. That's not to say VR does not have drawbacks. Health issues such as vision damage and social issues need to be carefully researched before VR is fully unleashed.

China's strong technical infrastructure makes it a breeding ground for cloud VR development. China has been vigorously developing cloud computing infrastructure and taking a leading role in network construction. According to the *44th China Statistical Report on Internet Development*, by June 2019, the number of fiber broadband users in China had reached 396 million, accounting for 91% of the total number of fixed Internet broadband users. Additionally, China has officially issued 5G commercial licenses.

According to Ministry of Industry and Information Technology (MIIT) data, by the end of July 2019, three of China's national telecom operators had developed 285 million Internet Protocol television (IPTV) users. China's IPTV development and decade worth of experience lay a strong foundation for the development of cloud VR.

The Chinese government values the development of VR technologies and has incorporated VR into many important national documents, such as the recent *Outline of the 13th Five-Year Plan for the National Informatization* and the *Guiding Opinions of the State Council on Vigorously Advancing the "Internet Plus" Action*. Some Chinese cities and government departments have released specific VR policies and will begin deploying VR, one of the country's key technologies, to promote the industry's rapid development. China's telecom operators are also accelerating the large-scale development of cloud VR. They put cloud VR into trial commercial use in 2018 and have worked with industry partners to provision VR services for users. In 2019, multiple provinces and cities officially launched cloud VR commercial services, further accelerating the technology's popularization. The support of national policies and enterprise investment form a favorable development environment for developing cloud VR. Since the reform and opening-up of China, its economy has rapidly grown, and people's consumption concepts have also changed. Firstly, people are more open to new trends and technologies (such as mobile payment, online shopping, online live broadcast, selfie, bicycle sharing, and high-speed railway). They are willing to try, adopt, accept, and apply these new things into their lives. Secondly, while the spending power is improving, people are pursuing a better experience, and they are willing to pay what is necessary to enjoy innovative experiences and next-generation products. These attitudes and spending habits favor the growth of cloud VR.

New technology always leads to the decline of a giant in favor of a new one. So, who will be the next giant? We can be sure they will not emerge in the search engine field, as industries are often changed by disruptors from other industries. Though we cannot foresee the new industry landscape brought by cloud VR, we can seize the opportunity to deploy it as soon as possible, lead this new revolution, and assume a more important position in the new era and landscape.

Virtual things can be achieved, and if you can imagine it, then it may become a reality.

The famous mathematician Leonhard Euler said that imaginary numbers do not exist in the real world. And although they do not exist, their discovery shows a leap of human cognition to a higher dimension. We believe that the emergence of VR will also revolutionize human society.

The movie *Ready Player One* illustrated the future of VR. In VR, all rules can be rewritten, and a new universe created. People can move between planets instantly and shuttle back and forth. They can control time (rewind 60 seconds in time), ignore gravity, and even dance in the air. They can also become heroes and save the world. In the VR world, people have established a set of social rules: they have their own professions, studios, companies, and even friends and loved ones. In the VR world, imagination is limitless and real. Everything that can be imagined can be realized and perceived by people around the world. People can gather together in the VR world by imagining virtual things such as King Kong, Godzilla, and Gundam, as well as those in movies, literature, ancient times, and even in the future. Our imagination is one of the most wonderful characteristics that human beings possess, and VR is the best facilitator of imagination. In reality, people only need a few VR devices in a small garage to do things that are beyond reality and imagination.

Now VR is open and waiting for us to explore. Every idea, no matter how big or small, may become the most valuable thing in VR. We are looking forward to witnessing the arrival of the new world belonging to us all.

Acronyms and Abbreviations

2D	Two dimensions
3D	Three dimensions
AAA	Authentication, authorization, and accounting
AMOLED	Active matrix OLED
AMT	Adaptive multiple core transform
AMVR	Advanced motion vector resolution
AP	Access point
API	Application programming interface
APK	Android application package
APP	Accelerated parallel processing
ASIC	Application-specific integrated circuit
ASW	Asynchronous space warp
ATMVP	Alternative temporal motion vector prediction
ATW	Asynchronous time warp
AVC	Advanced video coding
BIO	Bidirectional optical flow
BNG	Broadband network gateway
BRAS	Broadband remote access server
BSS	Business support system
CABAC	Context-based adaptive binary arithmetic coding
CAGR	Compound annual growth rate
CAR	Committed access rate
CAVLC	Context-based adaptive variable length coding
CCSA	China Communications Standards Association
CDN	Content delivery network
CG	Computer graphics
CO	Central office
CPE	Customer premise equipment
CR	Core router
CUDA	Compute Unified Device Architecture
DAA	Destination address accounting
DASH	Dynamic Adaptive Streaming over HTTP
DBF	Deblocking filter

DCT	Discrete cosine transform
DFS	Dynamic frequency selection
DHR	Dummy head recording
DLNA	Digital Living Network Alliance
DMVR	Decoder-side motion vector refinement
DNS	Domain Name System
DST	Discrete sine transform
EPG	Electronic program guide
EPON	Ethernet passive optical network
ERP	Equirectangular projection
FEC	Forward error correction
FoV	Field of view
FPGA	Field-programmable gate array
FPS	Frames per second
FS	Full search
FTTH	Fiber to the home
GI	Guard interval
GoP	Group of pictures
GPON	Gigabit passive optical network
GPU	Graphics processing unit
HDMI	High-Definition Multimedia Interface
HDS	HTTP Dynamic Streaming
HEVC	High-efficiency video coding
HGW	Home gateway
HLS	HTTP Live Streaming
HQoS	Hierarchical quality of service
HRTF	Head-related transfer function
HSI	High-speed internet
HSS	HTTP Smooth Streaming
HTTP	Hypertext Transfer Protocol
HVS	Human visual system
ICT	Information and communication technology
IDC	International Data Corporation
IETF	Internet Engineering Task Force
IMU	Inertial measurement unit
IP	Internet Protocol
IPoE	IP over Ethernet
IPTV	Internet Protocol television
KVM	Kernel-based virtual machine
L3VPN	Layer 3 virtual private network
LAN	Local area network
LCD	Liquid crystal display
LFU	Least frequently used
LM	Liner mode
LRU	Least recently used

MCS	Modulation and coding scheme
MCTS	Motion-constrained tile set
MIMO	Multiple input multiple output
MPD	Media presentation description
MPEG	Moving Picture Experts Group
MRL	Multiple reference line
MRS	Multi-resolution shading
MSE	Mean square error
MTP	Motion to photon
MU-MIMO	Multi-user multiple-input multiple-output
NAT	Network address translation
ODF	Optical distribution frame
ODN	Optical distribution network
ODU	Optical channel data unit
OFDMA	Orthogonal frequency division multiple access
OLED	Organic light-emitting diode
OLT	Optical line terminal
OMF	Omnidirectional media format
ONT	Optical network terminal
OSS	Operation support system
OTN	Optical transport network
OTT	Over the top
PDPC	Position-dependent intra-prediction combination
PMOLED	Passive matrix OLED
PON	Passive optical network
PPD	Pixels per degree
PPI	Pixels per inch
PPPoE	Point-to-Point Protocol over Ethernet
PQ	Priority queuing
PRI	Primary rate interface
PSP	Platonic solid projection
QAM	Quadrature amplitude modulation
QoS	Quality of Service
QUIC	Quick UDP Internet Connection
RAIL	Response, Animation, Idle, Load
RDOQ	Rate-distortion quantization
RSVP	Resource Reservation Protocol
RTCP	Real-Time Transport Control Protocol
RTMP	Real-Time Messaging Protocol
RTP	Real-Time Transport Protocol
RTSP	Real-Time Streaming Protocol
RTT	Round-trip time
SAD	Sum of absolute difference
SAO	Sample adaptive offset
SDK	Software development kit

SPS	Single pass stereo
SRD	Spatial relationship description
STB	Set-top box
STMVP	Spatial temporal motion vector prediction
TCP	Transmission Control Protocol
ToF	Time of flight
ToS	Type of service
TW	Time warp
TWS	Tile-wise streaming
UDP	User Datagram Protocol
USB	Universal serial bus
VLAN	Virtual local area network
VM	Virtual machine
VMM	Virtual machine monitor
VPLS	Virtual private LAN segment
VR	Virtual reality
VVC	Versatile video coding
WAIP	Wide angle intra-prediction
WDMlr	Wavelength division multiplexing 1r
WFQ	Weighted fair queuing
WMM	Wi-Fi multimedia
WPP	Wavefront parallel processing
XMPP	Extensible Messaging and Presence Protocol

References

1. China Academy of Information and Communications Technology (CAICT). Virtual Reality/Augmented Reality White Paper (2018) [R/O L]. (2019-01-23) [2019-10-02].
2. China Academy of Information and Communications Technology (CAICT). Cloud Computing Development White Paper (2019) [R/O L]. (2019-07-02) [2019-10-02].
3. Huawei iLab, China Academy of Information and Communications Technology (CAICT). Cloud VR+2B Scenario White Paper [R/OL]. (2019-02-22) [2019-10-02].
4. Metraux G S, Oster G. The senses considered as perceptual systems by James J. Gibson (review). *Leonardo*, 1968, 1(1): 89.
5. Champel M-L, Dore R, Mollet N. Key factors for a high-quality VR experience. *Applications of Digital Image Processing XL*, Proceedings Volume 10396. Society of Photo-Optical Instrumentation Engineers, 2017.
6. Fautier T. VR video ecosystem for live distribution. London: *IBC 2016 Conference*, 2016.
7. Kuzyakov E, Pio D. Next-Generation Video Coding Techniques for 360 Video and VR[R/OL]. (2016-01-21) [2019-10-09].
8. ISO/IEC JTC 1/SC 29. *ISO/IEC 23090-2:2019 Information Technology-Coded Representation of Immersive Media-Part 2: Omnidirectional Media Format*. Geneva: MPEG, 2019.
9. Kearney M, Osmani A, Basques K, et al. Measure Performance with the RAIL Model[R/OL]. (2019-08-30) [2019-10-09].
10. Zhu X C, Li X, Chen J. Next-generation video coding standard–HEVC. *Journal of Nanjing University of Posts and Telecommunications (Natural Science Edition)*, 2013, 33(3): 1–11.
11. Zhu X, Liu F, Hu D. *New Video Coding and Transmission Technologies*. Beijing: Electronic Industry Press, 2014.
12. Grois D, Marpe D, Nguyen T, et al. Comparative assessment of H. 265/ MPEG-HEVC, VP9, and H. 264/ MPEG-AVC encoders for low-delay video applications. *Applications of Digital Image Processing XXXVII*, Proceedings Volume 9217. Society of Photo-Optical Instrumentation Engineers, 2014.
13. Liang J, Chen G, Zhuang Y, et al. *Key Technologies, Architecture, and Applications of the Content Delivery Network (CDN)*. Beijing: People's Posts and Telecommunications Press, 2013.

14. Huawei Technologies Co., Ltd. Fusion Cloud V100R005C10 Cloud Computing IT Basics 01 [DB/010 L]. (2014-04-18) [2019-10-15].
15. Feng L. *Unity Shader Essentials*. Beijing: People's Posts and Telecommunications Press, 2016.
16. Bierling M. Displacement estimation by hierarchical block matching. *Visual Communications and Image Processing III*, Proceedings Volume 1001. Society of Photo-Optical Instrumentation Engineers, 1988.
17. Xu L. *Research on the Motion Estimation Algorithm for Sequence Images Based on Block Matching*. Jinan: Shandong University, 2007.
18. Video Experience Alliance (VEA). Virtual Reality (VR) Experience Standard Technical White Paper [R/10 L]. (2019-10-21) [2019-10-28].

Index

Note: **Bold** page numbers refer to tables and *italic* page numbers refer to figures.